To my very creative
friend, Sarah, a true

Magic Child !

Love,
Jane

Magic Child

All about Love and Power from the Inside Out

Jane Meyers

BookPartners
Wilsonville, Oregon

Copyright 1999 by Jane Meyers
All rights reserved
Printed in U.S.A.
Library of Congress Catalog 98-74025
ISBN 1-58151-020-9

Photography by Loma Smith
Photograph for introduction a family snapshot
Photograph for chapter 3 by Mark Ganba
Cover design by Richard Ferguson
Text design by Sheryl Mehary

BookPartners, Inc.
P.O. Box 922
Wilsonville, Oregon 97070

This book is dedicated to the immortal and irrepressible Magic Child in each of us, and to my beloved husband, Ron, whose soul songs celebrate and evoke inner magic.

Contents

Preface

Two roads diverged in a wood, and I—
I took the one less traveled by,
and that has made all the difference.
– Robert Frost, *The Road Not Taken*

 Magic Wand
Follow the path of your heart.

A Path through the Woods

I set out on the road that led to my career by going to Bridgewater State College in Massachusetts, where I graduated Summa Cum Laude with a Bachelor of Arts degree in English and a minor in Secondary Education. Later I got a Post-Graduate Diploma in Journalism from the Western Australia Institute of Technology. I taught school for nine years, six of those as a junior-high English teacher with a focus on writing. Having spent the first half of my life immersed in the educational system, I decided to take a different approach in my late thirties when my children were still little and I was starting to reinvent myself.

My path to becoming a therapist was a journey through the woods of personal experience and an eclectic choice of workshops and training, rather than a clearly defined formal degree program. From this background, I draw upon five pivotal influences: primal therapy, metaphysics, intuitive journaling, transformative dance, and Hendricks training.

In 1986, I discovered primal therapy, which involves tuning into one's body memory by paying attention to the breath and noticing places of body tension that "speak" of old emotional trauma. By staying with the feelings that arise through this breathwork, instead of trying to escape them, the client usually regresses in consciousness to an earlier time, often childhood, infancy, birth or before, when the trauma originated.

In a regressed state, a person can relive memories and emotions from long ago. Under the protection of the adult self, the younger self gets a chance to fully express emotions that were hidden because they seemed unsafe when first experienced. Often these expressions will come out in a little child's voice and vocabulary or as the crying sounds of an infant. The process is very intense and the reward is great. After releasing clogged emotions, the client experiences more inner space, which usually fills with a deep sense of peacefulness. This environment of freedom and serenity is the playground of the Magic Child.

I committed myself to weekly primal therapy sessions and also participated in weekend intensives for five years. During that time, besides clearing out old buried emotional trauma, I gained a familiarity with the emotional realm that is essential in my counseling practice and forms the basis for this book. I discovered that the fear of expressing uncomfortable emotions is only a feeling and the path to freedom and peace is through, not away from, emotional honesty.

After discovering this world of once taboo emotions, I began to encounter the world of Spirit within, which had also been obscured from my conscious mind. I was raised as a Catholic but had dropped my affiliation with the Church and its belief system and let the issue of spirituality idle on a back burner for years before I discovered metaphysical teachings (the study of nature's reality, particularly the connection between mind and matter).

In exploring the metaphysical belief that the outer world is a manifestation of the inner world, I found a new spiritual connection, the God energy inside of me. I now refer to this divine energy, or "godstuff," as the Magic Child. Although the Catholic teaching had always declared that God was present in everything, I had personally experienced God only as an outside force. Now, whether turning inward or outward, I find God everywhere. The Magic Child sees through all the masks of fear, recognizing the golden glow of God in every form of life. This guiding spiritual belief heavily influences my counseling practice, my writing, and every aspect of my life.

In 1989, I learned a journaling technique from Dr. Lucia Capacchione, author of *The Power of the Other Hand*, that enabled me to receive spiritual guidance from within. The technique involves writing and drawing with the non-dominant hand as a way to access information and feelings hidden from the conscious mind. This technique was my pathway to developing deeper intuitive knowing. My intuition has been an essential therapeutic tool. I have used it to sense the presence of emotions clients have hidden from themselves. I don't approach people with an outline of what they need to discuss or learn, to take their next steps. I trust my intuition to suggest the approach or the words that will invite those feelings into the open and beckon my client's hidden self to emerge.

My next major influence was Gabrielle Roth, author of *Sweat Your Prayers*. Gabrielle established her reputation at Esalen Institute in California, which represented the cutting edge of experiential therapy in the sixties and seventies. She calls herself an urban shaman because, like the shamans of primitive society who traveled through the underworld to heal people, Gabrielle, in a modern setting, leads healing journeys to the emotional underworld, through dance. By physically expressing all emotions, the dancer fully inhabits his or her body and moves through turmoil to peace.

Dance became the vehicle that helped me express emotional pain and taught me to celebrate all the varied parts of myself. I went on to study different transformative dance approaches from other teachers such as Pablo Bobbio from Argentina and Anna Halpern from Tamalpa Institute in California. Eventually, I made the transition from student/client to teacher/therapist through the doorway of dance.

While teaching dance classes, I discovered the increased intuitive sensitivity of a person who is physically grounded. This became apparent when I witnessed the results of following dance sessions with guided imagery and journaling. I had no training in visualization, and in fact couldn't do it myself when someone else was making the suggestions. However, in trusting intuitive guidance, I found a natural gift for using imagery to lead people on inner journeys to self-knowledge and healing. Guided visualization is the heart of hypnotherapy, which I later became certified to practice.

The final major piece of my training was certification in both Body-Centered Therapy and Conscious Relationship Transformation, under the tutelage of Drs. Gay and Kathlyn Hendricks at the Hendricks Institute. Practitioners learn to interpret the organic wisdom of the body using movement, breath, and integrity tools. The emphasis of both trainings is to learn to live from our spiritual essence and expand our capacity to give and receive love. By learning to tell the truth and keep our agreements we come into integrity, which frees us to create the lives we envision. This promotes greater vitality, intimacy in close relationships, and fun.

I consider the Hendricks training the most formative influence in my work. Their teachings helped me combine communication skills with the familiarity I already had with my body and emotions. They taught me the importance of expressing my emotional truths to all other people in my life. Through these studies, I discovered how the various parts of our personalities seem to have a life of their own and unconsciously direct our behavior.

The importance of being in integrity and taking responsibility for my life, instead of living like a victim, became very clear to me. Along with accepting responsibility, I learned to accept my emotions instead of just expressing them, and then move from that point to start designing my life. After completing the Hendricks Institute training, I knew I had the counseling skills and tools to assist people in making significant life changes.

These influences have been major ingredients in my professional and personal life; like a rich stew, I combine elements from a wide variety of counselors, workshop teachers, and books. Even when I wasn't actively seeking new ideas and tools, Life, like a master chef, added secret spicy ingredients on a daily basis, in the form of people and experiences. This book has been simmering inside the stewpot of my soul for nearly half a century, waiting to nourish your spirit.

Acknowledgments

I can fly higher than an eagle
for you are the wind beneath my wings.
—Larry Henley and Jeff Silbar

 Magic Wand
Know that you are never alone.

The Wind beneath My Wings

This book would never have been written without the support and influence of many important people in my life. I deeply appreciate each person's special gift to this book; collectively they have become—the wind beneath my wings.

My life is radically different and much more alive, as a result of the teachings of Drs. Kathlyn and Gay Hendricks. Many parts of this book are based on my experiences of applying their teachings in my own life and with clients. The Hendricks are working to change the world by empowering people, and their many students, like myself, will further this work in some unique fashion.

Bev Edelman, a woman who practices emotional honesty and radiates zest for life, was my first great teacher. She opened the doorway to my inner realm by introducing me to primal therapy and metaphysics. I count myself blessed to have Bev as a dear friend.

Lucia Capacchione, Gabrielle Roth, and all my other teachers gave me lights to explore the passageways of my inner world.

All the clients and students who have entrusted me to guide them on their journeys have expanded my wisdom and self-knowledge. Without their stories, this book would not have been possible.

Dr. Patrick Eleam, Cathy Pollack, Diane Sullivan, and all the other body-workers upon whom I have relied to midwife my body and mind into a spacious enough condition to birth this book have my gratitude.

Rev. Jody Miller Stevenson, my mentor, inspired me to begin writing my long dreamed of book and to keep going until it was completed.

After Dr. Lynda Falkenstein's verbal kick in the pants, I abandoned my dreams of writing a book, and actually began working on it.

My sister Kelly Pfautz and my dear friend Jai Deardorff gave me invaluable encouragement and editing direction in the early stages of my writing.

Loma Smith, my sister-in-law, was the first person to read my completed initial draft. Her reluctance to stop reading was a graphic testimony to her enthusiasm for the book. When she started using my ideas to make positive changes, she validated my efforts as an author. Loma's desire to help others love life shows up in her beautiful, love-rich photographic art laced throughout this book.

Loma, as a photographer, is part of the design team that has made this book the rich visual feast it is. My daughter Holly Hesse transformed my metaphors into playful cartoons, sprinkling the text with the light of humor. Mark Gamba, an extraordinary sports photographer, supplied the exciting canoe photo for the chapter on responsibility. Suzanne Stauss of Exhibit A Graphics conceived the design for photo presentation. I am indebted to this wonderful team.

Taffy Gleason is the editor of my dreams. Taffy comes alive creating order from chaos. Her insightful comments helped me see the places in my book that were contradictory or unfounded as well as the parts that quivered with power. Through her influence I was able to reorganize the previous drafts and express my thoughts with more clarity and power. Her faith gave me strength and inspiration whenever insecurity made me question the value of my writing. She was the compass that kept me steady right to the end of the project.

Kathy Arthurs, Dr. Patrick Eleam and Lynn Welsh Gamba assisted in the later editing stage, like relief pitchers, providing fresh insights and sharp eyes.

Thorn and Ursula Bacon and the staff of BookPartners are the talented professionals who transformed my work from a manuscript to a real live book.

My parents, Fran and Paul McConnell, whose relationship to God was their highest value in life, instilled that faith in me through word and example, giving me the spiritual and ethical foundation for my life. Their love supported me when I couldn't love myself, for they always saw the Magic Child inside me. Whenever I spread my wings, they encouraged and celebrated my efforts.

Rachel and Holly, my daughters, freed me to focus on writing this book through their willingness to be independent and to help with housework. They helped me stay in balance by enticing me to relate to them without badgering me for constant attention. My desire to mother these two beautiful and complicated young women, in a conscious way, has been one of the greatest propellers for my personal growth.

Even though we are no longer married, David Hesse loved me more than I knew how to love myself. He also financed the educational opportunities I needed to grow into the person I am, with the skills I have, for which I will always be appreciative.

Ron Meyers, my beloved husband, has helped me recognize and reach past limiting patterns and beliefs through his commitment to conscious loving. Ron's humor, honesty, encouragement and vision are inspiring and delightful. Though he had no children of his own to prepare him for fatherhood, he joined my family and offered Rachel and Holly paternal strength and support as well as incredible playfulness. I particularly value Ron's willingness to be publicly transparent, to let me write openly about him and about our experiences together. He has never asked me to hold anything back because he was too embarrassed to make it public. Ron has the liberating ability to love himself just the way he is. I appreciate his ability to see and love the Magic Child in me whether she is hiding behind a mask or shining for all to see.

My life is filled with people who are living miracles—the only variety of people that exists in my reality. I am thankful for all the moments I have lived and to all the miraculous people who have danced through life with me.

If you could learn to look kindly into the mirror,
you would see the Magic Child's golden light
shining through the mask
of self-judgment and limitation you wear,
and illuminating your true reflection:
the face of unconditional love.

Magic Wand
Find the magic inside your own heart.

Discovering Your Magic Child

Magic is all around us. If you pause for just a moment, perhaps you can sense its presence streaming inside your body. Can you feel it? The magic is invisible, of course, but it's the greatest power there is. This magic takes a tiny winged seed nestled within a pine cone and changes it into a giant Ponderosa pine tree. It's the energy that converts a hard gnarly bulb, buried in the ground, into a graceful daffodil swaying in the sunlight. We have a cellular familiarity with this magic because it transformed a microscopic cell into the complex human being reading this book. We humans tend to argue about what to name this magic, but everybody recognizes its power.

Some of us manage to live in the flow of this magic, happily achieving our dreams, while others, having lost their magical connection, stumble and struggle through daily life. If we want to experience full creative power and learn to love ourselves without limits, we must find our magic once again.

We all knew magic once. Do you remember what it felt like when you were a child? I used to create gourmet pies by shaping pebbles and mud into a dish with a petal garnish. How did you use your magic? Maybe you were one of those three-year-olds that sailed the seven seas in a cardboard box and became king or queen with the help of only a cape and a plastic crown. Perhaps you talked to the flowers and the animals, and could understand their replies. We knew as children that magic was real and natural. We believed we could be and do anything. We had no fear of failure.

Then somewhere between childhood and adulthood, in reaction to less-than-optimal life experiences, most of us stopped believing in ourselves and our innate power. We traded creativity and wonder for self-criticism and fear. The inner magic that once flowed so naturally seemed to vanish, disappearing behind the walls of our negativity. Disconnection from that magic left us feeling empty. In one way or another, life became a search to fill the hole we felt inside.

People try to fill the void in different ways. Feeling empty inside, we conclude that the space needs to be filled with something from outside ourselves. This is the beginning of power struggles as we focus all energy on getting whatever seems to be lacking, such as love, talent, money or opportunity. People avoid the despair of feeling empty by stuffing themselves with substitutes like work, sex, religion, causes, material objects, self-improvement, or substances. These temporary and ultimately dissatisfying solutions take us further from our magic essences and leave us feeling even emptier. We can never fill the inner void from the outside. The path to freedom is always through the frightening hole inside us. On the other side lies a wonderland of magic.

Most of us have trouble believing we could be magical. We feel so weak and unworthy, we can't imagine being completely wise, lovable and powerful. Since the magic required to transform us, in our own minds, seems to reside outside of us, we typically abandon our impossible dreams and outrageous potentials and cling resignedly to impoverished self-images.

Within each one of us there is a spark of life, a light-filled magic that is an indistinguishable part of the love energy that creates everything in existence, an energy many call God. I am calling this spark the Magic Child, to suggest the original innocent connection we all once had with the magic inherent in life. I believe the Divine Presence manifests in human form. The Magic Child is the aspect of us who still remembers that we are woven of Divine energetic fabric.

Although most of us lose contact with this wondrous aspect of ourselves at an early age, it never goes away. The Magic Child continues to shine within our hearts, regardless of our conscious awareness of it or our belief in its presence. This shimmering Being overflows with wisdom, love for self and others, and the creative power needed to enable each of us to reach our highest potential.

The Magic Child is a navigator who steers by the Star of Truth, and it can guide us safely through our earthly lives if only we turn inward, trusting enough to ask for help. This creative consultant can help us design and manifest circumstances beyond the wildest dreams of our conscious minds. No matter how much we, or others, believe we are defective and unforgivable, the Magic Child laughs gently at such foolishness and continues to emanate love. If you could learn to look kindly into the mirror, you would see the Magic Child's golden light shining through the mask of self-judgment and limitation you wear, and illuminating your true reflection: the face of unconditional love.

The Magic Child is our essence. When we look inside and find negativity, we are really seeing deceptive shadows of illusion. All humans are under the same spell, which is like an energetic prison surrounding the Magic Child. Instead of seeing beauty and possibility when we look at ourselves, we see defects looming before us.

By affirming the existence and invoking the assistance of the Magic Child, we undergo a conversion, a turning of the heart. This conversion from self-hatred to self-love is usually not quick or easy because self-criticism has deep roots. Most people, having learned to measure themselves against an impossible standard of "perfection," feel somehow inferior. The inevitable failure to meet that standard is a source of shame. Perfection is a widely variable mental construct, generally crafted and propagated to fill the needs of personal, social, professional, or religious authority figures. These standards of perfection are as deadly to a healthy sense of self-esteem as the mythical Greek Sirens who lured sailors toward shipwreck and ultimately death through their seductive song-promises of a perfect paradise.

We often develop our notions of perfection in childhood, imagining or being taught that if only we could meet our parents' needs, instead of inconveniently presenting our own, then they would love us completely and our family or even our world would be perfect. Critical parents actively foster this belief, but even accepting parents can pass it on, because in our culture ignoring one's own needs and feelings to care for another's is presented as saintly virtue. In my opinion, it is actually a seed of violence. Consider the inherent conflict. If we give to others while ignoring our own needs, we communicate a deep message to our innermost selves that we don't matter; we don't deserve to and cannot expect to have our needs met. The natural response to such messages is not an open-hearted outpouring of love and true service, but contraction withdrawal into deep grief and rage. Although many people will repress these feelings and continue on a path of service founded on victimhood or martyrdom, the feelings inevitably leak out, either outwardly in passive controlling ways or inwardly through the ravages of illness and depression. This kind of harm may be more subtle or indirect, but can be just as deadly as more blatantly destructive expressions. For this reason, I believe misplaced responsibility is a crippling legacy.

Young children often engage in magical thinking and are particularly prone to take on misplaced responsibility. Developmentally they are at the center of their universe and believe they are therefore personally orchestrating everything. From this childhood perspective, most of us easily believed it was possible to give our parents perfect lives by simply behaving more perfectly. We fantasized about becoming their dream child and struggled to be more quiet, to get straight A's, to dance more gracefully, or to hit the ball harder. Instead of rejoicing in our accomplishments, most of us focused on the gap between our accomplishments and what we felt we needed to do to be perfect and satisfy our parents.

The resulting shame over missing the mark was painful but didn't destroy our sense of control. We could still hold on to the fantasy that, by changing something about ourselves, we could earn our parents' complete love and acceptance. Facing the apparent truth that parental love is conditional seems to be too devastating for most of us as children. We don't have the understanding that their love is conditional because of their pain, not because we are in some way inadequate. Instead we wrap our essence, our Magic Child, in shame and go through life avoiding our true self, for fear of having to acknowledge that we really are unacceptable.

The way to free the Magic Child and begin to experience the joy of living our full potential is to begin to face and love ourselves exactly as we are. This means looking at our lives and lovingly accepting ourselves—despite having unconsciously created our present circumstances, even though we desired something better—and consciously choosing what we want to create instead.

In advocating self-acceptance, I am not condoning unhealthy behavior, but rather compassionate strength. In learning to love ourselves, we are not saying, "This is who I am and I'm not changing!" Love is responsible, and sometimes we must set boundaries or learn new coping skills. It says, "Summon the strength I know you have and let go of destructive attitudes and behaviors." Love is also forgiving. It says, "I know you have always done the best you knew how to do." Finally, love is empowering. It says, "I see the magic inside, the gifts meant for sharing. Please use those talents to create a more beautiful world." We can never spoil ourselves, or anyone else, with too much loving compassion.

Compassion makes room for new ways of living. When we can set aside resentment and self-criticism, loving ourselves and others exactly as we are, without demanding "getting rid" of unacceptable emotions or behaviors, then we usually feel freer to make positive changes. As our hearts open with self-love, creative expression is a natural result.

Although this sounds like a straightforward path, living a life of self-love is very challenging. I have found, through examining my own life and in working as a counselor, that people have common sticking places. These are conditions and situations where self-love seems impossible. From a sticking place, we tend to feel like victims and focus on what's wrong with ourselves and others, instead of expressing love and creative power.

This book is filled with personal stories, as well of those of friends and clients, intended to help readers navigate such sticking places. Unless I use a surname, all the names are fictitious, to protect people's privacy. In several instances I have even changed the names of places, for the same purpose.

My beliefs and perspectives are based on my experience in predominantly white, middle class, United States culture. People with other backgrounds may experience different cultural limitations and personal sticking places. If that is the case, use the sections of this book that beckon your Magic Child into the sunlight and leave the rest gently alone, like a pair of shoes that don't quite fit.

Besides stories, this book is packed with Magic Wands: principles that have changed my life and which, I believe, can transform yours, too. By putting these principles into practice, we can end the spell of fear that keeps us from fully loving ourselves and bringing forth all our gifts.

Ultimately, only total love can crumble the prison walls and dispel the illusory power of self-criticism. Although total self-love may seem impossible, it is not. The path may feel difficult, but the reward is great. Self-love liberates the Magic Child, who is then free to work miracles in our lives and fill us with unimagined joy. In reading, watch for insights about your own issues, patterns and sticking points, to discover ways you may have limited your own happiness.

My intention in writing this book is to help create a world where children are safe to unfold fully because we adults understand the importance of focusing on self-love while gently freeing the Magic Child from the citadel of our fear.

My husband, Ron, provided a wonderful example of love's liberating power. I share it at the outset of this book because it is the origin of the term Magic Child, and because it illustrates the joy that can transform your life, even if you are presently in great pain, if you set out on the path of self-love.

Ron Meets His Magic Child

One evening while playing the guitar, Ron strummed a haunting tune he had written twenty years earlier. Nausea and sadness enveloped him, as they always did when he tried to play that tune. The reaction never made sense, but was severe enough that he had always stopped playing the tune to end the uncomfortable sensations, and so had never completed the lyrics. This time, however, Ron accepted his feelings. He continued to play, allowing his emotions to grow more intense, while focusing on loving himself, along with his mysterious discomfort. Slowly, lyrics began to unfold, as if they had lain dormant, all those years, inside the pain.

I have a love way down inside
Feelings I want to show
I have a love way down inside
Feelings I want to grow.

Why are they so hard to sing?
Why do I keep them down?
What am I trying to do to me?
What do I want to be?

The nausea was a guard at the door of something he had rejected long ago. In going through the nausea, he had to face the next line of guards: unacceptable emotions. For whatever reason, Ron felt unsafe expressing those repressed emotions, believing something was wrong with them, and therefore something was wrong with him for feeling them. Because of that belief Ron had never been able to risk letting his deepest self emerge.

However, Ron was ready to make a change in his life. Courageously he faced his fear and prayed for truth and guidance.

Why don't you show me
How to find my fear?
I hear you shouting.
You have my ear.
Here's my heart
With my mind.
Whose love do I
Need to find?
Oooh the Magic Child in me.

Come on up! Come on up!
Come on up! Come on up!

What emerged, at last, was not a tormenting energy but a loving one. Ron's request for guidance transformed his emotions and he was reintroduced to his long-repressed Magic Child.

I am the sun that shines within
I am the feeling you wanted to know
I am the sun that shines again
I am the one whose love's aglow.

Why don't you call me?
I can help you be.
Why don't you call me?
I can help you see.
I'm the Magic Child in you.

As Ron realized that he was filled with magic, instead of misery, his song also became filled with wonder and love.

Now I feel you, now I see
Now I feel you so strong in me.
I love the Being that you are.
You know the feeling when you find your star?
The shade of white in the blackest sky,
The deepest sea in the ocean of time?
Oooh the Magic Child is me.

I have a love way down inside
Feelings I show; feelings I grow
inside it's magic; it's magic inside.

By moving into his fear and pain instead of repressing it or running from it, Ron discovered the wonderland hidden inside his heart. The Magic Child immediately started to shower him with love and miracles. Let Ron's story of self-love be an inspiration. You have this same power. The Magic Child is you! Take a chance! Put aside your self-doubt long enough to wave all the Magic Wands throughout the chapters and see what happens. Before long, you'll realize you are flowing with new life and surprising joy. You'll be part of a powerful sacred circle, filled with Magic Children, that is loving our world into a miraculous new day.

The only antidote to destruction is creation.
—Stephen Nachmanovitch,
Free Play: Improvisation in Life and Art

Magic Wand

Soothe the face of pain with love's creative caress.

In the Face of Violence

Our world trembles with violence and destruction. The newspapers are filled with stories of parents who lose self-control, then physically, sexually and emotionally abuse their own children. People filled with rage and self-loathing strike out at total strangers: kidnapping, raping and killing innocent children; destroying property; randomly slaughtering passersby; bombing crowded buildings. Even young children, mimicking their elders, have opened fire on unsuspecting classmates in bizarre killing sprees. Otherwise good people, impelled by ideological fervor or moral imperatives, discriminate against, attack, and sometimes even kill those who fall outside their idea of the right way to be, think, or act.

Laura Smither was a victim of senseless, random violence. She was one of my eldest daughter's best friends from Texas. A sweet, intelligent twelve-year-old with a passion for ballet, Laura was blessed with loving parents who placed family interests above all else. They all lived happily in an area known for good schools and community values. One spring morning Laura went out for a jog but didn't come home. After a heartbreaking month of uncertainty, her body was found decaying in a swamp.

When I first heard the news, I felt sick imagining Laura's terror and her family's pain. I thought about my own two daughters and wondered if they would remain safe in this seemingly violent world. For me, the only difference between Laura and all the other children who have died due to violence is that I knew her personally. I wanted to prevent anybody else from suffering as Laura and her family had.

Reflecting on society's current angry response to violence, I realized it is principally oriented toward protecting society and punishing violators. Certainly, this is a critical and appropriate response to violence. However, because physical jails only duplicate the energetic prisons of self-hatred that already confine violent criminals and abusers, the climate of violence remains even if the faces of the perpetrators change. Violent criminals need the control of external consequences, because they lack the ability to control their behavior from within. Necessary as these external measures are, they are only a surface approach. Reformation of both incarcerated and latent criminals requires a conversion of the heart and inner work leading to changed behavior.

In order to make a difference for the future safety of all children, we need to create a world where everyone can find love, even the individuals trapped inside the cycle of self-loathing and criminal behavior. I am advocating a societal commitment to the prevention of violence through conversion of hearts. For even in the face of violence, love has a powerful ability to transform people.

To achieve that, we need to enlighten our world from the inside out. Society will grow gentler as people learn to love themselves and turn their energy to creative expression. The more individuals learn to do this, including criminals, but especially parents, the more we can collectively transform this world into a safe and harmonious environment where everyone can reach full potential. In such an environment, people could focus on delightfully sharing their gifts with one another and no one would ever hurt another living being again.

I urge readers to begin creating such a world by internalizing the messages of this book. Discover the places where you may be withholding love from yourself and begin there. The effect of opening your heart on your own behalf is more powerful than you can imagine. As your self-love increases, look for ways to express your inner magic. This will have a powerful ripple effect upon the collective society. Recognize that love and creativity transform the violence that revenge and hatred can only reinforce. Put your philanthropic dollars into organizations that actively promote self-love and creativity, then watch our world grow gentler and safer.

The desire to seed our world with self-love and creativity has become the organizing principle for all my work: counseling, this book and any future ones, my tapes, and group presentations. I intend to be a contributing force to ending all forms of violence toward children by illuminating, for every person whose life I am privileged to touch, the life-transforming presence of the Magic Child trapped beneath all the negative judgments, fear, and anger that prevent each of us from living up to our highest potential. I long for every Magic Child to be able to dance freely in the sunshine and the moonlight until our world is no longer a violent place. Join with me, please, in envisioning such a creation.

Chapter One

*If we are one with God, one with all that exists,
then "who we think we are" has no limits
and every part of us is Divinely lovable.*

Magic Wand
Remember who you are.

Divine Connection

Before we can imagine ourselves containing a Divine Presence, like the Magic Child, we have to understand our connection with the Divine, the God energy permeating all that exists.

The term God may not work for some readers. To be consistent, I have chosen the name God for all Divine manifestations of God: Jehovah, Allah, the Great Mother, etc. If you are more comfortable using a different word for the Divine, simply translate, using any name that empowers you.

Many people are missing a connection to God. As we begin life, the Magic Child has not yet hidden or been imprisoned and so we find God everywhere.

Years ago my daughter, Holly, impressed this point on me on the way home from preschool one day. She looked at me very seriously and said, "It's okay if you don't have a friend to play with. You can just go outside and Mother Earth will be a friend to you." It takes Divine eyes to recognize sacred presence. This spiritual approach to life is natural to children, but by adulthood, many of us have unconsciously stored or imprisoned the Magic Child in darkened rooms of our inner mansions and so have trouble finding God's presence in the world.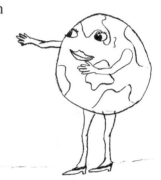

Human beings lose their instinctive ability to detect God shining through nature, circumstances, and people, for many reasons. Sometimes it atrophies because a child's parents no longer value, or never learned to value, the spiritual dimension of life and so fail to nurture the child's sense of the sacred. Other people, raised in religious families, may disconnect from the Divine when they are taught that God is judgmental and threatening. After years of feeling guilty for doing things that give them joy and worrying about hell, many kiss off this abusive type of God and the religion that promoted Him.

Women especially have turned away from authoritarian, patriarchal male Gods who demand subordination to men and deny women's collective power and individual worth. Other people have lost interest in a God who seemed to abandon them in their time of need. This mistrust may be present, but buried, even among people who profess belief in their God.

A client of mine, Molly, was a very religious woman who believed the Lord had guided her to me through the phone book yellow pages. Molly wanted to be hypnotized to lose weight, but as the journey began and I invited her to surrender to the power of God flowing through her as breath, she began to sob. Having dealt with childhood incest many years before, Molly was surprised by these tears. She had never come to terms with her feelings of betrayal and abandonment by God, who evidently had allowed this atrocity to occur. Though outwardly pious, she had severed her Divine connection.

I have counseled many people who have lost their connection with God. They go about their lives without noticing a sense of incompleteness, but when we talk on a deeper level, often their tears betray the loss they feel inside. I believe connection to the Divine is a basic human need, and that the Magic Child, inside each of us, is a sacred being who hungers for sacred nourishment.

Before we can nourish ourselves with Life's holy communion, I think we need to redefine our relationship to God. Many people have discarded the hellfire and brimstone God in favor of a God of love, but I believe we need to make an even more radical redefinition. I believe our connection with God is more intimate than any relationship we can imagine. It is even more intimate than union, which implies the joining of two separate entities. We are not separate from God. The Magic Child represents our true essence and that essence is Divine.

In thinking about who we are, few of us describe ourselves as part of God. Instead, we usually portray ourselves as fearful, limited beings. This thinking is the result of being governed by our conscious minds, which are limited to data absorbed through the five senses. Beneath the level of conscious thought exists the mind of the Magic Child. This unlimited mind recognizes other, non-sensory realities and, through intuitive prompting, reminds us of our Divine connection.

The mind of the Magic Child recognizes only one energy in all creation—love. Our conscious minds are more comfortable with categories, labeling people and experiences as either good or bad, belonging to God or the Devil. As we mature, most of us struggle to explain why good-intentioned people sometimes act in bad ways and why bad things happen to good people. We marvel when we notice a spark of good in bad people. All this confusion stems from the insistence of our conscious linear minds that life has to be divided into good and bad energies. The mind of the Magic Child extends way beyond limited human categories. Where human eyes find evil, magic eyes find a loving being who has been hurt and hides that pain under protective layers of fear and anger. Where human eyes see unfair experiences, the Magic Child discovers rich opportunity for a soul to grow in its capacity for love.

From the perspective of the Magic Child, love is all there is, so of course God has to be defined as love—and so do we. Despite the desire of our conscious minds to subdivide life into separate compartments with distinct labels, love cannot be diced up. We cannot distinguish ourselves from God, nature, or one another if, on the essential level of existence, everything is one identical energy of love.

By recognizing that we are one with God, part of the very same love energy, we can finally learn to love our whole selves. This has been difficult for most people to do because the Magic Child, that Divine essence, has been hidden from view. Without the Magic Child's presence, our lives typically feel lackluster and gray, as if love's fire has gone out in too many inner rooms. Having forgotten our true, magical identity, we feel unlovable.

We feel powerless, too. We can't fashion more positive lives if we believe that our circumstances, however dissatisfying, are better than we deserve and are beyond our power to influence anyway. Recognizing our oneness with God, the creative power of life, dispels the illusion of unworthiness and helplessness. Then, we can love ourselves and accomplish anything we set out to create. The Magic Child has no limits. Recognizing our Divine connection is the Magic Wand that can restore creative power, self-esteem and the ability to live life fully.

Gregory was a client in his fifties who had never married and was on the verge of a nervous breakdown over losing a woman he thought he loved. He had been raised as one of six children in a Midwestern Catholic family. Once a successful builder, he watched his life come crashing down around him when the market fell, and he went bankrupt. Having failed to recover financially, Gregory felt rudderless, as though there was nothing about him that was valuable. His father's constant refrain, "You're just a bum!" seemed to have come true. Nothing seemed to bolster his self-esteem, until, during a hypnosis session, I told him the following story. As you read it, substitute girl, if you are female. Perhaps someone you trust would read it to you, while you are relaxed.

Once upon a time, there was a beautiful boy, a magical boy. He was God's boy. God looked at this boy and saw nothing but goodness, magic, and love. Everywhere the boy looked, all he could see was God. He found God in the bugs in the creek, in the fish in the stream, in the flowers by the path, in the snowflakes falling from the sky. This boy knew that everything, including himself, was God. Nothing existed except God.

But as this boy grew, his parents, teachers, and siblings told him the same lies they had been taught to believe in. Although they were God's boys and girls too, they had forgotten their connection to the Divine. Now instead of finding God everywhere, they found fear. When they looked at God's boy, they were afraid to let his magic shine. Perhaps he would get hurt. Other people wouldn't understand. Perhaps he would need too much from them, and they wouldn't have enough to give him. To make him smaller and less significant, they began to tell him the lies. "You're a bum," they said. "You're no good and will never amount to anything. You only think of yourself. That's bad. You're bad."

At first, God's boy was confused. Then he felt angry, but he wasn't allowed to show that. Mostly he felt very sad. But he wanted love, and he thought he had to believe the lies or he would be all alone. Fear was already growing inside him. So he betrayed himself. Even though, deep down, he knew he was part of God and could never be anything less, he accepted the lie that he was no good, and not a part of God.

After that, the boy felt mostly shame. He didn't want anyone to find out that he was bad, so he hid behind a mask of being smart, rich, and in charge, hoping nobody would notice how bad he really was. This worked for awhile. But, in time, he was stuffed so full of self-hatred and pain that there was no room inside him to stuff anything else and he exploded. Nothing worked anymore. All he could do was cry. No matter what he did, he couldn't make the pain get back inside. There was nothing left of the mask to scrape together and put over his true face. He didn't know what to do.

At last, one day, he looked in the mirror. This time when he looked, he saw past the tears and the mess. He saw God's boy looking back at him. God's boy had gentle, compassionate eyes. "I love you," said God's boy and, for the first time in a long, long while, the man looked at himself, at God's boy, and said, "I love you."

The love he felt began to spread inside, starting like a warm ember in the belly and growing larger and warmer—a hearth fire filling him with peace and well-being. The memory came back so strong, the knowing that he was God's boy, made entirely of love, just like everything and everyone else.

Reflecting on the shambles of his life, he understood that real and painful as his physical experiences seemed, they had to be an illusion subject to transformation. As manifestations of God, both he and his life circumstances had to be created from love, once the veil of illusion was pulled away, because God is always love. Reality was an expression of love, nothing more, nothing less. Joy began to bubble up, and lighten his whole body. How long a time since he had felt joyful! God's boy took some deep breaths. Breathing out, with a sound, he expelled the lies from his body. He had come home to God.

After this session, Gregory was shaken, but for the first time felt optimistic. "I finally feel like we're getting somewhere," he said. Because we are all expressions of God in our essence, we cannot achieve a vibrant self-love when estranged from God. Spiritual reunion is a prerequisite for self-esteem.

For those uncomfortable with the word "God," unlimited Divine connection may not seem appealing, but this needs to be examined carefully. Those who have fled the confines of organized religion without being able to articulate a new attitude of spirituality avoid using the word "God." Do you do that? For some time, I did.

My path to discovering oneness appeared when I rejected the view of God presented by the religion of my youth. At first, I just stopped thinking about God. Once the directing force in my life and a primary relationship, God now became an outdated guide book gathering dust on my mental shelf. Discovering abstract terms for the Divine, like The Universe or The Life Force, enabled me to conceive of that energy as something inside that formed my essence. This energy was benevolent but faceless. Although I was sensing the presence of the Magic Child, we weren't yet on speaking terms.

Then one day, while driving, I had what felt like a vision. The whole sky seemed filled with loving energy, the Life Force, permeating everything that existed, including me, and it had a face. This face reached across the safe, impersonal distance between me and the Divine. This energy felt so alive and personal it required a name, so I returned to childhood terminology. God was alive once again, but in a much bigger way, because there was no sense of separation. Now, in talking about God, I refer to a being that is alive and present within me. This God energy is all loving, all powerful, and all creative. It is both the fabric of all life and the very personal Magic Child.

Why do we so easily forget our Divine connection? An ancient myth, paraphrased here, describes how this happened.

In the beginning, everything was God and God was all that existed. God, as love, was flowing with self-love and creative power. When combined, these two qualities created an image of self called "Other." God and the Divine Reflection "Other" let the love flow freely between them. Through this process, the creativity expanded and more reflections sprang into being. At first, all were perfect reflections of total light and love. In time, a game was created with the intention to create even more to love through the use of disguises.

God, the Spirit, would hide inside a different form, and then attempt, from inside, to love the form enough to penetrate the disguise, recognize self as the original Spirit of love, and reclaim the creative power of that love. The hide-and-seek field Spirit chose for this game was itself a Spirit in hiding, called Earth.

So it is that each of us, shining reflections of the One Divine Spirit of Love, come to Earth disguised as a body, rich with physical senses. This sensory apparatus so mesmerizes us with pleasure and power that the limitation illusion goes unnoticed. The game is to expand awareness beyond physicality—what we see, hear, and touch—and find the Divine light shining everywhere.

The Upanishads, ancient holy texts of the Hindu religion, remind us:

There is a light that shines beyond
all things on earth beyond us all
beyond the heavens
the very highest heavens
This is the light that shines in our Heart.
Chandogya Upanishad 3.13.7

The infinitely creative Divine mind invented a very challenging game, the Earth Game. Penetrating the disguise, recognizing the light of love, the Magic Child, and thereby winning the game are not easy tasks. Inside the disguises, using only the data gathered by our conscious minds, all of life is divided into "me" and "not me." This is called a dualistic view of life, one of the major illusions, or veils, we must learn to see through. It teaches us to believe we are separate from one another, and everything else that grows on the earth, from the time we begin living inside our mothers' wombs to our deaths. Of course, the Divine can only be imagined as "not me."

By comparing ourselves to God instead of identifying with God, we always perceive ourselves as lesser, subordinate. In comparison to God, we seem small and weak and confused, while God seems great and powerful and wise. From this viewpoint, we can never imagine ourselves as one with God. See—that's what makes this such a challenging game!

A handicap of the Earth game is that those marvelous brains, able to dissect, analyze, categorize, and harness much of the physical world, cannot leap beyond logic and answer the deeper questions of life. Yet, still insisting on rational explanations for situations and events that do not have reasonable expla-nations, we make up meanings and call them real. Faced with the violent death of a child (like Laura Smither), widespread famine, or the destruction caused by other natural disasters, we invent logical, sensory explanations. We conclude we are: at the mercy of physical forces we have not yet learned to control; victims of the decisions other people make; or pawns in the hands of a God with secret information. It isn't that our explanations are wrong. On the physical plane much of life is outside our control. The point is that life's more important meaning comes from a non-physical, non-rational dimension. If we fail to recognize this then power will seem to reside in "not me" and, feeling alone and helpless, we will overlook the Magic Child shimmering inside, waiting for acknowledgment, eager to increase the flow of magic in our lives.

People who have liberated the Magic Child usually feel alive, empowered, and connected, not alone and separate. To free the Magic Child, instead of relying on sensory data and our rational brains, we need to delve into the knowing of the intuitive mind. Sadly, many of us have lost touch with our intuition. The only thinking style we know how to use is logical and linear. However, access to the whole mind can be regained. The intuitive mind of the Magic Child is like the cosmic answer book. Through it we can experience unity with all life. Through intuition, we can discern what is right for us, discover things about life and other people without being told directly, easily figure out how to create whatever we want, and know we are one with God.

Albert Einstein, the father of modern physics, proved that all matter is actually energy. We now know, scientifically, what has long been understood by mystics and people living in harmony with the Earth. Innate intelligent energy flows throughout the universe expressing itself in varied physical forms, but remaining in essence the same connected energy field. Every one of us is an expression of this energy.

In elementary school, we were taught to divide all reality into the categories of animate or inanimate. Anything inanimate, by definition, was considered lacking life and intelligence, so people were free to manage it as a resource. Either we could identify signs of breath, growth, or intelligence or it was inanimate. Yet, if everything is innately intelligent energy, there is no such thing as an inanimate object. Everything is equally part of the life force. When we step beyond the bounds of five-sensory reality and use the power of the intuitive mind, this becomes clear.

Rocks are just one example of an inanimate life form. Yet I have held some rocks in my hand and sensed the life energy flowing through them. Just holding them seemed to prompt new insights. While traveling through Utah, I saw rocks rise up from the earth in forms resembling clusters of humans that seemed to be steeped in wisdom. For me, rocks are as alive as everything else that exists. Humans are simply unskilled in communicating with other life forms, because we have not been taught how, and we have been blinded by the illusory belief that much of life's matter is not really alive.

A Connection Perspective

We can more easily free ourselves of this limiting life view if we understand the way cultural perception has evolved over the span of human existence.

Until sometime in the first year of life, human babies do not experience themselves as separate from their mothers. Similarly, in ancient times, people felt intimately connected to all life, which many called the Great Mother. The Australian Aborigines, one of the most ancient peoples of the Earth, believe the life patterns set by the Creative Ancestors exist as seeds dreaming within the Earth. They believe we can intuit these patterns and so discover who we are and how we are meant to live. *The Essential Mystics: The Soul's Journey into Truth,* edited by Andrew Harvey, includes an Aborigine song that suggests this connection:

Tree...
he watching you.
You look at tree,
he listen to you.
He got no finger,
he can't speak.
But that leaf...
he pumping, growing,
growing in the night.
While you sleeping
you dream something.
Tree and grass same thing.
They grow with your body,
with your feeling.

Native American Indians also retained a belief in the sacred unity between God, humanity, and the Earth. Black Elk, a holy man of the Ogala Sioux tribe, said, "The first peace, which is the most important, is that which comes within the souls of men when they realize their relationship, their oneness, with the universe and all its powers, and when they realize that at the center of the universe dwells Wakan-Tanka, and that this center is really everywhere, it is within each of us."

In the 1850s, Chief Seattle, a highly respected leader from the Pacific Northwest, made a now famous speech during treaty negotiations in Washington, D.C., which poetically expresses this world view.

*I know the sap that courses through the trees
as I know the blood that flows in my veins.
We are part of the earth and it is part of us.
The perfumed flowers are our sisters.
The bear, the deer, the great eagle, these are our
brothers.*

*The rocky crests, the meadows,
the ponies—all belong to the same family…
The shining water that moves in the streams and rivers
is not simply water, but the blood of your grandfather's
grandfather…
The air is precious. It shares its spirit with all the life it
supports.
The wind that gave me my first breath
also receives my last sigh…
The earth does not belong to us. We belong to the
earth…
The earth is our mother.
What befalls the earth befalls all the sons and
daughters of the earth…
All things are connected like the blood that unites us.
We did not weave the web of life.
We are merely a strand in it.
Whatever we do to the web, we do to ourselves.
We love this earth as a newborn loves its mother's
heartbeat.*

The Celtic peoples were labeled pagan by Christians because they worshiped God in the earth. The following, and several other references used in this book, are from *Essential Mystics*. The same source credits the ancient *Welsh Black Book of Camarthan* for this tribute:

I am the wind that breathes upon the sea,
I am the wave on the ocean,
I am the murmur of leaves rustling,
I am the rays of the sun,
I am the beam of the moon and stars,
I am the power of trees growing,
I am the bud breaking into blossom,
I am the movement of the salmon swimming.
I am the courage of the wild boar fighting,
I am the speed of the stag running,
I am the strength of the ox pulling the plow,
I am the size of the mighty oak tree,
And I am the thoughts of all people
Who praise my beauty and grace.

In the influential Western world, most people have forgotten their link to Earth and all other life forms, as well as the Divine connection. That isn't necessarily all bad. Just as a human baby needs to experience itself as separate from its mother in order to begin discovering personal abilities and talents, this segment of humanity, in exploring separateness from God, learned to develop the powers of the five physical senses and the logical mind. This exploration has led to advanced understanding and powerful applications in every field of science, possibly a very good thing. However, it has also led us to create technology designed to serve our self-interest without regard for the effects on other people and life forms on our planet. With dawning awareness that we have poisoned our own nest, buds a realization that we are not separate after all.

The exploration of separation began with the advent of patriarchal societies in the pre-Christian era, where men replaced women at the head of social structures and where the chief, or only, God was depicted as Father instead of Mother. Just as the baby experiences father as "not me," so people in these societies viewed Father God as separate. At the time this shift was happening, human fathers were patriarchs, stern and absolute rulers of their families, not tenderhearted "daddies." People experienced themselves as God's people, subject to His Divine rule, eligible for, and dependent upon, His Divine protection. Like earthly rulers—only more so—this God was strong, wise, and just, but also strict and remote. Most of all, God was the absolute authority. People prayed for His help, lived in fear of His wrath, and charged into battle to fight His causes.

One of the innovations of Christianity was that Jesus consistently spoke of God not as his King, but as his Father. The Father he described was not a patriarch but a loving provider who wanted to care for His children and teach them to be loving as He was loving. This relationship eventually became an important part of Christianity, although for centuries, Christians, like other religious groups of the time, continued to think of God as a more powerful version of the kings of their own countries. At a time when territorial power struggles were widespread in Western civilization, whenever European and Moslem rulers wanted to claim more lands, they inspired the populace by flying God's flag at the head of their battle formations.

The world today seems less obsessed with conquering lands already claimed. The birth of the United States inculcated democracy more widely into the human consciousness, like a dandelion grown strong enough to send its seeds all over neighboring yards. The democratic principle proclaims that all people, not just kings, are entitled to life, liberty, and the pursuit of happiness, and are responsible for, and entitled to, self-governance. In our times, at least in Western civilization, people seem more concerned with that goal. Society is examining ways to generate happy, functioning, responsible members. There is increasing recognition of the importance of the family in accomplishing this. In such an environment, the view of God as a loving Father is very attractive.

The problem I see in this relationship with God is that people tend to perceive themselves as little children, still weak and dependent, too small to know what's right and prone to make big mistakes that require intervention by a savior. Most parents expect their children to grow up eventually, accept full responsibility for their actions, and realize their full potential. We don't envision them growing up still helpless and dependent on us. We don't expect to provide for them or rescue them as adults. Why would God be a more co-dependent parent than we humans are?

Christianity has exerted a huge influence on the world. Yet the principle gift of Christianity seems to have been largely overlooked. Father John O'Donohue, Catholic priest and author of *Anam Cara: Wisdom from the Celtic World*, talks about the meaning of the Incarnation, Christianity's principle doctrine, when he says, "I believe that the modern Western expression of Christian religion endorses and implies a division between soul and flesh, and between individual and nature—a division that is really false. If you look at the Incarnation—which is Jesus the God becoming man—what you see is that when God became human, the Divine embraced every aspect of that which we consider human. Or to put this truth in a metaphorical way, the flesh of Christ enfolds the bones of every human event."

In my reading of the Gospels, Jesus teaches that we are all one. He tells people that whatever He has done we can do, and even greater. How would this be possible if we were not all part of the same power source: infinitely creative love? In reference to Jesus, St. Paul's letters in the Christian Bible state, "In Him we move and breathe and have our existence." We exist within the mystery of God, not someplace outside, or even below on some Divine organizational chart. Yet despite these teachings, Christians, like most people who are stuck in five-sensory thinking, act from the belief that God is better, higher, and, above all, other.

By choosing to keep Jesus as "not me," relating to Him as more than just a human, Christians, and all other groups who place their God on a pedestal, accept certain limitations. While it is possible to feel totally loved by God, it is impossible to claim love's full creative power. Instead, God, as the authority, always has the final say. Human creative plans are subject to God's approval or they don't work out. Since God is viewed as all-wise, people have to believe their ability to know or create is limited. Mythology, worldwide, abounds with stories of unfortunate mortals who dared claim they could know or do what only the gods were supposed to be able to do and who were harshly punished for their audacity. Full power for humans is off-limits.

With this type of Divine connection, people feel only partially responsible for their lives. They can influence the quality of their lives through hard work and good behavior, but they have no power to orchestrate—mysterious harm may still befall them. Mainly they have to surrender to God's greater power, proclaim their lack of control and accept whatever happens to them as God's will. This view of life encourages the interpretation of success as proof of Divine favor and failure as either a test of character or Divine condemnation. People live like victims and justify doing so by mentally wrapping themselves in the robes of martyrdom. This provides a sense of meaning but it doesn't empower anybody. The Magic Child stays hidden when this belief prevails.

When people believe they have no power to create the kind of life they want, they often give up. Their energy is depressed because they are angry about being insignificant pawns in God's arrogant game. Some people focus on the promises of a better deal in heaven, which consigns life's potential to the future. I believe we can create the lives we want, in the present, by liberating the Magic Child, and recognizing our unity with God, each other, and all life. There is no outside force controlling or preventing our happiness. The saying "We have met the enemy and he is us" is quite true. The enemy is our illusory belief that we are separate from ourselves, each other, and God.

The good news is that the necessary shift out of limited consciousness is in motion. Besides the societies I have already mentioned who never forgot the Divine connection to life on Earth, Eastern religions have always taught that the goal of human existence is to experience oneness with God. They developed technologies, like yoga and meditation, to awaken the human mind to awareness of unity with God.

In the *Shveteshavatara Upanishad* is written:

Like oil in sesame seeds, like butter
In cream, like water in springs, like fire
In a firestick, so dwells the Lord of Love,
The Self, in the very depths of consciousness.
Realize Him through truth and meditation.

During the sixties and seventies, many people in Western societies were exposed to the beliefs and practices of Eastern religions as well as to those of other peoples with non-dualistic views. The possibility of being one with God filtered into the mainstream of Western society.

Meanwhile, Western technology hooked up the global village, and people began to realize humanity is interconnected and interdependent. Physicists developed quantum theory and began to prove, using high-powered microscopes and advanced mathematical calculations, that reality extends far beyond the realm of the five senses. Their experiments proved all energy is connected and every particle affects the whole. With the advent of space travel, people got an outsider's view of the earth and began to appreciate her fragility. To remember the words of Chief Seattle, "We are just a strand in the web and what we do to the web we do to ourselves." The ancient spiritual ideas about connection are being validated through the scientific method. I am excited by these trends.

The Secret Life of the Magic Child

The importance of understanding this Divine connection is that our ability to love ourselves and to create the lives we want on this Earth is totally dependent on who we think we are. Do you remember that phrase from childhood, "Just who do you think you are?!" Usually it was hurled as an accusation because we had stepped outside the bounds family or society had imposed, and it implied we better get back inside that particular boundary. Most of us accepted this as the price of being part of the group, but to step back within the limits, we repress the part of us that has caused a problem. Instead of celebrating individuality, we lock the Magic Child in a dark room of the inner mansion and put a sentinel of shame outside to prevent love's attempts at liberation. If we are one with God, one with all that exists, then "who we think we are" has no limits and every part of us is lovable. The sentinel of shame needs to be dismissed so the delightfully individual Magic Child can expand into his or her full space.

My belief in the Magic Child, shimmering with the Divine fabric of love, is reinforced through my work. When clients explore the subconscious, they often find God inside themselves. Sometimes they picture God in a traditional form, like Jesus, and I watch their faces transform with a radiant inner light. My client Esther was a ministerial student who had been meditating on a daily basis for a year, mentally constructing a lovely garden where she waited for Jesus to appear. In hypnosis Esther found a deeper garden, made of crystals, and it was there that she met Jesus. Tears of joy rolled down her cheeks as she faced God, expressing as Jesus, right inside herself.

Other clients perceive not a God figure but a Divine quality, personified in symbolic form. Susannah, a beautiful woman in her early twenties who was sexually abused as a child, habitually chose partners who were weak-spirited, violent men. Her life had been spent in frightened accommodation; she hid any aspect of her own spirit a man didn't like. Deep within, Susannah discovered Divine strength, personified as a huge bear. She seemed to grow taller as she accepted what some Native Americans would call "Bear medicine" as her own.

Sam, a client in his mid-twenties who spent time in prison for a rape he committed when he was eighteen years old, still struggled with unwanted sexual fantasies and behaviors. Completely frustrated by what felt like inherently bad character, he felt powerless to change. In his inner realm, Sam discovered a little boy who had been sexually violated by his mother at a very early age. This child, who was angry, scared and very sad, had been completely hidden from Sam's conscious mind, and couldn't express anger directly toward his mother. Instead, the anger turned inward toward himself and outward at society. The little boy was too wounded to believe he was good. I led Sam to an inner place that lay deeper than his pain. On a peaceful beach in the sunset, he was approached by a shining Being of Light. Afterwards, Sam's face was aglow. His voice was hushed with awe as he told me what had happened. "The Being came to me," he said, "came right inside. Then it told me, 'I am you'." I knew Sam had met the Magic Child.

Jerry had a similar experience. He was a client in his forties who was feeling deep pain after the breakup of a relationship he thought would be permanent. He had been delving into his own issues and uncovering painful childhood wounds. He felt small and helpless, on a journey through darkness. Unable to go on alone, he finally asked for help while under hypnosis. The response of a holy presence caused him to draw his breath in sharply. "It was just inside me!" he whispered. "It was really hot." Tears ran down his face, like a baptism, as he trembled with the love he felt inside.

I have felt this sacred awe myself, on more than one occasion, sometimes within the context of a story, sometimes simply as energy. One time, in the stillness following a powerful emotional release, I was filled with a memory of being a Native American medicine man who had just died. Buried in a mound of dirt, I saw the funeral and mourning activities of the tribe in the periphery of my awareness, while my attention was absorbed in communing with the earth. No edges separated my body from the dirt. I felt totally peaceful, seamlessly connected to the earth and vibrantly alive.

Other times, energy has streamed inside me, conveying a certainty of my ability to fulfill my soul's intentions. In those moments, all the seemingly real limits of earthly experience, such as shortages of time or money, clearly feel like illusions. Even after returning to the waking state, I retain a more muted version of this knowing and am able to move through the day acting on these deeper understandings.

Connection Metaphors

For those who still have difficulty accepting the idea that we could be one with God, consider the meaning of connection. From within the limits of five-sensory reality, it means God, life, or the web all represent a mosaic and each part of life is a tile in that mosaic. A tile is part of the mosaic, but not the whole mosaic. We are parts of God, but not God. That is the five-sensory view.

This mosaic image focuses our attention on the individuality of each tile. The five-sensory mind is convinced that distinctions are real because they are apparently measurable. But the magic mind does not make distinctions, except on a superficial level.

The holograph concept illustrates the magic mind's perceptions. In that model, every portion of the holograph contains the whole. In cloning experiments entire organisms can be replicated from a single cell because each cell contains the whole code. I believe that God is a holograph and each seemingly separate one of us is a part of the holograph, indistinguishable in our essence state from the whole.

The ocean provides another image. We are each like a drop of water in the ocean. The ocean consists of many drops and yet, unless separated from the ocean, one drop is indistinguishable from the ocean. When we separate ourselves from our Divinity through our thoughts of inadequacy, we are like the drop removed from the sea. If we keep aware of our connection to the whole, like the drop that forms part of the ocean's power, we have all the creative power, all the love, we can ever need.

Ultimately, we cannot define the Divine connection in a satisfying way because human language has limitations. The language of logic is based on distinctions and categories. Metaphors are often more helpful than definitions because they flow from the imagination rather than from the narrow perimeters of the conscious mind and so have more power to touch our deepest remembering. When we use metaphoric speech, we are using a language of association. When we read Robert Burns's simile, "My love is like a red, red rose," logic is set aside and we experience his love as an exquisite flower. The poets and mystics have always turned to metaphor, which is the Magic Child's native language, to express mystery. The monk and mystic Bede Griffiths described the frustrations of linguistic limitation in *Return to Center*. He wrote:

> *But does this mean that here all differences and distinctions disappear? Does this mean that I am God? Here I must remember that what I am trying to describe is a mystical reality, which cannot properly be expressed in human terms. I am straining human speech in order to try to bring it within the grasp of my mind..If I try to find words to express that transcendent Reality, I have to use images and metaphors, which help to turn my mind toward the truth, and allow Truth itself to enlighten it.*
>
> *I can say that that eternal world is like the white light of the sun, in which all the colors of the rainbow are present and in which each retains its own distinctive character. Or I can say that it is like a symphony in which all the notes are heard in a single perfect harmony, but in which each has its own particular time and place. Or I can say that it is like a multitude of thoughts gathered together in a single mind which comprehends them in a single idea embracing all. Or going deeper, I can say that it is like a communion of persons in love, in which each understands*

the other and is one with the other. "I in them and thou in me, that they may become perfectly one." This is as far as human words can go.

In *The Way of Passion* the great Islamic Sufi poet Rumi wrote about the uselessness of describing the Divine in words or separating the essence of humanity from the Divine.

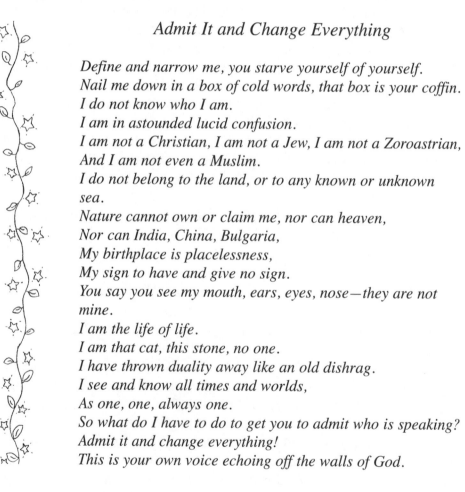

Admit It and Change Everything

Define and narrow me, you starve yourself of yourself.
Nail me down in a box of cold words, that box is your coffin.
I do not know who I am.
I am in astounded lucid confusion.
I am not a Christian, I am not a Jew, I am not a Zoroastrian,
And I am not even a Muslim.
I do not belong to the land, or to any known or unknown
sea.
Nature cannot own or claim me, nor can heaven,
Nor can India, China, Bulgaria,
My birthplace is placelessness,
My sign to have and give no sign.
You say you see my mouth, ears, eyes, nose—they are not
mine.
I am the life of life.
I am that cat, this stone, no one.
I have thrown duality away like an old dishrag.
I see and know all times and worlds,
As one, one, always one.
So what do I have to do to get you to admit who is speaking?
Admit it and change everything!
This is your own voice echoing off the walls of God.

The Magic Child's Liberation

Ron initially had trouble accepting the idea of Divine connection. "With the Christian beliefs I was raised by," he told me, "I just can't get to a place where I can believe I am God." We talked about how this is impossible for our conscious minds. Although convinced I am completely connected to God and fully responsible for creating my life, I still make a distinction between myself and God.

Although one with God in essence, in everyday life, I too easily lose awareness of that essence and operate from the limited, five-sensory viewpoint of my conscious mind. This self still believes I am separate from God, simply a tile, and gets caught in feeling undeserving and unlovable, in doubting my ability to know what is right for me and to manifest my dreams. In that place of consciousness, I can't think of myself as God either. But when I identify with the Magic Child I understand this mystical connection. Through longing for God, I recognize the true self that the Magic Child is reminding me about.

In his *Book of Hours*, the German poet Rainer Maria Rilke speaks for the Divine, the Magic Child, calling us to know our own selves, through the longing of our hearts.

I am, you anxious one.
Don't you sense me, ready to break
into being at your touch?
My murmurings surround you like shadowy wings.
Can't you see me standing before you
cloaked in stillness?
Hasn't my longing ripened in you
from the beginning
as fruit ripens on a branch?

I am the dream you are dreaming.
When you want to awaken, I am that wanting:
I grow strong in the beauty you behold.
And with the silence of stars I enfold
your cities made by time.

If we can liberate the Magic Child, who comprehends unity with God, then we can start living our lives as God would live them. Our only obstacle to complete love, abundance, and personal satisfaction is an unwillingness to think and act as God. If we could all make this shift, we could create the kind of world God would create: a world of loving acceptance, unlimited abundance, and creative possibility. In such a world of Magic Children at play, there would be no violence.

Please, remember who you are. Liberate the Magic Child. Our world is waiting for you to come all the way home to creative, loving consciousness of your truly magical identity. The journey isn't long or hard—all it takes is a shift in your thinking.

Wondersparks

1. What is your relationship to your God? If you perceive your God as different than you, as "Other," what purpose does that separation serve for you?
2. If you have rejected the God of your youth, what is your current relationship to the sacred?
3. Have you made a conscious choice to believe in a new way or are you in a holding pattern without a particular belief? In that case, what are you waiting for?
4. Do you trust your God with your life?
5. How would your life be different if you woke up tomorrow as God?
6. Would you love yourself and others more if you knew you were God?
7. Would you give yourself the riches and the satisfactions you've been wanting?
8. What gift is your Magic Child waiting to give our world?

Elixirs for the Mind

Seat of the Soul, by Gary Zukav. If I were going to live on a desert island, this is one of the books I would bring. Gary shows how humankind is evolving from a species relying on external power, based on five-sensory perceptions, to a species that uses spiritual power. His explanations are clear and provocative.

Coming Home: The Return to True Self, by Martia Nelson. If I could only take one book to that desert island, this would be the one. The author not only explains the Divine connection but also uses that understanding to foster self-love and creative power.

The God Game, by Father Leo Booth. The difference between religion and spirituality is clearly explained by this Episcopal priest who, through the pain of alcoholism and the grace of recovery, discovered a living God.

The Feminine Face of God, by Sherry Ruth Andrew and Patricia Hopkins. Whether you are a woman who feels relegated to second-class religious citizenship or a man who has been exposed to only the masculine view of God, this book offers a refreshing feminine perspective on the experience of the sacred. The authors have interviewed many women and share a variety of approaches to the sacred, including integration of spirituality, the body, and sexuality.

The Essential Mystics: The Soul's Journey Into Truth, edited by Andrew Harvey. This beautiful book is rich with mystical wisdom from eight different world traditions. Harvey honors them all, explaining their unique contributions. It is a rich lore of inspiration for me.

Anam Cara: Wisdom from the Celtic World, by Father John O'Donohue. O'Donohue offers sacred nourishment in the Celtic tradition, which finds spirit everywhere, through all the physical senses. His words are rich with compassion for all of life, even those experiences that can be most challenging, like relationships, work and death.

Rilke's Book of Hours: Love Poems to God, translated by Anita Barrows and Joanna Macy. This is a collection of beautiful mystical poetry of spiritual yearning and discovery. The Rilke poems that I have included in my book all come from this source.

Manifest Your Destiny, by Dr. Wayne Dyer. I would put this book into my desert island knapsack. Dyer helps readers understand how, as expressions of the Divine energy, we are inseparable from all that is and are constantly engaged in a process of creation, which allows us to become more conscious.

Chapter Two

We will finally feel at home
when we regard our body
as a sacred expression
of our soul's love and creativity.

Magic Wand
Treat your body like a beloved friend.

Body Truth

The dualistic belief that our bodies are somehow separate from the essence of our souls leads to deep inner discontent, a sense of internal warfare. If soul is the God part of us, and the body is something else, then is the body an obstacle to experiencing the Divine connection? Is it our earthly task to overcome the weakness of the flesh and the illusions of the ego so that we may leave our troublesome, uncooperative bodies behind and enjoy the bliss of the spirit world? This view encourages us to think of the body as a burden, at best, and a foe, at worst.

Another equally harmful approach is to ignore our bodies. We reluctantly tolerate earthly form while "in exile" from the spirit world. If we think of life as an educational process for our souls, our bodies seem somehow separate and inferior. If we focus on spirit as something other and better than our tangible selves, it's as if we ride a mental rope swing so far beyond the human experience that we fling ourselves outside the earthly realm altogether. Our bodies may remain here, but because we're not honoring them, we miss the whole point of incarnation and spend our lives feeling alienated.

I think we need a radically different approach to our bodies, one that is soulful and respectful. To do that we need to think in terms of images that suggest intimacy and unity rather than separation. What if we were to approach the body as a beloved friend? What if we began treating our bodies not as prisons, or even temples housing the good part of us, but as our goodness, our essence, in sensual form?

Father John O'Donohue, author of *Anam Cara*, a book that describes the image-rich tradition of Celtic spirituality, said, "The soul is not in the body, but rather the body is immersed in the soul, which radiates out all around the body." Gay Luce, founder and director of Nine Gates Mystery School, said, "The body is like an antenna for God.…There isn't anything about our bodies that is not this antenna, this tuning fork for the Divine." The mystical English poet William Blake, who found the Age of Reason lacking in spirit, wrote, "Man has no Body distinct from his Soul for that called Body is a portion of Soul discerned by the five Senses, the chief inlets of Soul in this age." In the early sixteenth century, Mirabai, India's most famous woman saint, wrote the following poem, published in *Women in Praise of the Sacred:*

> *O friend, understand: the body*
> *is like the ocean,*
> *rich with hidden treasures.*
>
> *Open your inmost chamber and light its lamp.*
>
> *Within the body are gardens,*
> *rare flowers, peacocks, the inner Music;*
> *within the body a lake of bliss,*

on it the white soul-swans take their joy.
And in the body, a vast market—
go there, trade,
sell yourself for a profit you can't spend.

The poets and mystics give us a sense of the relationship between the limited physical self we experience daily and the Magic Child who is somehow more. I like to think the soul, the Magic Child, is expressing itself in material form as a body. When we die, I think the soul lets go of that particular expression, but while we live, our bodies are every bit as holy, just as much our truth, as whatever we imagine our spirits to be. We will finally feel at home when we regard our bodies as sacred expressions of our souls' love and creativity. This level of self-honoring can only evolve if we begin to treat ourselves, expressed in bodily form, the way we love our most intimate friends—tenderly and respectfully, eager to know both the secret tears and the hidden dreams, the emotional world of the body. There is an organic unity of earthly body and Divine spirit. Only in loving and listening respectfully to the whole, can we experience inner magic.

In order to love ourselves as spirit-drenched physical beings, we need to understand the legacy of body-hate that has prevented this attitude. If the senses are, in fact, the chief inlet for the soul; if our bodies are, in fact, rich with hidden treasures, tuning forks for the Divine—how did the body fall into such spiritual disrepute? The division between body and soul started with the Greeks and mushroomed with the spread of Christianity. The dualistic illusion says we are spirits, belonging to God, who is also Spirit. All that stands between us and God is this weak, sinful flesh that we are trapped inside. In the Bible, especially the letters of Paul, encouragement to put aside matters of the flesh abounds.

In medieval times, Christians carried this idea to extremes. Intent on becoming more "spiritual," they punished the bodies that kept blocking their way to sainthood. It was common practice for these Christians to wear coarse, uncomfortable hair shirts and to whip themselves on a regular basis. Priests encouraged these behaviors as well as other physical and emotional humiliations.

With all that self-abuse, bodies still could not be tamed. Gluttony, sloth, and most especially lust, three of the "deadly sins," were rampant. Even the most publicly religious members of society were secretly plagued by "lures" of the body. So the Catholic Church mounted a concerted attack to purge society of fleshly influences.

Sexuality was considered the most powerful entrapment of the flesh, so anything that promoted sexuality had to be squelched. Women were labeled as a menace and were blamed for tempting men to yield to the fleshly passions. Men, naturally attracted by female beauty, were not expected or required to be accountable for their behavior. Eve's role in causing humanity's separation from God in the garden of Eden was held up as proof that women were a danger for men aspiring to be spiritually pure. For women, born "handicapped" as the more sinful sex, the only hope for salvation was total denial of sexual desire.

Anything that promoted physical pleasure was viewed as an evil temptation by people who held this mindset. To dance, especially for women, was to flaunt the dangerously sexual body, so dancing was bad. Puritans, who certainly had a formative influence in United States culture, were perhaps the most fanatical group. Even clothing was a fleshly pitfall, so people had to wear plain dark clothes.

Compounding religious attitudes about the sinful body is the Western scientific attitude, which dates back to René Descartes, who is considered the father of modern philosophy. Descartes was primarily a mathematician. He recognized that everything in existence could be doubted except the process of doubting, therefore the one who doubts must exist. This is the origin of his famous saying "I think, therefore I am." From that premise the world's values were eventually reconstructed.

Descartes believed that the material universe, including the human body, was totally mechanical, following logical laws. He explained away mystery and consciousness as the intervention of God, whom he considered First Cause. His philosophy is important, because since that time, in the Western world, soul, expressed as consciousness, has been the realm of religion while the material world has been the realm of science. The body became just a piece of equipment, available for study, dissection and separation.

Between the religious view that the body is an impediment and the scientific view that the body is a piece of machinery, those of us who have grown up with these Western influences tend to think of our bodies as "other." Bodies, seemingly on their own, contract diseases that hurt us. We "take them into the shop" for repair, but cannot always get them fixed. Efforts to change habits and lifestyles seem to be thwarted by bodies that possess an independent mind, stronger than our conscious will. So we eat cupcakes though intending to eat salads, drink alcohol while saying we want water, and sit watching television, ignoring plans to exercise.

Even while we think of our bodies as "other," our self-image, particularly for women, is totally entwined with the way our bodies look. Of course they never look right, because we compare them to soft-focus photographs of magazine models with air-brushed, flawless skin and computer-enhanced figures.

These self-critical attitudes lead to discontent and alienation. How can we feel at home when our physical forms are the enemy, engaged in obstructing the work of our souls? We have to change this belief. Our bodies are not adversaries. The Magic Child is the soulful essence of love expressing in the physical realm.

Before the time of Descartes, soul was perceived in everything. Because it cannot be measured, Descartes essentially cast it out of the material world and tossed it to the priests for study. Since this separation, soul, as a spiritual idea, has been stripped of its earthiness. All that was left of soul in the scientific realm was the aspect that could be measured, that was referred to as mind, and that was thought to reside in the brain. Intelligence became not a quality of soul but a complex electronic function that could be measured by scientific tests. Aspects of intelligence such as intuitive knowing, which could not be measured, were dismissed as unimportant—simply "women's intuition" or "old wives' tales."

But now, as scientists gain the tools to probe more deeply into the body, they are discovering that mind is not restricted to the area of the brain or to logical function. They are starting to recognize that mind resembles soul, but their scientific code discourages many of them from calling it by name.

In *Healing and the Mind*, the companion volume to a Public Broadcast Station (PBS) series, journalist Bill Moyers documents interviews with a variety of doctors and scientists, including Candace Pert, Ph.D., a professor at the Center for Molecular and Behavioral Neuroscience at Rutgers University. Pert studies the chemical relationship between the mind and the body, the exchanges between peptides and receptors on a cellular level that we experience as emotions and physical responses. Moyers asked, "What is the mind?" Pert replied: "The mind is some kind of enlivening energy in the information realm throughout the brain and body that enables the cells to talk to each other, and the outside to talk to the whole organism....The mind is not confined to the space above the neck. It is throughout the brain and body."

Larry Dossey, M.D., is an expert on alternative healing and one of the authors included in the text *Healers on Healing*, edited by Dr. Richard Carlson and Benjamin Shields. He says, "In our culture we have said mind is local. It is confined to the brain....The local approach to the mind means that minds are multiple—one mind per each...human brain on our planet....But this way of looking at mind breaks down when we examine the way minds actually behave. In fact the mind steadfastly refuses to behave locally, as contemporary scientific evidence is beginning to show....Brain-like tissue is found throughout the body. Receptor sites for chemical endorphins have been discovered in many places outside the brain....Endorphins are actually made at sites distant from the brain. So, even from the conservative perspective of modern neurochemistry, it is difficult, if not impossible, to follow a strictly local view of the brain. Furthermore...the mind appears to have burst not only the bounds of the brain to invade the entire body, but it seems to have escaped the body altogether. There is much data suggesting that mind is at large in the world, that it is not a place at all."

Dossey describes experiments where information has been transmitted accurately across great distance with no device but the power of mind. In some experiments, the information has been received several days before being transmitted. This shows that mind is not limited by space or time. Dossey continues: If minds are not in a place in space or time, then they are unbounded; if unbounded, then they are not separate. This means they cannot be individual, as we have always thought. True, mind may act through individual brains, just as a radio signal can act through a receiver. But that isn't the complete story. Fundamentally, mind must be one, not many."

Candace Pert also says, "Clearly there's another form of energy that we have not yet understood. For example, there's a form of energy that appears to leave the body when the body dies. If we call that another energy that just hasn't been discovered yet, it sounds much less frightening to me than 'spirit.' Remember, I'm a scientist, and in the Western tradition I don't use the word 'spirit.' 'Soul' is a four-letter word in our tradition. The deal was struck with Descartes. We don't invoke that stuff. And yet too many phenomena can't be explained by thinking of the body in a totally reductionist fashion,…as just chemical and electrical gradients."

So according to science, one mind is expressing everywhere, and perhaps the body possesses an energy that can only be explained as soul. If this is all true, and I certainly believe it is, then our relationship to our bodies has to change. If we treat our bodies as beloved friends, then perhaps we will learn their native language. Our bodies, totally infused with mind, are innately intelligent and capable of direct communication. For that reason, I have coined the term "bodymind" to connote the spirit-drenched nature of physical form. Bodies use a language of physical sensations, symptoms and gestures that are all directly linked to emotions. If we pay attention to such bodily communication, listening with a friendly ear, an intuitive ear, we can access valuable and reliable information. If we ignore either the signals from our bodies or the emotional meanings embedded within those signals, we will fail to thrive upon this physical earth plane.

Because society has disdained the physical and extolled the power of reasoning, many people only value concepts. Ideas are certainly important. They are the seeds of creation. But just as seeds need to be planted in the ground and watered to grow, so ideas need to be grounded in the body and moistened with emotion before they can develop in a positive way. Many people are pot-bound. Distracted by all their wonderful ideas, these folks overlook the importance of the physical and emotional planes. Without more soil and water, their ideas can't flourish. This is true regardless of the spiritual merit or creative genius of the individual ideas. Ironically, for those who love ideas and reason, growth requires turning to the more mundane realm. If you're wanting to expand but feeling stuck, you may be pot-bound. By engaging your body in emotionally rich conversation, you may experience a new growth spurt and begin to thrive instead of just survive.

Intimate Conversations

Body communication is very different from analytical discussion. Bodies offer perspectives that will often seem strange to the rational mind. I remember a particularly startling conversation with my body. Like an unappreciated friend, my body set me straight on how my own attitudes were causing my problems. This conversation happened during my first training with Kathlyn Hendricks, which involved learning to listen to the body's messages. For nine months, I had been on an allergy diet to eliminate a severe problem with intestinal gas. The diet was working and the symptoms had stopped for quite some time. During the training, the symptoms flared up again, even though I was still on the diet. Although puzzled, I was learning to take responsibility for my life in a more complete way and so began wondering if my body's response could have anything to do with unconscious emotions or attitudes.

Kathlyn described how she had discovered a connection between an allergic sneezing response and anger. I was curious to learn if the gas was a coded message from my body. When I asked the question, using Dr. Lucia Capacchione's non-dominant hand journaling approach, my body spoke right up.

"I am the nether world of digestion, the place of acceptance or not, the place of nourishment and distribution. I, the body, have the power to digest food as well as experience. I, and none other, decide whether to do this. I am a sovereign power, indivisible from the mind; not a subterranean saboteur, but rather part of your 'me.' I am rejecting the food you put into the body because we have, as one unit, decided it is important to lodge a protest. This world is far too difficult to digest. Experience cannot be easily understood. So many things out there are bad for us and to us."

This response revealed a victim who had been experiencing herself as separate from life. The next question was, what did my body want?

"A seamless attitude to life and to food; to know I am nourished by everything I encounter. There is nothing that is potentially non-me. It is helpful to eat with reverence and remembrance of this, and more slowly, not just shoveling food in to quell the hollerings of hunger."

Within two days, the gas problems vanished and I went back to eating the restricted foods without further problems. I had learned an important lesson about listening respectfully to my body, and seeking my body's advice.

I now often help clients converse with their bodies. Kellie came to see me while pregnant with a second child. Her first daughter had almost died at birth because the placenta had grown into the uterine wall and wouldn't expel. Kellie was afraid this might happen again. I used the tool of hypnosis to lead Kellie into a conversation with her uterus. In that exchange, Kellie sensed her uterus saying it had clung to the first baby, fearing it might be taken too soon. Kellie had undergone five abortions before that birth. This current message indicated she had not fully grieved her unborn children or dealt with the guilt she had felt at the time. In a sense, the uterus was representing the part of her that had been unwilling to have those abortions. This healing conversation was an avenue for Kellie to make a deeper peace with herself, a full-bodied peace.

Another client, Peg, wanted to improve her vision. Facilitated by hypnosis, she was able to speak with her eyes. This was not an easy conversation because she had to let her eyes reveal the horror they had seen, which had been too terrible for Peg to retain in conscious memory.

"My little brother is four and I am five. It's dark in our bedroom. The door opens and a light shines on his face. He has one eye open and he's terrified, frozen, like a bunny rabbit. This is what I don't want to see (at this point her lip began to curl and tremble and her eyes started fluttering rapidly). A man comes in the room. He's an alcoholic that my parents sometimes left us with. I see red—it's blood. He's doing something to my brother. I can't see. I'm supposed to help him. I'm his big sister."

As Peg's eyes released these tormenting images, tears of fear and pain spilled out, along with more clarity about what had happened. The man had fondled her brother and sexually violated him, the same things he had done to Peg on other occasions. As these memories came into focus, Peg re-experienced intense terror. Her voice locked with the old fear that making a sound would draw the abuser back to her. This piece of the memory released her tears of guilt and grief. As a child, she had believed it was her job to protect her little brother but had kept quiet fearing another attack on herself. Her guilt over failing to protect him had been locked in her eyes all these years. It had been more accept-able to unconsciously give up her vision than to remember what she viewed as such a terrible, selfish failure.

Of course, Peg was not to blame in this situation. She and her brother were both little children with no power to protect themselves from this abusive man. As an adult, reliving the memory, Peg was able to realize this. The tears that poured from her eyes were like baptismal waters, washing clean the guilt she had carried so secretly, and unnecessarily, for so long.

I don't know if Peg's vision improved because she felt complete and ended therapy. Listening to body wisdom does not guarantee a miraculous cure, but ignoring body wisdom definitely interferes with healing. Sometimes the inner urge to cure ourselves physically disguises the more important hidden agenda for emotional healing.

Regina was an ecologist who came into my office complaining of depres-sion and excruciating headaches. She was working fifty to one hundred hours per week, struggling to save a beautiful land preserve.

Using hypnosis, I invited her body to share the feelings embedded in the headaches. Imagining a beautiful meadow and a guide that radiated love, Regina realized she avoided this loving guide because she believed love hurts. She said anything she loves always dies even though she struggles to prevent death. Suddenly, her beloved little dog Lucky, who had died three years earlier, despite her best efforts to save him, came scampering into the meadow of her mind with a stick, ready to play. Torn between delighted surprise and anguished fear that he wasn't real, Regina laughed and cried simultaneously. I invited her to describe the part of herself who felt like a failure when she couldn't keep all life trapped in physical form.

"She's all hard edges. She looks tense. She feels tight and moves jerky. She seems mad."

I asked if this character got many headaches. Regina laughed, "You don't have to ask, just look at her. There's no way anything can move in there."

Approaching her body like a dear friend required Regina to look at this image with tenderness. The eyes of love penetrated the dense outer forms and revealed the more vulnerable inner layers. As Regina looked with love at her hard-edged aspect, she discovered a fragile child inside.

"Oooh!" she began to cry. "There's a little tiny girl in there." Then, laughing, "It's like the Wizard of Oz. She's trapped inside the armor." At this point she began to sob. "I feel so sorry for her. If only she could get out, she'd be in the meadow with Lucky."

As we focused more love on the tiny trapped girl, a wondrous transformation began. Lucky tried to get the child to play stick with him but there was no response. Regina realized the child couldn't even see Lucky because she was too small to look out the eyeholes of the hard-edged armor she was trapped inside. This dream-image armor seemed to be box-shaped and so Lucky dug a tunnel into the armor-box and pulled the little girl out to freedom. As Regina cradled the girl, letting her sleep, she focused love on the empty armor, which was not altogether a bad thing. It had kept the child safe. Regina felt appreciative and awed by the girl's skill at creating such a protection. In the light of love, the armor now began to transform and become part of the meadow, with part of it melting into "the prettiest gold dress that fits the little girl perfectly."

Regina's body seemed to be saying that her desperate clinging to life in material form, whether it be a little dog or a land preserve, was the source of her headaches. Only the warmth of love could pry loose that fearful grip and ease her pain.

Not only do our bodies have feelings, they have memories as well. In fact, the bodymind never forgets. The conscious mind seldom holds more than a handful of early childhood memories, but the body stores everything that happened in childhood, and even before. Bodies remember birth, prenatal times and even conception. Many influential core beliefs are formed during these preverbal phases of development. As we explore recurrent situations and behaviors that we want to change, our bodies can reveal valuable insights and significant memories from our earliest experiences.

Because these memories are hidden from our conscious minds, direct inquiry is ineffective. Hypnosis is a tool that gently lures the stored feelings and experiences into the open. The hypnotic process is a bit like the way I imagine time travel would be. Guided by the voice of the therapist, a person gradually leaves the level of awareness where the conscious mind is in control. The conscious mind usually remains present, but it's as if it were behind one-way glass. It can observe all that is being remembered but can't interfere and dominate the conversation the way it normally does, with its endless analysis and critical, inhibiting viewpoints. The person leaves the more familiar thought level and moves into an undefined, dreamlike mental space, using intention as a compass. Often, the intention is an instruction to go to the origin of the problem. Then, like someone awakening in a different time and place, the person begins to notice sensory data. As the data accumulates, clarity about the new time and place emerges.

One client, Michael, was blocked in getting a creative product out into the marketplace. Though sensing that the obstacle was inside, his conscious mind couldn't uncover it. He was willing to have a deep conversation with his body, so, using hypnosis, I guided Michael back to the origin of this block. That open-ended induction led Michael into uterine waters and feelings of abandonment and deep grief. By focusing his awareness on these emotions, Michael discovered, to the surprise of his conscious mind, a memory of a lost twin. His body had revealed the memory of grief following the twin's death. Michael was consciously aware that his parents had expected twins right up to the time of birth. They had chosen names for two babies. When no twin was born, everyone dismissed their expectations as a mistake.

In fact, regressive therapies have revealed that blighted twins are a somewhat common occurrence. Sometimes the surviving twin even has body parts, such as fingernails, of the lost twin embedded in cysts in odd places of his or her body.

In the hypnotic moment, Michael was not analyzing the data on whether this experience was possible. His body was unfolding the layers of sadness, despair, betrayal and anger locked in memory. Michael felt the emotions as intensely as he had originally felt them. I helped him stay in the moment and move through it. His body revealed conclusions he had drawn, and positions he had taken, as a result of his brother's departure.

Michael had interpreted his twin's death as betrayal. Believing the twin had abandoned him and reneged on a promise to be there helping him, Michael came into life believing he was insufficient for the tasks of living, and he was mad about it. Life was already the wrong experience.

As the conversation continued, Michael regressed even further. He remembered that when his brother had died, both twins agreed that the one not born could be of more help in non-material form and that he would stay close and help the other throughout his physical life. But after the death, Michael's sorrow and anger blotted this agreement as well as the twin's willing presence from Michael's conscious mind. From that point onward, experiences like never being able to please his father despite steady efforts seemed to prove he was not enough on his own. One failure after another reinforced his sense of inadequacy.

Michael realized he had gone beyond ignoring his brother's helping presence. Many past and present problems now seemed like angry, subconscious challenges to the missing twin. The game's setup became clear: if the disaster was big enough, his brother couldn't save him, which would plainly expose the twin's betrayal and prove Michael's helplessness.

This was a painful conversation between Michael and his body. But once the long-held anger and grief had been expressed, Michael experienced lightness and a profound connection to his brother. Realizing he was not alone, Michael began consciously asking for help and his project began flowing once again.

Another client whose life was adversely affected by prenatal experiences was Donald. A very thin man and slight of stature, he impressed me as someone with only a tentative agreement to be on the planet. Tormented by obsessive urges to seek sexual satisfaction with prostitutes, which he often acted upon, Donald was ashamed and fearful. He knew this addiction could destroy his marriage, and he was confused about why, despite his good intentions, the desires persisted.

Donald's body conversation led back to the uterine environment and the moment of his birth. His body's memory revealed amniotic fluids filled with maternal anger toward his absent father. Just like nutrients, the mother's emotions travel freely to the fetus, who is incapable of differentiating between "me; mine" and "not me; not mine." So for Donald, the world seemed like an angry place. Emerging from the birth canal expecting the world to be filled with anger, Donald entered an environment that felt "harsh, blinding, hard, and cold" and he was burdened by an anguished impression that his mother did not want him. Donald's tears flowed as this bodily memory of rejection flooded his conscious mind. With the memory came an intuitive understanding that his insatiable sexual urges issued from deep, unacknowledged longing to find unconditional love in the welcoming, accepting arms of his mother.

These are just a few examples to illustrate the potential richness of healing conversations with our bodies. The question remains—how do we learn to listen to our bodies? The body speaks through physical sensations. This language can be decoded only through the intuitive mind of the Magic Child, so we have to develop our intuition to communicate with our bodies.

Engaging Conversation

As we enter into conversation with our bodies, we need to offer spaciousness and patience as well as an attitude of curiosity. If our body "says" queasy stomach, we will not further our understanding of this message by angrily chomping antacids to rid ourselves of the annoying discomfort. Instead, I'm suggesting we simply love the stomach, complete with its discomfort, and wonder what it may be trying to express, all the while patiently waiting and listening.

I am not advising you to avoid all medicines, doctors, or medical procedures. There may be times when a pain is too intense and discomfort or responsibilities prevent us from sitting quietly and asking for insight. By the time we have progressed from discomfort to illness or severe injury, few of us have the kind of inner relationship and self-healing skills that would make medical assistance unnecessary. We don't have to be stoic and solitary, shunning all help. We can use medicine, while continuing to maintain an attitude of loving wonder.

Once curiosity draws us into conversation with our bodies, the second part of communication is listening. Poet Anne Sexton said, "Put your ear down to your soul and listen hard." Intuitive messages don't come through the way we get information in the five-sensory world—direct and logical. Instead an idea may simply pop into our heads. Such thoughts may, at first encounter, feel like a favorite pair of shoes, totally comfortable and right. Other times they may seem like a starlet dressed in gaudy sequins and a garish orange wig showing up for Thanksgiving dinner—completely unexpected and bizarre. However, even these oddball thoughts, if we welcome them at the banquet table of our awareness, may—under all their strange costuming—contain important new ideas or directions.

It is tempting while first learning intuitive listening to discount thoughts that arise as "just imagination." This is a habit learned from a society that over-values logical thinking. Imagination has a bad name because it implies something unreal, not based on five-sensory, present reality.

A contemporary approach to explaining the different ways our minds work, which may be overly simplified, is to describe two regions of the brain: the left and right hemispheres. According to this model, the left brain governs logical, linear, rational thought while the right brain is the realm of the creative imagination. Because society and the educational system emphasize the measurable, controllable talents of the left brain, many of us grow up believing that this way of thinking is real and imagination is the opposite. Many people are so used to being confined in the "offices" of the left brain, they no longer believe life can be approached from a different perspective. "Get real!" they say. "Life doesn't work like that." A middle-aged accountant named Andrew, who held that attitude, was astonished to discover the world of his imagination.

Andrew told me that he was a totally left-brained person, that he did not even have a right brain, or if he did, it had atrophied to the size of a peanut. My reply, that he most certainly did have a right brain, and he could access it through hypnosis, intrigued him. He made an appointment immediately.

During Andrew's first session, we surveyed the vast and familiar region of his left brain for awhile, just to get him comfortable with his inner landscape.

Then we wandered over to the unexplored territory of his right brain. In imagination, Andrew could see his right brain like a field before him, but couldn't go there. What prevented him? He was at the edge of a cliff and could only get across by jumping. When I reminded him that in the safety of the imagination he could fly, he jumped off the edge.

Soon Andrew was mentally wandering through a new world. He went into a coffee shop, where he became absorbed in philosophical discussions with other patrons. Then he found a piano, an instrument he had always wanted to play, and began to play as if he had always known how. He picked up a saxophone, too, and played with great joy and accomplishment.

Finding an easel, Andrew began to paint. Somehow he stepped into his painting, passing through a doorway in time, into a world that felt like medieval Wales. He visited an interesting cast of characters and felt a great sense of peace there.

The painting was the most intriguing part of Andrew's journey, because it developed over several sessions. He developed the painting, mentally, portraying details of the Welsh scene from the first session. In subsequent weeks, the landscape began to take on a life of its own. Soon Andrew started writing a fantasy novel based on his inner world.

This exploration changed Andrew's "real" world by awakening many talents he never suspected he had. He started taking saxophone lessons soon after and made plans to study piano later. Although he loved playing sax, his energy for the fantasy novel carried him like a tidal wave. He wrote passionately, going further into that world every spare moment, until the story had mushroomed into a trilogy.

Not only did Andrew unleash his creativity, but his newfound comfort in the inner realm of the imagination gave him the security he needed to explore buried childhood pain. As he dealt with unresolved issues and gained a sense of peace about them, he noticed they were woven into his novel. Through the story, he was healing those parts of his life. Within six months, a publisher was eagerly waiting the completion of the trilogy. The part of the story Andrew shared with me was spellbinding. I can't wait to curl up with his book! More importantly, Andrew felt more relaxed and full of life than ever before. His accounting business kept increasing, the more relaxed he grew, and his relationship with his wife and children improved. He found a sense of well-being so profound that not even tax season took it away! Andrew has a new, more expansive and empowering definition of reality.

Imagination is a realm removed from the physical senses, but is not therefore negative. The word stems from the Latin "magi" which means wise ones. Magic has the same root. The wise Magic Child uses the magic language of intuition. To access our inner wisdom, intuitive fluency is a must. Trusting imagination is the first step to that fluency.

When we use imagination to solve problems, we are creating ideas that did not exist in our conscious minds. Some of these ideas will be practical, some not. These ideas, I believe, come from unbounded mind, in which we all participate.

Kellie imagined that her uterus was expressing certain feelings about her baby and about the previous abortions. There is certainly no way to prove that the uterus had these feelings. Many people would automatically dismiss the insight because it can't be proved as fact. In so doing, skeptics would miss the opportunity for healing that Kellie experienced. The value of an intuitive insight is measured by how a person feels as a result. In accepting her uterine feelings, as an intuitive expression of her body, Kellie opened a door to an inner room in her heart that had been sealed off. As her tears flowed, she was able to let go of the grief and guilt she had not dealt with previously. After the release, Kellie felt lighter and freer. If a thought does not lead to a feeling of greater energy, it is probably not a true intuition.

I want to stress the very personal, intuitive nature of the body's responses. Remember how my body expressed discontent with victim consciousness through the physical symptom of gas? Several years later I had another bout with gas, identical to the first one. Examining my life for victim attitudes didn't yield significant insights, so I used the journaling technique again, this time with different results.

My body now spoke about needing more space inside and asked me to clear the toxins from my body, the clutter from my home, and the chaos from my schedule. Not surprisingly, this all happened at a time when I was feeling overwhelmed. My daytimer was crammed with activities, projects were piling up on my desk, and my body felt bloated and uncomfortable. The two differing body "diagnoses" revealed how bodies speak in metaphor, using symptoms instead of images to convey messages from the knower within.

When a person is first learning to listen intuitively, sometimes the messages of the body are not clear. We are new at understanding this poetic language. We need to be patient and increase our tolerance for standing inside mystery with a loving heart.

Another problem for new listeners is interference. The internal critic is skilled at jamming the channel with responses indicating that the answer to everything boils down to our essential unworthiness and ineptness. The critic's messages always lower a person's energy, creating feelings of shame.

That doesn't mean your intuition won't offer you frank criticism. Like any dear friend, it courageously shares the uncomfortable truths nobody else will acknowledge. One client, a woman named Marie, was grieving the death of her maternal grandmother whom she had not visited in years because the grandmother was unpleasant. In dealing with all the family confusion surrounding the memorial arrangements, Marie realized she had unconsciously repeated her mother's pattern of creating distance between herself and any family member with whom she had unresolved emotional issues. Marie felt tremendous grief, because it was too late for her now to be with that grandmother on the physical plane. She was keenly aware of her responsibility in this matter, but did not experience shame. Instead, she felt the power to break free of the destructive pattern. This sense of freedom raised her energy level, even though she couldn't immediately shake off the grief. She accepted it as an appropriate emotion and felt it fully.

Besides noticing whether a thought raises or lowers our energy, we can also identify intuitive thoughts by a sense of recognition. Sometimes an idea arises that seems so obvious we discount its intuitive quality because we should have known it already, or perhaps we did know it before and forgot. This just means the idea was blocked from our conscious thinking and we retrieved it using intuitive skills.

In the case of an idea that seems obvious, that sense of recognition is a quality of the intuition. The idea feels so right to us, like the comfortable pair of shoes, that we judge it obvious. The judgment is irrelevant and will only block us from using our intuitive answers. The comfortable feeling we get from the idea is what matters. We feel good about the idea. It makes sense to us and we "believe" it will work.

Ideas aren't always obvious. Sometimes, as in the analogy of the gaudy starlet at Thanksgiving dinner, ideas seem very strange, but we like the way they feel. When an idea is not flowing from intuitive mind, we will feel uncomfortable with it, as if the thought is discordant to our soul.

We can also be uncomfortable with a thought because it seems too big. Thoughts about our own greatness may make us squirm if we are committed to feeling like victims. By listening with love to these ideas we can burrow underneath our self-hatred to recognize the spark of aliveness that such thoughts generate in our souls.

This intuitive approach to listening works, whether we are communicating with our bodies or focusing on external situations. For example, in wondering about a business situation, or a relationship, we may receive intuitive messages which, taken seriously and acted upon, will guide us well. The more we follow our intuition, the stronger and more reliable it becomes, somewhat like a path across a field that we traverse day after day, making it easier to find as footsteps wear away the grass.

The unique aspect of communicating with our bodies involves the body's way of speaking through physical sensations. The body usually speaks softly at first. A tightening in the throat may be a quiet indication of anger or of a thought we're afraid to express. If we ignore the tightening, the body speaks a little louder. Maybe now we feel a big lump in the throat and experience difficulty talking. If that still doesn't get our attention, we may get a sore throat. Taken to the maximum volume, the body might have to speak through a serious disease in the throat. One benefit of learning the body's mode of speaking is that our lessons become much gentler. The body's delicate taps on the shoulder become our teachers instead of its more serious and often painful attention-getting counterpart: a two-by-four whack on the head.

Before I discovered the connection between mind and body, whenever I felt a tightening in my throat, I would confidently predict the onset of a sore throat. Sure enough, one always arrived. After I became familiar with hidden emotions I realized that the throat tightening coincided with anger I was afraid to express. Eventually, I was able to use my body as an ally. When I noticed a tightness in my throat, I would check for anger. My body was a patient teacher who taught me to recognize angry feelings despite years of ignoring them so completely I didn't know they existed. With my body's help, I began learning to express my anger and stopped getting as many sore throats.

Furnishing a Loving Space

In order to stimulate conversation with our bodies, there is one more thing we can do besides wonder and listen with love and openness. We can create a space for communication. Friends talk more freely in private spaces. They like cozy chairs by a fire or a quiet corner of a garden with a comfortable bench. We can furnish an inner environment that encourages the body to talk by using techniques that quiet the chatter of our conscious minds. Each person will find some techniques more appealing than others. In my opinion, there is no hierarchy of methods because all, in some manner, elicit body truth. Whatever approach best facilitates communication is the best choice for each person.

I have already shared several examples illustrating the powerful conversations that happen during hypnosis. I think self-hypnosis can be learned, and is helpful, but a skillful guide is more likely to encourage you, to nudge you into the places that seem too scary to venture into alone, and to help you as you explore the more frightening memories.

Other approaches work well at home without a guide, once you have some level of proficiency. Instructional books are available for every technique, but a teacher offers a more powerful path to mastery. My book is not meant to replace other books or teachers; it's meant to expose you to a variety of "cozy rooms" designed to encourage deep conversation with the body.

Meditation

Meditation is one of the most time-honored paths. There are many styles and techniques of meditation, all with books and teachers to guide a novice to mastery. The benefit of meditation is that it stills conscious thoughts and allows the person to sink into a quiet place of non-doing awareness and acceptance. Most meditative practices involve noticing the breath, which is a physical expression of Spirit flowing through form. By focusing on the breath, we can gradually diminish mental chatter as our awareness of Spirit expands. When I have slipped into the deepest meditations, first the mental noise abated and then emotional complaints dissolved, leaving only a sense of love and deep well-being streaming through my physical form.

My friend Jim Pasmore shared a story that illustrated the quiet simplicity and rich benefits of meditation. While hiking through the woods, Jim spotted a beautiful tree that seemed to beckon him closer. He sat down, leaning back against the tree, imagining the feel of the life force running through it. As he sat, Jim's awareness seemed to meld with the tree's awareness. He began to notice the surroundings from the tree's perspective. The tree seemed to be a custodian of silence. For decades it had stood in the same spot, simply being, observing all the life around it. Just as the tree absorbed carbon dioxide from the atmosphere and returned oxygen, the breath of life, Jim imagined that the tree absorbed the toxins of frenetic activity and breathed out the spacious air of silence. He returned reluctantly to the world of human affairs, but his activity was now graced by stillness and reverence, a deep appreciation for all that lay in his path.

We all need meditative interludes. Nature is only one doorway to this inner peace. Some people travel inside themselves through a piece of music, some through a beautiful picture or a provocative line in a book. For others, some activity is the vehicle, such as yoga, dancing or fly-fishing. We all have to find our own entryways to meditative space.

Jon Kabat-Zinn, Ph.D., is one of the experts interviewed by journalist Bill Moyers in *Healing and the Mind*. Kabat-Zinn, Director of the Stress Reduction Clinic at University of Massachusetts Medical Center, teaches meditation to the patients who enroll in his clinic. People come to him to deal with the painful conversations they are having with their bodies. They discover that meditation is a powerful tool for listening because, in focusing on the breath, they learn to be attentive to the present moment instead of mentally racing back and forth between the past and the future. Kabat-Zinn says, "Your life is the sum of your present moments, so if you're missing lots of them, you may actually miss much of your children's infancy and youth, or beautiful sunsets, or the beauty of your own body. You may be tuning out all sorts of inner and outer experiences simply because you're too preoccupied with where you want to get, what you want to have happen, and what you don't want to happen."

As patients learn to be present in the moment without judgment, they gain a new ability to overcome the resistance that blocks communication and tune in to the painful sensations of their bodies. Kabat-Zinn says, "You learn how to work with the pain, to befriend it, to listen to it, and in some way to honor it. In the process of doing that, you wind up seeing that it's possible to feel differently about your pain. Sometimes, when you focus on this, the sensations actually go away....But you're not trying to make the pain go away. This is a fundamental point that people sometimes misunderstand at first....We actually move into the stress or pain and begin to look at it, and to notice the mind's reactions, and to let go of that reactivity. And then you find that there is inner stillness and peace within some of the most difficult life situations. It's right in this breath, and it's right in this experience. You don't have to run away to get it someplace else."

Sometimes people receive intuitive messages from their bodies while meditating. This is not always the case, but by creating a climate of attentiveness and non-judgment, we enhance the possibility that, in general, our bodies will feel welcome to speak to us.

Another benefit of contemplative-style meditation, when instead of emptying the mind, we focus on a single positive thought, is the opportunity to attune ourselves on a cellular level to an enriching idea. It may be something our body has shared with us, like when my body asked me to have a seamless attitude to life, to know nothing was potentially non-me. Such ideas are too big to digest consciously. In meditation, we can spread ideas out through our whole beings. In this way, we honor communication from our bodies by seriously ruminating over the body's messages. It's also an effective way to share new ideas with our bodies.

I encourage my clients to support their hypnosis work through meditation, taking themselves back to the inner realm and contemplating the images and messages revealed during their session. I personally find significant change impossible without taking time to internalize it in the quiet atmosphere of meditation. This spiritual body-building is even more critical than physical exercise. In meditation we strengthen the intuitive "muscles" that allow our bodies to communicate soul messages clearly to both our conscious and subconscious minds.

Journaling

Another way to initiate conversation with our bodies is to journal. The conscious mind is so accustomed to monopolizing our attention that getting intuitive messages while thinking can be impossible. By engaging the body through the physical task of writing, messages that our conscious minds have been blocking may suddenly emerge on the page. The technique I enjoy using was developed by Dr. Lucia Capacchione. Her book, *The Power of the Other Hand*, contains many exercises based on the technique of drawing and writing using the non-dominant hand. Capacchione discovered that this process lures the wild, intuitive, creative, and repressed voices into the open, sidestepping the conventional, predictable, rational side of the brain.

In brief, her method is to make a picture expressing a sensation, emotion or situation you are experiencing, using the non-dominant hand. Then, allowing that picture to represent whatever energy is trying to communicate, begin speaking with it. Using your normal writing hand you write a series of questions, one at a time. A typical set of questions is: Who are you? What are you feeling? How did you get that way? What do you want? How can I help? To answer each question, you write—without censoring, criticizing or correcting—whatever comes to mind using your non-dominant hand.

My first workshop with Capacchione was early in 1989. The exercises at that workshop were profound. At the time, my chest was all congested and I didn't know why. Raw feelings poured onto the page. In one exercise, I released pent-up childish anger, splattering brown scribbles and naughty words like "poophead" all over my paper. In another exercise, I drew the tiniest possible baby picture. "Baby" was feeling very frightened.

I have the fears that I will go to the bottom of the pond.
Do you mean you're afraid you will die?
I am.
Why do you think that might happen?
When I bad I get a (s)panking.
But you're only a baby—nothing you do is bad.
That is how the mother should tell me.
But Mommy didn't tell you that?
She threw the brush at me (I remember my mother sometimes spanked me with a hairbrush).
I didn't know. She shouldn't have done that to you. You're a good baby.
Boo hoo hoo Boo hoo I cry and I are sad and I need some cries.
It's okay to cry, Baby. You don't have to be happy or strong or all finished being sad—or even go in your room. Is it hard for you to cry?
I is choking on my sads. It is very very biggey. I is scared about de chokes.
Is there something you'd like me to do to help you?
I is needing of the space to cry when I is sad.

I needed to recognize the presence of these emotions clogging up my body, although I remember listening with awe and envy as another workshop participant read the seven-point metaphysical program for improving vision that flowed from her writing. Non-dominant journaling became my morning practice for the next five years. During that time, the dirt road to my intuitive side became a highway. Messages come not only from frightened, angry parts, but also from the wondrous Magic Child. These words of Divine wisdom, flowing from my pen, were more inspiring to me than anything I ever read in somebody else's book. Because the process always began with a drawing, a side benefit was unlocking my artistic ability. I highly recommend this technique. Start with any sensation, emotion, situation, or even dream character that has you mystified and use the basic questions, or get one of Capacchione's books and let her walk you through the process, one exercise at a time.

Art

Many consider art the exclusive domain of individuals known as "artists." Ordinary people shun artistic expression, assuming theirs won't be any good, and, in doing so, shut themselves off from a wonderful, innate, non-verbal tool for expressing inner magic. Why have so many people in this culture lost their artistic confidence? Typically, it happened in elementary school, where art often became equated with drawing in a realistic style. Our grades proved we had no artistic ability, even if we'd never been taught how to draw realistically. Internalizing the message, we left art to artists. Nobody seemed to notice that many artists don't have a realistic drawing style; we just accepted that art was for them, not us.

I believe everybody has artistic ability. How could a being like the Magic Child be incapable of making art?! When I was teaching art to preschoolers, no child ever complained about lack of ability. Unwarped by judgment, children approach art with enthusiasm, happily slapping paint onto paper without concern for getting it right.

I encourage you to experiment with this modality, especially if you're convinced you won't enjoy it, because it is such a powerful doorway to the inner realm. Art can be a form of meditation when used for centering, especially using a form like a mandala. It can also be a vehicle for expressing emotions, either those you are feeling or those you have buried. I have used art to put my dreams in concrete form, which helps me to understand them. Sometimes images, which have emerged when I have just allowed myself free artistic expression, have held a symbolic power that helped me believe in my own possibilities or realize the depth of emotion I felt about something.

The images can also be a way to effect an emotional transformation as we play with creating more satisfying images. I remember a particularly powerful experience of artistic transformation. At a Hendricks training, I was drawing my emotional experience of being in the womb. The aspect that was present for me at that point was very negative, and I was making a mess of the art paper with my angry strokes, even tearing it. Finally I had vented all the feelings and I began to imagine a new prenatal experience for myself. I shifted into a peaceful nurturing emotional space and began moving gently, humming softly, and drawing intuitively. The picture that emerged was a contented fetus in a womb. I hung it on my wall at home to remind me that I can recreate that experience of nurturing for myself.

Music

Like art, music is an area that many third-grade teachers taught us to avoid, through their disapproval and shaming of off-tune efforts. And like art, music is an innate human gift. Maybe everybody doesn't have an equal talent or doesn't instinctively know some of the musical skills, such as staying on pitch, but most people can learn most skills, and the more important aspects of music don't have to be learned. Sound moves through our physical bodies and carries emotion with it. The Magic Child is making itself heard. That's why singing in church is such a powerful experience, or joining in with the crowd at a concert. Plenty of people who are too shy to sing publicly will belt out a tune in the shower, where the sound of water outside harmonizes with the sound coming from within and creates a healing experience of resonance. Sound has the power to release trapped emotion, yet like the feelings people in the Anglo-American culture so readily stuff, sounds are commonly repressed as well. Contrast, for example, the joyful, raucous sounds of the dance in Hispanic culture, or black American congregations singing in church.

You don't have to be a gifted singer, musician or songwriter to use the tool of music to express emotion and access inner magic the way Ron did. You may not have the talent to produce the songs that become famous, but you can create a cozy room for conversation to discover what is inside you. Let your sounds and songs flow freely.

Dreams

Dreaming is another way our bodies communicate. They whisper to us nightly, but we often don't remember our dreams at all, much less the details of them. When we do remember, our dream conversations often confuse our conscious minds because dream language is full of imagery and emotion instead of logic. The art of interpreting dreams is ancient, and books and teachers on this subject abound. I found *Living Your Dreams* by Gayle Delaney, Ph.D., very helpful. Delaney explains that the subconscious mind produces dreams and understands dream meanings. She says that we can learn to participate actively in the dream production, and as we do, dream messages will become clear to our conscious minds.

Delaney refers to the dream version of the intuitive voice as a "dream producer." She uses a process of dream interviewing to interpret the messages of dreams. She asks the dream producer questions about intuitive associations with the dream symbols, because an image can have very different associations for different dreamers. She avoids textbook interpretation of the meanings of symbols. Most dream characters are aspects of the dreamer's own psyche revealing information about the dreamer rather than about the person whose character the producer is speaking through. The dreamer's viewpoint is pivotal to understanding why the character has been given a role in the dream.

Delaney emphasizes the value of attending to dreams. She says our dream producers are reaching out, wanting to help solve problems and transform our lives.

Direct Contact

In each of the preceding techniques the body silences the logical mind and draws out the quiet messages from the Magic Child. In the techniques that follow, the focus is on the body itself. The body-centered approach often leads to powerful insights and emotional release, but this is not the primary goal. There are three main categories of direct contact: bodywork, breathwork, and movement.

Bodywork

In bodywork, a practitioner or friend touches, soothes or manipulates the body of another person. Through the healing power of touch, the person's body begins to unwind. In a state of relaxation, imagery, memories, emotions and insights often flow freely. Direct physical contact releases old destructive patterns and new choices can be physically planted. Nurturing touch softens physical resistance and allows the bodymind to soak up the transforming rays of love being applied directly, skin to skin.

Every body deserves and requires touch, and I particularly recommend this approach for people who seem to be strapped to the wheel of logical control. If you find that your rational mind is unwilling to abandon the helm no matter what technique you use, try some bodywork. Because the goals of bodywork are nonverbal, the logical mind has nothing to produce, and may finally get bored with making lists and wander off. Regardless of whether this happens, the work is happening on the level of touch and can be effective even if the rational mind continues talking.

I think bodywork is also an ideal starting point for people who have not yet learned to communicate with their own bodies. Without this skill, a person can feel overwhelmed by emotions and life situations and may avoid techniques that require active participation. The advantage of bodywork is that, in most forms, the client doesn't have to exert any effort. By simply inviting nurturing through another's healing hands, the individual may experience enough comfort and release to gradually take a more active role in the healing process.

There are many forms of bodywork. Massage, Rolfing, Reiki, Alexander training, and chiropractic are just a few. To describe them all in detail would require a book of its own, if not a short encyclopedia. Let your intuition "do the walking" and find a form that appeals to you.

Breathwork

The breath is a physical manifestation of the life force moving through the body. I like to imagine it as the breath of God reaching deep within me, communing with the Magic Child. A steady focus on breathing can lead to deep relaxation or meditation. We can also activate its power to enliven and cleanse us emotionally, on a cellular level. On the physical level, breath brings oxygen to all the cells and eliminates some toxins.

In the introduction, I described in more detail some of the regressive results that breathwork may lead to. In my opinion, a trained facilitator greatly enhances the possibilities for emotional exploration and release. Knowing that someone is close by to witness and, if necessary, strengthen or soothe, allows an individual to travel more deeply into the inner realm.

Movement

Whereas bodywork is often a passive experience, movement is, by definition, active. By physically moving our bodies, we stir both our thoughts and our feelings, because the mental and emotional planes, combined with the physical, comprise the integrated organism called a human being. Only when all these planes have been activated can we fully experience the streaming of Spirit throughout our energy fields. Because the body is often treated like an unwanted stepchild, with emotions being the equally unpopular sibling, many of us gravitate toward sedentary positions and logical analysis. Movement is an excellent tool for correcting the imbalance because physical motion creates ripples in all of our energy fields.

Most of us have experienced the ripple effect from the physical to the mental plane. Have you ever gone for a walk "to clear your head" and understood a problem from a new angle when you returned? By removing attention from conscious thoughts and putting it on the body, we get off the hamster wheel of familiar ideas and wander into the unlimited field of possibilities. The more vigorous or precise the physical

movement, the more completely we need to focus. A high diver has to be totally present to execute a successful dive. A basketball player needs to be attentive to the game at every moment.

The ripple from the physical to the emotional plane is also familiar to most of us. Has worry or frustration ever driven you to play an extra vigorous game of racquetball or to clean your house from top to bottom? The physical activity discharges the pent-up emotion, leaving the bodymind calm and peaceful.

In spiritual terms, physical exercise stimulates the flow of the life force, what the Hindus call "kundalini" energy. As this force flows more vigorously, it awakens all the energy centers of the body. Inspiration and compassion are just two of the powers unleashed as the kundalini rises.

The Eastern world has developed certain forms of movement specifically designed to release this powerful energy force. The Hindus, over many centuries, created a system known as yoga, which means yoke, suggesting a link between the body and Divine mind. Yogic postures are crafted to release the kundalini energy and bring the practitioner into awareness of the bodymind connection. In various Asian countries, comparable systems known as martial arts were developed. Tai Chi Chuan, Chi Gong, and Aikido are just a few of them. Buddhists cultivate mindfulness through the simple movement of walking with all attention focused on each step. The mindful walker notices the sensation of each foot caressing the earth, of balance shifting from hip to hip, and sends thoughts of appreciation toward the earth that receives and supports each foot. What all these systems share in common is the power of focused movement.

My personal movement preference is dance. While any style of dance can create that ripple effect in the mental and emotional planes, I like natural movement. By that, I mean allowing the body to respond to music without the constraint of a correct form. This organic approach shifts the focus from disciplined performance to sensuous pleasure and exuberant expression. In such an environment, emotions and insight readily flow. I often use dance as a prayer form, allowing my body to dance my feelings and longings or to track the energy of Spirit moving through me. Because dance is a type of movement that seems disproportionately avoided in our culture, and because it is my favorite, I intend to focus on this form of direct contact.

The Secret Dancer

Perhaps, in part, because the negative medieval association between dancing and sexuality still hangs about in our collective unconscious, many people are reluctant to dance. This is a cultural limitation rather than a natural state. Small children instinctively move to music. They never stand still wondering if they can dance. While professional dancers have strong, disciplined bodies, all bodies are capable of dancing. I've seen a man in a wheelchair dance with every body part he could still move. My dance students have included gay men struggling with AIDS, a seventy-four-year-old woman with cancer, people weighed down by obesity, and many individuals who had never before danced. All of them were able to dance because dancing is as natural as walking. Even the most dance-phobic adults will at least tap their feet to a strong beat in the privacy of their homes or cars, as if inadvertently exposing their residual skill. What happens between childhood and adulthood that sends the dancer into hiding? Aside from absorbing the inhibitions of the collective unconscious, personal experiences force most dancers into secrecy. Luckily, that self-imposed banishment doesn't have to be a lifelong sentence.

Simone was a thirty-year-old married client who had recently moved to town with her husband and baby. She was uncomfortable with the decision to settle down in a place far from her family of origin. Feelings of disloyalty haunted her, intruding even during lovemaking. Hypnosis helped Simone to discover a small child crouched in a tight corner of her consciousness. The little one within complained that she had no space to be herself. Her parents were just too controlling. We gave the little child hypnotic messages about deserving her own space. For the first time, Simone was able to imagine a safe space, now that she had connected with the part of her that needed it. When I asked the little girl what she wanted to do in that safe space, her instinctive reply was "Dance!" I believe that we need to take these inner messages literally and act upon them, to show the intuitive self we value the information we receive, so, even though Simone was unaccustomed to dancing, I asked her to move to the music. Her face was joyful as she danced around the room, taking up space. The next time I saw her she was much more relaxed and happy.

Beatrice was a client in her forties who had taken refuge in alcohol and in a series of affairs, rather than end a long, dissatisfying marriage. She was a gentle spirit who did not trust her intuition or her ability to be successful without a husband. Her father was a domineering, critical man whom Beatrice still struggled to please. During a therapy session, I asked Beatrice to dance. She was frightened by the suggestion, but she complied. She moved like a pinned butterfly, afraid to risk anything but the barest movements. Suddenly tears began to flow. Beatrice was remembering her family's ridicule when, as a four-year-old, she declared that she was a ballerina. "What if you were right?" I asked her. More tears. In the end, that fragile butterfly of a ballerina soul was stirring softly inside her again.

Frequently the dancer retreats during adolescence with the advent of formal dances. Suddenly dancing is no longer simply an expression of the body's joy and aliveness but something that has to be done right. Peer conscious and lacking confidence, many young people run from the possibility of looking foolish and never get out on the dance floor. Tom, a client and a grandfather, remembered, during hypnosis, how he avoided the risk of looking foolish by labeling dance as "girl stuff." During junior high dances, Tom stayed safe and manly by horsing around with "the guys." He went on, in that hypnosis session, to find a bodily memory of free, rhythmic, African movement. After hypnosis, when I asked him to dance, he moved the body he had previously judged to be old and stiff, with fluidity and delight.

Some people avoid dancing because they're disconnected from their bodies. Transformational dance teacher Gabrielle Roth refers to such people as "absentee landlords of the body." The body is walking around but nobody's inside. People who have been sexually abused often internalize the abuse and experience their own bodies as the enemy. They don't want to be in a body because they have experienced it as a very unsafe place. Dancing is difficult for someone who's hanging out a safe distance from the body.

Trella was a client who was struggling with extra weight and memories of painful abuse. During therapy one day, I played the theme from *The Last of the Mohicans*. The chorus is "No matter where you go, I will find you, if it takes a long, long time. No matter where you go, I will find you, if it takes a thousand years." Even though Trella did not have a stereotypical dancer's body, I have never witnessed more beautiful movement. I felt chills all over my flesh as I watched her spirit dance its way home to her long-abandoned body.

Caroline was a woman in her late forties who signed up for an all women's dance class I offered. An unhappy, dull-eyed woman, she avoided eye contact with everyone. Caroline, who was sexually abused as a child, had very low self-esteem. Dance allowed her to experiment with creating safe boundaries. She would challenge herself to look at a partner, knowing she could move or look away from that partner at will. Over time, Caroline increased her ability to look someone in the eye and she began having more fun dancing. Her eyes acquired more sparkle and she made positive life changes as well.

Many people in our society prefer the safety of the intellect, often because that was the only part of them that was valued by their families. Since the head doesn't have too many movement options, head-dwellers don't usually gravitate toward the dance floor.

Nick was another of my dance students. A bachelor in his forties, he was a brilliant man who loved to analyze books, people, situations and life in general. He signed up for the dance class on a whim and discovered another world within himself. In the dance class, I played a wide range of music, and students were able to express familiar emotions and emotions they were unaccustomed to feeling or expressing. They were also able to experiment with physical contact and eye contact, and expand their comfort zones. As the class progressed, I noticed that Nick had more energy and playfulness. He started going to dances and having fun with women he met there. Nick talked for years afterwards about that class being the most transformational experience of his life.

Celine was a client who loved the peace of the spiritual plane that she experienced in frequent meditation. She was a highly efficient office manager, who seemed to have an uneasy truce with the physical plane. She made enough money to pay bills but seemed disdainful of money and the world of work, resenting material necessities that dragged her from the meditative realm. I asked her to choose movements to express her internal conflict over wanting to rise into the planes of pure energy and having to do all this stuff on Earth. When she exaggerated two gestures that represented her conflict, her movement metamorphosed into a beautiful dance that was uniquely hers. Through dance she realized that she could bring meditation insights into the world of form and she could integrate these two realms in a graceful sequence instead of an awkward conflict-ridden transition.

Besides the "threat" of bringing the person back to the body, dance can also immerse a person in spirit. Many world cultures have recognized dance as a powerful doorway to spiritual experience. Patel, a man from India who participated in one of my dance classes, experienced incredible energy and freedom

through dance. He likened it to an opening of all the energy centers such as yogis feel. I believe some people avoid dancing because they're subconsciously afraid to let the flow of Spirit in their lives be stronger than a trickle. When Spirit fills the dancer completely, control is lost. Most of us are less than eager to surrender our tight grip on life and risk letting Spirit take charge.

My introduction to the ecstasy of dance came not through the beat but through the pen, in February 1989, during a journaling workshop with Lucia Capacchione. She led the group in a visualization to find our heart's desire. We were each supposed to imagine being in the center of our heart, holding a sword to ward off all the voices of doubt and failure. In those days I couldn't visualize, so when the exercise was over my mind was blank. Capacchione then asked us to draw, using the non-dominant hand, a picture of ourselves doing our heart's desire. I was not optimistic. There was no picture in my mind. Besides, I only knew how to draw stick figures.

I started drawing anyway, wondering what might emerge. Not surprisingly, stick figures came out, but, unlike previous drawings, these figures were powerful and flowing. The figure representing me was dressed in a swirling gown of purple and magenta and stood, arms extended, facing a second figure in green who was flying free above. The words were even more dramatic. "I want to dance and heal with dance, set free to fly with dance the crying children within." I stared at the picture and the words with mouth agape and heart swollen with desire. I was stirred by this revelation of purpose and yet was completely mystified.

I had never taken a dance class. I had seen a few modern dance performances and occasionally attended the ballet, but I usually had to fight off sleep during the shows, unless costumes or the story line captured my attention. I liked dancing to rock and roll at parties, but I had just celebrated my fortieth birthday, and most of the parties I went to featured birthday cakes with fewer than five candles and lots of little children. So how was I supposed to use dance to heal?

Ten months later I attended a transformational dance workshop led by Gabrielle Roth. That experience was so powerful that my dancing spirit rushed from her hiding place and began to connect all my internal dots. Soon, amazing as it seemed, I was teaching dance, remembering its power, using it to transform my life and the lives of others. Over the years, I have helped many people take initial steps toward experiencing the joy and power of dance.

If you'd like to give your dancing spirit a chance to emerge, here's a simple method. Put on music you enjoy and just start moving your body in any way that feels good to you. Challenge yourself to move as many parts of your body as possible. Shoulder blades, elbows, knees and knuckles all move; spine, hips and pelvis move too. In our culture, many people have a locked pelvis and even lose spinal flexibility with age, in part because they never move their backs. Each individual vertebra is capable of movement if it hasn't already calcified and fused. With practice your spine can move like a sinuous snake. The spinal fluid will be circulating and you'll feel a much greater aliveness in your body.

While dancing, vary the body part you lead with. For example, let your elbow lead the movement, or your bottom. Change the level you move at. You can dance while you're lying down or in a squatting position. See how many parts of your body you can move at once. Play with restrictions. Dance without moving your arms at all, or your legs. Dance to fast music. Dance to slow music. Play a variety of musical styles. In teaching classes, I play with emotional opposites as well as a variety of styles, to inspire a wider range of movements and open different energy centers.

Celebrate your willingness to dance, even if you still need to do it in private. If you feel ready, consider dancing in front of somebody else. The power of a witness, whether it is one person or a whole class, vastly intensifies the benefit of the dance. Through dance we are able to express parts of ourselves we have difficulty loving. For example, a person may be uncomfortable showing anger in life but willing to dance it. Since dance is a form of play, we can sometimes find the courage to stretch into an emotion or aspect that we're not ready to welcome into our daily lives. In doing this before another person, we give that part a deeper message of acceptance. As long as we choose a respectful witness, we can experience being accepted from the outside, and this facilitates self-acceptance.

Just knowing that someone is witnessing the dance creates this experience of acceptance. When the witness is a dance partner, and eye contact is maintained throughout the dance, the effect is even more powerful. This is intimacy from the inside out. Intimacy can be thought of as "into-me-see." By sharing ourselves with a dance partner we expand our ability to experience intimacy. Initially this closeness seems dependent on our partner's openness, and of course this is important. Through dancing with multiple partners, the dancer discovers the key to intimacy is comfort with self-disclosure. The more parts of ourselves we dance into the open, the more freely we can share ourselves with the people with whom we desire close relationships.

The intention of my dance classes has always been to bring forth the whole self through movement with an intimate level of acceptance. This form of dance has given me a lasting feeling of comfort with movement and greatly stretched my sense of self. Some of those stretches still linger in memory, like the dance where a gentle-spirited man and I explored cockiness. Although neither of us normally acted in cocky ways, both of us could express that attitude in dance. We had wonderful fun, playing with this unfamiliar energy. Another time, in dance, I felt shy and virginal. Experiencing this old feeling was like pulling a beautiful lace doily out of a trunk in the attic.

Dance also offers a way to express shadow material. For example, I have danced rage and violence, fear, seductiveness and unbridled sensuality. Dance, within a group setting, has been a vehicle for finding greater self-acceptance and wholeness. I feel like there is more of me in my life now than there was before I started dancing. Dance has been my channel for the deepest conversation with my body. Like a seed slowly unfurling, through dance I have disclosed my deepest secrets to myself. A poem I wrote to accompany a dance exemplifies the transformation available through dance.

Dancing Seed

We begin
as a seed
a tightly wound
kernel of possibility
great winged beings of light
glimmering inside the folds of fear
that keep us small and hopeful.

The darkness of the earth
presses in upon us
until we crack open.

Then softly, shyly, we begin to stretch,
unfurl our leafy wings
ease with grace through the damp ground
into the spacious light
where we spread our wings
against the limitless blue sky
that kisses the ground from which we emerge.

Joyfully we dance
in sun and rain and wind

rooted in the earth
until the day our roots have been danced free
and our widespread wings
take us into the sky
on a journey just beyond our dreams
a winged seed of freedom.

The day will come for all of us when we are no longer rooted to this earth, expressing in human shape. But until that day comes, we are privileged to inhabit these sensory-rich, poetic, communicative Spirit-forms known as bodies. Surely this is not a mistake. Regardless of what kind of relationship we have had with our bodies up until now, let us turn inward and make a new commitment to intimacy. By attending to the needs of our physical forms and listening hard to the whispered messages they hold for us, we can make the most of this earthly experience. With the physical, mental and emotional planes connected and activated, we will feel the power of Spirit rushing through form, the Magic Child dancing free.

Wondersparks

1. What is your relationship to your body? Is it in your way or do you have a friendly relationship with it? Does this relationship satisfy you?

2. Do you listen to the quiet voice within or do you tend to ignore or discount those messages? Does that approach work for you?

3. If you decided to treat your body like a beloved friend, how would your life change?

4. Here are some Wondersparks in motion! Think of an area where you feel stuck. Ask: What is needing to be expressed, born through me, right now? Put on some slow, beautiful music. Then get your body into a tight ball, imagining you are a seed deep in the earth. Gently and very slowly begin to unwind, like a seed becoming a shoot, then

a blossom, imagining that you are gradually revealing all the treasure that is you. Ultimately you will be standing, wide open, moving freely. Then ask the question again. What is needing to be expressed? Take the first intuitive thought you get as your answer.

5.   This is an exercise I learned from Kathlyn Hendricks. Try it when you feel torn in two directions. Focus on one emotion or attitude, for example, feeling pressured to hurry and get things done. Find a way of moving and a gesture that you can repeat over and over, which express this feeling. Next, do the same with the opposing feeling, such as wanting to rest. Now move through the room, alternating the two movements, exaggerating each one, playing with speeding up or slowing down the movement, speeding up the intervals at which you switch between movements. If you focus on the movement, rather than analyzing what should be happening, you may discover new perceptions about the conflict, from your body's point of view.

Elixirs for the Mind

Energy Anatomy, by Caroline Myss, Ph.D. This also belongs in my desert island collection. Actually, Myss's book is called *Anatomy of the Spirit*, and *Energy Anatomy* is a comprehensive audio course of her work. Dr. Myss has worked for more than sixteen years as a medical intuitive, studying how our thoughts and emotions get stuck in particular parts of our bodies, causing us to lose power energetically and manifest illness. She correlates her observations with great spiritual traditions, finding parallels and universal truths in the Christian sacraments, the Jewish Tree of Life, and the Hindu chakra system, framing these systems in fresh new ways. Her down-to-earth stories riveted my attention and I enjoyed her blunt, humorous style. I keep listening to these tapes, learning something new each time.

At the Speed of Life, by Gay Hendricks, Ph.D., and Kathlyn Hendricks, Ph.D. This text explains the body-centered approach to therapy, a fundamental summary of the Hendrickses' revolutionary work.

Working Inside Out, by Margo Adair. Adair combines clear explanations of how the intuitive mind operates with beautiful relaxation inductions that you can tape or have a partner read, designed to empower you in many areas of life.

Healing and the Mind, Bill Moyers, ed. Based on the PBS television documentary, this book bridges mainstream and alternative traditions, presenting cutting-edge technical information in language an ordinary person can understand.

Heal Your Life, by Louise Hay. This is an older book, but still interesting. Besides sharing the powerful story of her own healing, Hay correlates a list of illnesses with suggested emotional causes. Her list isn't meant to replace intuitive authority, but to channel thinking in a new direction.

An Operator's Manual for Successful Living, by Nicholas Martin. Martin, who believes that humans are spiritual beings expressing themselves through body, mind and emotions, explains how each of these component parts functions, in clear language in a good operating manual. He then presents a list of specific skills, and challenges many people face, and offers innovative exercises to deal with them.

The Power of the Other Hand, *The Creative Journal*, and *Recovery of Your Inner Child*, by Lucia Capacchione, Ph.D. These books offer interesting journaling exercises to guide you in self-growth. The first book explains how Capacchione discovered the power of non-dominant–hand therapy and a theory of why it works.

Serious Creativity, by Edward de Bono, Ph.D. An international leader for thirty years in the field of creativity development, de Bono teaches practical, effective techniques for generating creative ideas in any situation. His approach is widely used in corporate settings and is equally helpful for individuals. This is a great tool for generating the best ideas of the Magic Child.

Drawing the Light from Within, by Judith Cornell, Ph.D. If you want to explore your artistic ability, Cornell teaches you simple techniques to make your artwork pulse with light. More than an art manual, her approach involves tuning in to the spiritual element of the inner artist.

Drawing with Children, by Mona Brooks. The director and founder of an art school for children, Brooks has taught many children and adults how to look with an artist's eye and duplicate what is seen on paper. The before and after drawings in this book are astounding. This book was my guide for learning how to draw in a more realistic fashion and I used the technique successfully to teach many children.

Freeing the Voice, by Kristen Linkletter, and *The Healing Voice*, by Joy Gardner-Gordon. Although I have not personally read these two books they have been highly recommended to me for helping people to free their Magic Children to make a joyful noise!

Living Your Dreams, by Gayle Delaney. Full of clear explanations about the dreaming process, and innovative ideas for interpreting your dreams.

Dream Gates, by Robert Moss. In this audio series, Moss, a dreamer trained in the shamanic style, presents many different approaches to dream interpretation, as well as visualizations to lead listeners into the dreamscape.

Sweat Your Prayers, by Gabrielle Roth. Drawing on a lifetime of luring students past fear into the ecstasy of dance, Roth shares her philosophy and basic rhythm method with readers, in language so poetic it dances across the page.

The Serpent and the Wave, by Jalaja Bonheim. This book, based on a spiritual acceptance of the body, offers a Western perspective on the power of movement and abounds with powerful movement meditations. The author is a movement therapist and performing dancer, who has extensively studied Eastern philosophy and classical Indian dance.

Come Home to Your Body, by Pamela J. Free. This Feldenkrais practitioner offers movement techniques for awakening the body's wisdom.

The Power of the Mind to Heal, by Dr. Joan Borysenko. In this audio series, Dr. Borysenko presents the idea that our minds hold the key to physical, mental, and emotional healing. She guides listeners to reach into the pain of life experience and find the inner well-spring of strength and wisdom that brings healing transformation. She draws on modern psychology, many spiritual traditions, and deeply moving stories to help listeners reach their higher selves.

Chapter Three

The ability to see yourself as a gift
is the deepest benefit
of taking responsibility for your life.

Magic Wand
Claim full responsibility for your life.

The Power of Responsibility

Imagine you are in a small craft traveling on the River of Life, a great waterway with many tributaries. Some are quiet ribbons of blue, meandering through serene valleys; others are filled with wild, white water rapids, exploding into the air and crashing against the shore. If you want, you can have a compass and paddles, even charts, and books on navigation. You can also choose to sit in the boat and simply experience the ride.

Everybody will hit a white water patch now and then, but certain people will spend most of their time riding the rapids. Some will do it because they like the excitement. Others will end up in the rapids again and again because they choose not to learn to navigate or even to carry paddles.

Responsibility is the paddle that allows you to choose a direction in life. By acknowledging your role as conscious creator of your life, with all its experiences, you get to stay in the steering seat, holding the paddle. You will still hit rapids occasionally, and situations will come along that were unanticipated or that seem to be beyond your ability to control. But you will still have the paddle. You will not be at the mercy of the rapids totally. The opposite choice is to ride along without steering aids. The people who make this choice are the victims of life. They go wherever the river takes them, never charting a course, never steering to avoid rapids, never accepting responsibility for repeatedly landing in the rapids. They continuously point their fingers, blaming others for all their problems or making excuses about why they are stuck.

Most of us slip into victim thinking occasionally. From that perspective, life seems beyond our control. Feeling helpless, hopeless, and overwhelmed, we marinate in the emotions of fear, sadness, and anger—victims, who have no power.

Victims aren't much fun to be around and often people judge themselves harshly when recognizing victim tendencies in themselves. However, victims are not bad people, simply individuals with disempowering outlooks who haven't yet realized there is another approach to life. If you have begun to recognize your own victimlike attitudes, please don't use this section to beat yourself up. Instead celebrate your dawning awareness. Forgive yourself for not recognizing the importance of healthy responsibility earlier and look forward to the creative power that you are already closer to exercising as you start becoming conscious of the ways you behave like a victim.

One of the main ways that we humans get stuck in victim thinking is by focusing on fault. Because we never purposely create negative situations or relationships, we are unwilling to accept blame for the negativity we experience. We're so conditioned to think that somebody must be at fault that we look for someone else to blame—another person, the government, or even God. The fallacy comes in confusing fault and responsibility. They are not the same. A responsible person assumes, "Whatever happens in my life must have something to do with me, even if the connection is subconscious, even when it's part of my soul's agenda."

As I explained earlier, some events have no rational explanation. A person gets cancer, loses a home in a hurricane, or endures the murder of a loved one and the question "Why?" doesn't generate a satisfactory answer. In such times, we need to assume this is not the business of the personality but rather an affair of the soul. As we look back in years to come and reflect on the strength we developed through adversity, we may get a glimpse into the soul's lesson plan. Until then we have to accept the mystery. On the other hand, there are many life circumstances that feel unrelated to us on the personality level, which actually have a strong subconscious connection.

Patsy Ellen was a middle-aged woman who always felt excluded by her triathlete husband. She enjoyed gentle excursions into nature, while he couldn't have fun without pushing himself to excel, and she complained that he always expected her to push her own limits. They had difficulty playing harmoniously together. For a long time Patsy Ellen had felt frustrated, and hopeless about their relationship. Then one day she wondered if she was responsible for any of their problems. But, she asked herself, why would she create a situation where she constantly felt like, and labeled herself as, an inadequate wimp? That question unlocked a memory that surprised her. When she was a child, Patsy Ellen's adored big sister had been a tomboy, while she had been a bookworm. Clumsy, with failing eyesight that hadn't been diagnosed, Patsy Ellen was treated like a pariah by both her sister and her sister's friends if she tried to join their ball games. Sitting in my office, Patsy Ellen's eyes flowed with tears at this memory. She was shocked to realize this still bothered her and, even more, that she had managed to recreate a similar situation with her husband.

Sometimes people wonder why anyone would choose to recreate unpleasant circumstances. They are sure they would never do that intentionally and so don't understand how they could be responsible. The key word is "intentionally." We create these situations subconsciously, usually to have another opportunity to resolve the elements that didn't work for us the first time.

In Patsy Ellen's example, she carried unresolved pain about being excluded because she wasn't an athlete. In duplicating that situation with her husband, she got to try again to be accepted and included by an athletic person who was important to her. She also recognized her own tendency to push through physical fears by forcing herself to take on athletic challenges. She hadn't realized that her husband's pushing mirrored her own.

When adults become conscious of a familiar pattern being replayed, we have a chance to change the dynamics. Patsy Ellen realized that approval and acceptance from outside was less important than self-acceptance and she could now mercifully embrace the childish part who still felt unloved. Such empowering choices lead to real healing. But the door to that healing begins with taking responsibility.

Patsy's insight wouldn't have happened if she had not stopped complaining about the situation and asked the responsibility question. Complaints and excuses keep us stuck, with no paddle in sight. We don't find out how our situation is connected to us and we don't get to do anything to change it for the better. Think about the language of excuses. Most people use them sometimes and some use them all the time. "I can't help it; I can't possibly do that because…; Nobody ever told/taught me that; My parents didn't raise me right; We were poor and didn't have the chances other people had; This illness has the better of me; My spouse doesn't treat me the way I want to be treated; My children are out of control and don't respect me; The government is run by fools who tax away all my earnings; The economy is terrible and I can't get ahead," etc.

All of these statements may be true. Regardless, without deciding to take responsibility for our own lives, we will remain victims. Perhaps our parents didn't have healthy child-rearing skills. We couldn't do much about that as children. Now, however, choices are available to us. Instead of spending a whole life absorbed in self pity, or angrily reacting to everything our parents stood for, or mindlessly following their programming, we can accept responsibility and choose to live differently now. If we weren't taught something as a child that seems important to know, we can learn now.

If nurturing was not on our parents' skill list, we can nurture ourselves and choose to associate with nurturing people. Self-help books and professional therapy are widely available options for letting go of old traumas. Although a spouse, employer or friend may be abusive, if we examine our choice to be with such a person, the way our own behavior feeds those dynamics may become evident and we can then take steps to change the situation or relationship.

Even though the economy may seem terrible, we need to just accept it as a fact and work within that framework instead of complaining about it. Many of us lose precious life energy whining and resisting life because it's showing up as the wrong experience. The starting place has to be acknowledging exactly what is true, wondering if the situation has any connection to our behavior or beliefs, and then choosing how to proceed. At least that's the starting point if we want to travel the River of Life with a paddle in hand. By stubbornly defending our victim status, we remain disempowered. The Magic Child, who is innately powerful, cannot emerge.

Why wouldn't everybody automatically grab the paddle? There are benefits to riding without one. Sometimes we feel too helpless and convince ourselves that we can't change because we're so defective. But a part of us always knows the Magic Child as our true essence, and this part can be filled with rage that the victim-self has accepted such a demeaning self-image. Rather than experience that self-directed rage, we may resign ourselves to unfair fate while wishing for a different situation. Instead of facing our own anger, we may exhaust and paralyze ourselves with self-criticism or else try to ignore the "truth" of our inadequacy by concentrating on what's wrong with everybody else, attacking before personal faults can be revealed. We cannot afford to be seen as wrong, if we fear we are wrong in the core of our being, because any mistake might expose the extent of our defects. This is a costly attitude.

An older widow named Claire complained about her neighbor during one of our counseling sessions. Claire had asked Joan, who lived in an apartment above her own, to care for her little dog while she went on vacation. Joan agreed to feed, walk, and play with Claire's dog every day, but refused to let it spend time in  her own apartment, which is what Claire had hoped would happen. In the past, the dog had run through every room of Joan's apartment, urinating on beds to mark his territory.

Instead of appreciating the help that Joan offered, accepting responsibility, and apologizing for her dog's past behavior, Claire found a way to blame Joan. "My dog only did it because you got a female dog," Claire had told Joan accusingly. "He never did that before you got that dog." Claire, in her own mind, saved herself from being wrong, but it cost her a positive relationship with her neighbor.

For many of us, the word responsibility has a negative connotation. We think of an angry parental voice demanding to know "Who's responsible for this mess?" The responsible person, of course, would get in big trouble. Or we think of taking on extra duties at work or home or in volunteer settings (usually because nobody else will do the job and we are unwilling to be responsible for setting firm boundaries). In such a context, responsibility is just a burden. Who would want that?

Responsibility is also commonly misinterpreted in a co-dependent way. We are not responsible for other people's feelings and choices. Anyone having this kind of confusion about responsibility is likely to stay busy catering to the needs and trying to control the feelings of others, while ignoring personal needs and feelings. Taking responsibility for another and avoiding responsibility for self is not healthy.

If we interpret responsibility in any of these negative ways and avoid accepting it, we forfeit any conscious say in our own lives. "Victims" don't get to choose a direction in life, have no say in whether their important relationships are harmonious, and can't control their financial well-being or health. The only tools available to victims are hope and prayers for rescue. A joke, whose origin I don't know, illustrates the attitude of a victim who expects salvation from God.

A certain town had been experiencing heavy rains for several weeks. The flooding was so serious people were told to evacuate their homes. Raymond refused to leave his home. He had trust in God and knew God would save him. He stayed inside praying. After awhile, rescue workers showed up in a boat right outside his first floor window. "Raymond," they called. "Climb out the window and get in the boat. Your life is in danger."

"I'm not leaving," he replied. "God is my savior. He won't fail me." The rains continued. Sometime later another boat arrived. This time the

boat was outside the second story window. Again the rescue workers shouted to Raymond to get in the boat and save himself. "No need to," Raymond answered confidently, "God will save me."

The rain kept pouring down. Finally a helicopter hovered over the house where Raymond was clinging to his roof. "Raymond, get in the helicopter or you'll drown," they pleaded.

"My faith is steady," was the staunch reply. "God will deliver me." Well, Raymond drowned. When he arrived at heaven in a state of shock, sputtering with outrage, he insisted upon seeing God. When he got his audience, he demanded to know why God had let him down. "I trusted you to save me," he complained. "How could you let me die?"

"Raymond, Raymond," God replied wearily, "I sent two boats and a helicopter; what did you want me to do?"

Greek playwrights sometimes used a theatrical device called a *deus ex machina*, or "god out of a machine." When a situation got too difficult to unravel, the playwright would have a god descend from the sky in a machine, something like a hot-air balloon, to solve the problem. An external solution, an outside power, it could not be planned on, only prayed for. Most of us are like the ancient Greeks in this respect. We want a miracle worker, a genie, a fairy godmother, to solve our problems for us. "Heal me," we say to our doctors and our therapists. "You make me better." And of course they can't. The healers have many wonderful tools, but only the Magic Child has the authority to create wellness where there was disease, freedom where there was imprisonment, life where there was apathy and dejection. This happens when we accept responsibility for our lives, choose how we want them to be, and then take whatever steps are clear to us in the moment.

From limited ego awareness, we don't usually know how, or why, our problems are happening, or how to solve them. If we can accept ourselves as one with God, a true Magic Child, then we can, through an intention to be responsible, exert that same creative power that brought all life into existence, and choose a direction for our lives. The mystery in all this is that we can know our essence is Divine yet we cannot maintain that awareness in every moment. The limitations of conscious thought obscure a deeper knowing of exactly what is best for us and how to accomplish our goals. Much of our lives are spent operating in the dark, trusting intuitive clues. So at the same time we, as God-beings, claim responsibility for our lives, we also, as beings of limited awareness, have to surrender control to an all knowing God-self, the Magic Child. This seeming contradiction is built into the human experience. We are unlimited beings in limited form. Many of my clients' stories illustrate the transition from victim to responsible party.

Nancy was a woman in her mid-forties dogged by depression. On the surface there was no justification for such feelings. Her husband's job fulfilled all their financial needs and, since the children were grown, she was pursuing her own career, doing work that she loved. Nancy's biggest complaint was that her husband's frequent business trips prompted feelings of abandonment when he left and remoteness when he returned. Nancy's alcoholic father had not been emotionally present and, although she was aware that the situation with her husband triggered those old feelings, she still felt emotionally trapped.

As we explored this, and other concerns, it became clear that Nancy was angry over her parents' failure to provide emotional nurturing. In hypnosis she saw herself as a baby crying forlornly in the crib, ignored by her parents. I suggested imagining her adult self picking up and comforting the baby self. Nancy refused to do this. "That's their job!" she protested. "Why should I have to be the one to understand their problems and take them off the hook? As it was, I had way more responsibilities than a child should have. I can't do this for them. I would betray myself if I did."

Nancy eventually realized that even though her parents had failed in this responsibility, they could never make up for it now. Only she could do that by taking responsibility for her own needs. In later hypnosis sessions, she did pick up the child. In life, she began to feel more in charge and less depressed.

Even if our parents were emotionally healthy and had good parenting skills, none of them could meet every need we had. At some point we all have to accept that childhood was the way it was and parents can never go back and do it right. In some cases, the parents we are angry at for their inadequacies back then are still unable to love us in the way we need. But even if they have changed and are now more mature and loving people, we can't change what happened in the past. What we can do is take responsibility in the present. We can decide to pick up the crying child that lives in our heart and offer love and caring. We can offer the adult guidelines and boundaries that the child may never have received and give messages that build healthy self-esteem in place of old critical messages. If we don't do these things, nobody ever will. Regardless of whether someone, like our parents, should have taken responsibility and didn't, now the responsibility is ours.

A step beyond that is to accept whatever experience we had as the right experience. Nancy had trouble with this idea. "Nobody should have to put up with what I went through. That was wrong!" Of course, the ways many parents treat their children are mistaken at best and sometimes cruel. Still, if we can accept what happened at that time, under those circumstances, with those particular people, as the right experience, we will be free of the backward-focused anger over things that cannot be changed.

"Supposing all that has happened to you was actually the right experience," I suggested to Nancy. "What would be the gift of it all?" That was a hard question for her. The following week she came back with a tear-filled answer. "The gift," she replied, "would be me, exactly as I am." The ability to see yourself as a gift is the deepest benefit of taking responsibility for your life.

Jenny was a fifty-year-old client who had owned a successful business for years but since the death of her husband had lost the ability or desire to concentrate on it. She had also experienced serious medical problems shortly after his death and the medication caused weight gain, a new experience for this normally athletic woman. When Jenny crawled into a quiet corner of life to heal from all the trauma, she brought lots of donuts, and so gained even more weight. Then, no matter what diet she tried, she couldn't lose weight or focus on business. She had set clear goals and even knew the techniques to accomplish them, but something held her back.

In hypnosis, we explored this block, which Jenny described as soft and pink, somewhat pliant, but firmly in place. Eventually she intuited that this was an experience inside the womb, shortly before her birth. She remembered wanting to get out but not being able to push through. Although the obstruction obviously gave way at some point, Jenny realized her initial frustration led to a pivotal assumption.

Impatient to get out of the womb, Jenny never realized it was just a matter of waiting for the right time and circumstances. Instead, she had concluded that her wants made no difference because she was not in control of her life. In this primal instance, the power lay in the womb, which she believed had to authorize the timing of her birth.

This belief became a template for Jenny's life. Her motivation to perform had always been to meet other people's requirements: mother's, employer's, husband's. Never had she set goals just for herself, and accomplished them. Now, with her husband gone and no boss around, there was nobody left to direct her life, unless she did it herself. This was a key realization for Jenny. Soon she was exercising, eating healthy meals and getting her business back in order.

George, a client in his fifties, was suffering from high blood pressure. His doctor hoped my techniques would relieve that medical problem. In hypnosis, George consistently imagined his inner child as a crippled boy. George had never worn braces or had any other physical deformity as a boy, but he had accepted negative messages from authority figures in his youth. George was dyslexic in an era before dyslexia was identified as a problem, and his teachers had labeled him stupid and good-for-nothing. Singled out as his mother's whipping boy, he felt incapable of doing anything right. Believing it was beyond his power to create the kind of life he wanted, George had settled for an "okay" life. After all, everything is hard for a crippled boy.

George's work was learning to love the child within. As he grew more able to accept himself with all his feelings—even the "unacceptable" ones like anger or sexual urges—the boy of his imagination grew stronger until he could run and play like other children. In conscious life, George started exercising and reduced his blood pressure. Communication with his wife and children improved, and the business, which had been limping along, became very successful. As George became willing to be fully responsible and fully capable instead of crippled, there seemed to be no limit to what he created.

Jim was crippled by a belief that his character was inherently flawed. A client in his late thirties, Jim had an industrial strength, bulletproof inner critic. No matter what progress he made in therapy, the critic bounced back, seemingly stronger than ever, reminding Jim that nothing would ever make a difference because Jim was "defective goods." Left alone, according to the critic, Jim would make a hopeless muddle of anything he tried. If he did things he really wanted to do, other people would get hurt, because Jim was an irresponsible, selfish person who would just disappear into the woods with a backpack, abandoning his young family forever.

Jim was depressed and miserable, angry about being so stupid, about not having done things right, about still having problems in his life. He was really angry at his parents, who taught him to be critical, and at the internalized voice serving as their ongoing representative. Jim, however, could only acknowledge that anger toward his parents in an intellectual way. On an emotional level, everything was his own fault. Along with the anger, he felt incredible sadness over not being appreciated and valued. The sadness and the repressed anger left him depressed and hopeless, not knowing how to alter his life.

In order to change, Jim had to take responsibility, claiming his own life and replacing the critic as lord and master. He had to begin to lovingly teach himself new habits of thinking to replace those habitual, harshly critical patterns. Whenever Jim encountered the critic in hypnosis, there was a frightened little boy directing things, under the critical mask. That child was not the part of Jim that belonged in charge. Jim had to confront a basic issue of responsibility. Accepting his inner critic's dim view of himself had been a great excuse for not achieving his potential; it created a limitation of success in all areas of his life.

Our own magnificence is terrifying to most of us. In his inaugural address, Nelson Mandela, President of South Africa, quoted Marianne Williamson's famous words:

Our deepest fear is not that we are inadequate.
Our deepest fear is that we are powerful beyond
measure.
It is our Light, not our Darkness, that most frightens
us.
We ask ourselves, who am I to be brilliant, gorgeous,
talented, fabulous?
Actually, who are you NOT to be?

You are a child of God.
Your playing small does not serve the world.
There is nothing enlightened about shrinking
so that other people won't feel insecure around you.
We were born to make manifest the glory of God that is
within us.

It is not just in some of us; it is in everyone.
And as we let our own light shine, we unconsciously
give other people
permission to do the same.
As we are liberated from our own fear,
our presence automatically liberates others.

The little boy in Jim was afraid to be great, and, masquerading as the critic, convinced Jim to not even try. As Jim focused more on his purpose in life and connected with the Magic Child, the critic's voice became less constant and strident. By nourishing himself with positive messages and taking concrete steps to accomplish goals, Jim felt much better.

We are not being responsible adults by giving power to parts of ourselves, such as the critic, that are not qualified for a particular task. Many people abdicate power over their lives to their child-selves and then complain that they want to be responsible but just can't seem to get the job done.

Eddie was a client in his mid-thirties who, after about fifteen years of having a wad of chewing tobacco in his mouth all day long, sincerely wanted to break the addiction. We worked together for weeks with no success, even though he was ashamed of the habit and highly motivated to quit. Finally, we discovered that an angry inner teenager was chewing the tobacco. The teen, furious because many aspects of Eddie's life were the "wrong experience," wouldn't cooperate with any of Eddie's goals. By recognizing the teenage part of himself doing the foot-dragging, Eddie was able to take control as the adult. He stopped chewing immediately and completely and has not experienced any further urges to chew.

Maya was a forty-year-old client battling to extricate herself, by divorce, from the seemingly limitless greed and anger of her husband. The legal process seemed to be lasting forever, as he showed up over and over with new demands. The court system appeared to be oblivious to his manipulations and deceits and Maya was intensely frustrated. She was willing to let go of almost anything to end the relationship, and yet was unwilling to let him pick clean the carcass of her life. Using the non-dominant hand art technique I described in chapter 2, Maya pictured herself, enmeshed in this situation. The self she drew was very tiny, swathed in "nice girl" pink, drowning in black muck. Through the drawing, we realized Maya couldn't find a solution because she was too little and too nice.

Sometimes we just can't envision ourselves as powerful enough to handle certain situations. One approach at such times is to surrender to our God-selves and trust. Other times, I think we need to pull the power into our conscious awareness. One way to do this is to connect, on the inner plane, with an energy that we believe will provide the needed strength, and then, in our imagination, merge with that energy. Depending on the task at hand as well as personal heroes, an individual might call in such beings as Jesus, the Buddha, Joan of Arc, Albert Einstein, Rosa Parks, or Mahatma Gandhi.

Maya wanted to invoke powerful female energy, so we chose Kali, the Hindu goddess of destruction and rebirth. Aligning with this energy, she made a new picture, with bold strokes, covering the entire page. "I am Maya, The Empress," she declared. Shivers ran through both of us as this Empress energy streamed through Maya. I played Peter Gabriel's song *Shaking the Tree*, and Maya danced The Empress fully into her body, claiming Gabriel's refrain for her own: "This is my day, woman's day." The scared and helpless little girl had been consigned to a safe lap in her imagination. This situation was not the little girl's job to handle. The powerful woman who left my office was the person responsible for reclaiming her life. She later reported the positive outcome and how empowered she had felt taking charge of the situation. What a handicap needing to be perceived as nice had been! From then on, Maya was determined to have The Empress be a reigning power rather than a visiting dignitary in her life.

We don't avoid responsibility intentionally. Usually we are so trapped inside a part of ourselves like the nice child or the critic that we don't realize there is more of us available to take responsibility. The self acting in charge is afraid to let go of control, afraid something terrible will happen to us. Only with great love and trust can we relax the grip these parts have on our lives. In taking responsibility, we recognize ourselves as an essence. This essence is the great self, the Magic Child that exists on a deeper level, the "me" that always is, regardless of the part I may be acting from at the moment. In perceiving ourselves as glorious essence, and the individual parts of ourselves as the masks they are, we gain the power to choose our response. We become response-able.

Steps for Change

To experience the power of responsibility, begin with intention. Tune into a quiet place inside and declare the intention to be responsible. Declare this to yourself and any witnesses of choice, Divine or human. You may want to sit quietly, on a regular basis, and contemplate the idea of being one with life, one with God. Think about what that means to you.

As more experiences come along, assume that whatever is happening is tailored to your needs. If it isn't something you like, instead of asking irately, "Why is this wrong experience happening to me?" examine the situation with curiosity, as feedback life is presenting. Think about whether it illustrates some way you are avoiding responsibility. Consider whether anything in your past or present may be requiring life to unfold in just this way. Is some part of you angry and unwilling to be responsible? Which part is that? Ask whatever other questions occur. Be open to any ideas that pop into your head in response.

If people start offering criticism and advice, instead of assuming they are malicious and interfering, treat their words as important clues to the issue you're exploring. Examine your anger, fear and sadness. Are these emotions keeping you from assuming responsibility? Study the people that irritate you. Are you like them in some way you'd rather not acknowledge? Could there be some way they avoid responsibility that sheds a light on your own tendencies? As the connections become clear to you, be prepared to change your attitudes and behaviors. Step by step, give yourself positive messages and take whatever concrete steps become apparent. As you do this, expect life to start coming into alignment with your conscious desires. That is the power of responsibility.

Wondersparks

1. Did something happen to you that was not your fault, that was not the right experience, and that serves as an excuse for not accomplishing your personal goals?
2. How old is the aspect of yourself that is running your life?
3. Who is the beneficiary of your life energy? Do you make choices based on what is right for you or based on somebody else's requirements?
4. If you knew you were responsible for your life and powerful enough to exercise that responsibility fully and gloriously, how would you be living differently right now?

Elixirs for the Mind

The Conscious Heart and Conscious Loving, by Gay Hendricks, Ph.D., and Kathlyn Hendricks, Ph.D. These relationship experts clearly explain, using many stories, how we avoid responsibility for our lives, outlining the payoffs and costs for doing so.

Energy Anatomy, by Caroline Myss, Ph.D. Learn how to take responsibility for your own energy system by discovering your power leaks.

Chapter Four

Surrender is the rope
by which we pull ourselves out of the pit
of five-sensory options
into the unlimited world
of the Magic Child.

Magic Wand
Surrender to your higher power.

Sweet Surrender

The word surrender conjures up images of bedraggled soldiers admitting defeat, their heads hung in shame, yielding control of their country's destiny to a conquering army. In wartime settings, surrender was a terrible event for the losing side. Surrendering parties feared starvation, looting, destruction and captivity at the hands of the conquering force. Because that memory floats in our collective consciousness, few of us are eager to surrender to anybody for any reason. Yet, to enjoy the fullness of life, we must learn to do exactly that—surrender; not to an outside force this time, but to the Magic Child, God's "internal representative."

In giving control of our destiny to the Magic Child, we can expect miracles instead of abuse, joy instead of suffering. Years ago, in a song called "Sweet Surrender," singer/songwriter John Denver encouraged listeners to let go of struggle and he described the wonders and carefree life awaiting those who turned their power over to a higher force. He painted a picture of being in a magical flow "like the fish in the water, like the birds in the air."

The song reminded me of a favorite Biblical passage (Luke 12:24-27), in which Jesus tells his followers what to expect when God is in charge.

> *Don't worry about whether you have enough food to eat or clothes to wear. Look at the ravens. They don't plant or harvest or have barns to store their food and yet they get along all right, for God feeds them…Behold the lilies of the field—they don't toil and spin, and yet Solomon, in all his glory, was not clothed as well as one of these.*

Like battle-weary soldiers, most of us exhaust all other avenues for success before considering surrender to God. Marianne Williamson, author of *Return to Love* and other books, describes how she used to go from one crisis to the next. Only when sufficiently desperate, would she fall to her knees and turn the current mess over to God. The rescue would be miraculous but soon another crisis would force her back on the knees. Finally she realized, "I do better on my knees. Why don't I just stay there?!"

Surrender works better as an ongoing policy than a crisis management tool because it's the rope by which we pull ourselves from the pit of limited five-sensory options into the unlimited world of the Magic Child. In daily living, we are constantly challenged to remember we are powerful, individualized expressions of the Divine instead of the helpless, confused victims of life we often feel like. Even with the intention to be response-able, we still get stuck, interpreting life from the limited information our physical senses provide. From this perspective, our role in creating life the way it's showing up is usually unclear, and we see no path out of the confusion.

When we get stuck, there are really only two choices. The first, the victim option, is to protest the experience, using tools like anger, blame, whining, self-destruction, and denial of any personal responsibility for being in the situation. The second choice is to surrender to the Magic Child who comprehends the big picture. This Divine aspect of ourselves always knows how we got into any particular mess and how to change what's happening. By surrendering to this all-knowing energy, the limited mind, which we're always in tune with, can relax and stop worrying or even panicking over a messy situation.

Letting go requires confidence in the Divine. Imagine that the surrender process is like turning over your belongings to professional movers. If you trust them to do the job, you can relax and attend to other things. How absurd it would be if, after hiring them, you kept getting ahead of them trying to hold up the boxes they were carrying, just to make sure they did it right. Your "help" would only cause the movers to trip or get frustrated. Soon they'd quit and let you run around with the boxes by yourself. When turning our lives over, we need to trust the creative power of the Divine to accomplish things that we already know are beyond our ability.

In letting go of worry, our whole being unwinds and can slip into harmony with life. Then needed solutions can pass freely, liked winged angels, into our material world. Unseen hands are all around, reaching out to help if we will only open ourselves to the help. When we stubbornly hang onto the remote control, pressing the worry or panic button, to feel like we're doing something, our entire bodymind system tenses and contracts. The miracles can't get through the tight barrier created by fearful tension.

I remember driving home from a weekly primal therapy session on a rainy night in Texas, years ago. Those sessions always left me feeling peaceful, more spacious inside from releasing long buried, tightly held traumas. After a year of therapy, I was getting inklings of new emotional possibilities, maybe due to the inner space being cleared out. Despite a desire and a commitment to let go of past pain, my emotional grip was still pretty tight. I was particularly clutching a need to be perfect and to control everything, especially my children's behavior.

But, alone in the car, at that moment, loose in the empty space inside me, I flipped on the radio, and unexpectedly tuned into KHVN. The dial was set on KPFT, the local listener-sponsored station, which was having a quarterly marathon fund-raiser. As the deejay encouraged listeners to call in with pledges, KHVN was seeping through in the background with a special message for me. A song softly posed a question: "How would it be if you let your life flow?" Then it gave the answer: "You would glow; you would glow." Stunned, I turned up the radio, hoping to hear the credits for this beautiful song, but they were never mentioned. The song vanished back into the heavenly ethers, and I never heard it again. Over the years I have discovered the truth of that message. When I surrender, my life flows easily and miracles show up as needed. When I worry and fret, my life bumps and grinds along like an old jalopy that needs a tune-up and every little thing becomes a struggle.

Picture the image of a small child struggling to tie his shoes. The mother watches those clumsy efforts, respecting his desire for independence, knowing all the while she could tie the shoes easily if he wanted her help. God is like that mother. As long as we are intent on being the doer, God patiently awaits our invitation for help, content to let us learn through frustration and struggle, while also willing to create a miracle in our lives. The choice is ours. The child does need to learn independence from the mother. We, however, do not need to create separation from the Divine in order to learn and grow. We could let go of the belief that life has to be a struggle in the "real world" and let our lives flow with magic instead.

The Bible contains a beautiful image of the way our lives can flow. The Twenty-third Psalm describes God as a shepherd who takes good care of his flock. The King James version of the Bible refers to God as The Lord. As a twentieth-century American feminist, I find the image of relying on The Lord of the manor for my needs rather distasteful. The idea that the Lord would provide all good things, i.e., take care of all needs, and would open his great house to the people must have been a powerful and comforting promise to commoners who looked up to the aristocracy. I can certainly appreciate the power of that image for the audience for whom it was created and was expressed in the Twenty-third Psalm:

The Lord is my shepherd
I shall not want
He maketh me to lie down in green pastures
He leadeth me beside the still waters
He restoreth my soul…
Surely goodness and mercy shall follow me
all the days of my life
and I will dwell in the house of the Lord forever.

I love to realize that my Divine self makes me lie down to rest, since that's the lowest priority on my To-Do list, as I busily struggle to accomplish all the very important business of my life independently. I forget there could be an easy way: magical help from the God within. We do not have to struggle. Life can have the easy flow of being shepherded from one luscious pasture to the next if we simply surrender to the Magic Child.

Aurobindo, a modern Hindu mystic, cited in *The Essential Mystic*, describes the ease that can be ours when we surrender to our God-self.

But a time will come when you will feel more and more that you are the instrument and not the worker. For, first by the force of your devotion, your contact with the Divine Mother will become so intimate that at all times you will have only to concentrate and to put everything in her hands to have her present guidance, her direct command or impulse, the sure indication of the thing to be done and the way to do it and the result. And afterwards you will realize that the divine Shakti not only inspires and guides, but initiates and carries out your works; all your movements are originated by her, all your powers are hers. Mind, life and body are conscious and joyful instruments of her action, means for her play, molds for her manifestation in the physical universe. There can be no more happy condition than this union and dependence; for this step carries you back beyond the borderline from the life of stress and suffering in the ignorance into the truth of your spiritual being, into its deep peace.

The Surrender Instruction Manual

Surrender is an intention and a process. The first step is always intention. Remember you are a Magic Child, an individualized expression of the everywhere present Divine energy. As long as you are tuned into that aspect of your being, you are able to handle everything. Intend to surrender your life to that God-being.

Surrender all the aspects, even the outcome you want. From our limited consciousness, we don't even know what we need. So, having expressed an intention to surrender, ask that wise Magic Child to guide you in setting goals. "God, I want to be an instrument of your love in this situation. Help me formulate goals that will be for the highest good."

Goals are important in setting a direction, but without surrendering the goal-setting process, we may focus on the wrong goals. For example, we might convince ourselves that we want to buy a different house and yet, our guiding wisdom may indicate the deeper desire of a making our current home more harmonious. Even while thinking a goal is clear and right, we may discover through surrendering that God provides something better. A well-known song by the rock group The Rolling Stones presents this quite clearly: "You can't always get what you want, but if you try sometimes, you just might find, you get what you need."

Once you feel sure of a goal, surrender the means to achieving it. The victim-oriented, limited mind can only see three options. One is, "I have to do it all myself. If I don't make it happen, it won't." The second option is, "Somebody else either has what I need or has the skill to get it, and my job is to cajole, force or otherwise manipulate them into giving it to me or doing it for me." The third option is despair, "I'll never get my needs met. I'm helpless to change my life." These are all stressful, struggle-filled approaches.

For those who understand surrender, coupled with the power of positive thinking, there is another option. By focusing on a goal and maintaining a confident attitude and trust in God, miracles can happen.

Positive thinking by itself can help, but the pressure to control the outcome is still on our limited mind. Initially, this is a very empowering experience, for someone who has previously approached life as a victim. But as my husband,

Ron, says, "I feel if I take my eye off the ball for a minute, the ball will deflate!" People can ride high on the power of positive thinking and creative thought for quite awhile, but in time, exhaustion often sets in. The solution is to surrender to a higher power who knows how to orchestrate your life with ease. The Magic Child is just waiting for your cue.

In surrendering to this miracle maker you can say, "God, I am willing to work hard and ask your help in doing what I need to do. I surrender. You can be in charge here. Just talk to me in a way I can hear and I'll listen. Show me how to proceed, step by step. Thank you for your loving, creative support."

If your life is already in a shambles and you're surrendering as a last resort, try a prayer like this. "God, this is a mess! I don't know what to do and am not having fun. I'm willing to step aside and let you take over. Please help. I surrender. This is my goal but I don't know how to accomplish it and am not even sure this is the best goal. I believe you can create an outcome that will work really well for everybody and will even be fun! I believe that all I have to do is surrender and you'll take over just like you promised. Thank you for being here for me."

Sometimes we hesitate to pray, believing past prayers have gone unanswered. "If there is a God," we sulk, "how come my loved one died? How come I had such a terrible childhood? Where was God when I was in need?" Our lives are filled with unexplained pain.

Through adopting attitudes of connection with God, you may discover some pain was due to belief in separation from the Divine. However, we'll probably never be enlightened enough to avoid all thoughts of separation. There will continue to be times when we interpret our experiences in ways that cause us pain. This is, ultimately, part of our learning. In these times, the Magic Wand of surrender will bring us back to peaceful union and creative power.

Most clients I work with have some unhappy childhood memories, even if they came from good homes. Many people have had horrible childhood experiences. All of them, as they awaken to their shining essence, discover gifts that have been formed in the crucible of their childhood pain.

This discovery is dependent on letting go of our five-sensory insistence that we know how life should have been, should be now, or should be in the future. Through surrendering the often painful "shoulds" to God, the magic pattern of our experiences becomes clearer and peace fills our souls. We are able to stay in the present, understanding past experiences and trusting that our future ones will also be "right."

If you are someone who can't trust God right now, try this type of prayer. "God, I don't know where you are or if you are. I haven't been able to feel you in my life, and I'm angry about that. I've tried to muddle on without you, determined to make it on my own, resenting being alone. Sometimes I've done okay, but I'm not having fun, really, and I mess up too often. I don't want to live this way anymore. I'm ready to make a leap of faith, to jump off the mental ledge I've been clinging to and trust you'll be there to catch me. I want to feel you inside me. I want to believe I am one with you. Help my lack of faith. Catch me! I'm falling towards you, messed-up life and all!"

After making your own prayer of surrender, be where you can be quiet and listen for any immediate instructions. Sit and meditate, go for a walk, or take a relaxing bath. The next step, inspiration, or instruction will often occur quickly, but if it doesn't, just get back to work. Trust the process.

Surrender does not require that you give up all effort, scrap all goals and sit on the couch in a bathrobe eating chocolates, waiting for further instructions. While you're waiting and expecting a miracle, you have to keep working, following your best instincts in the moment to formulate and reach your goals. Simply do your best, and let go of all worry or self-judgment. Surrender does not demand self-punishment for not having known how to do the right thing in the first place. Lovingly acknowledge that your five-sensory mind is limited, by design, and turn the controls over to the wise mind of the Magic Child.

This approach is not an instant cure for all doubts and fears. When the disgruntled, complaining, despairing thoughts of limited consciousness jump like big dogs onto the living room couch of your mind, acknowledge them and put them where they belong. Don't try to pretend such thoughts don't exist, because clearly they are there, getting muddy paw prints all over the couch. Don't scream hatefully at them, thereby creating more negative energy.

Think of them as misbehaving pets or "dog-thoughts," then lovingly but firmly tell them to get off the couch because you've just cleaned it. Don't berate yourself for still having these types of thoughts. Discipline yourself to focus on the positive outcome that you're expecting, the surprising way in which your goals will be achieved.

You don't have to be able to imagine how this will work out (especially if it seems impossible) or even the details of the end result. Approach the miracle of surrender like a child at Christmas, bursting with curiosity, not anxiety, about what is in the package under the tree. Trust that the giver has put something wonderful inside. Your job is to keep the "dog-thoughts" off your couch and trust that help is on the way.

The final step is to say thanks. It is best to start thanking as soon as you surrender; you know the solution is already in progress. By thanking from the outset, you reinforce a positive attitude of expecting a miracle.

Summary

1. Intend to surrender to the Magic Child.
2. Ask for help in setting goals.
3. Surrender the means to achieving the goals.
4. Surrender the outcome.
5. Be quiet and listen for instructions.
6. If thoughts of worry intrude, love yourself, and then stop worrying!
7. Expect a miracle.
8. Say thanks even before the miracle shows up in physical form.

Miracles will appear in every aspect of our lives—physical, mental and emotional—if we truly surrender. On the physical level, we have to be willing to let go of other people, situations and the condition of our bodies. Mentally we need to let go of rigid ideas, beliefs and limitations. Finally we need to release attachment to feelings and attitudes on the emotional plane, as the following stories will illustrate.

Surrendering Situations, People and Body Conditions

The lowest point in my husband's life occurred when he was forty years old and CEO of a highly successful manufacturing business he had built from scratch. Just two years earlier, Ron had been nominated for NASA Contractor of the Year. Now, through circumstances beyond his control, he had been forced to close the business and was struggling to avoid bankruptcy. Unable to finance the stringent cleanup procedures the government was demanding, he was also awaiting trial on an environmental felony charge.

The woman he was then married to was suffering from serious stress-induced health problems. Awash in shame and frustration, Ron felt like every finger was plugging a different hole in the leaky dike of his life. He didn't know where to turn or what to do. Although he was not a religious man, at that moment he prayed a simple and profoundly serious prayer. "You take it," he told God. "I can't do it anymore." Ron said he never made a more fervent statement. Beyond caring about how his life would work out, he just surrendered.

In that moment, Ron had an awakening. A voice inside him called, "Hello!" The sound resonated throughout his body, as if a church bell had been rung inside his chest. Although he was startled and confused, at some deep level Ron realized that the Spirit of God that dwelled within had just revealed its voice. It was several years later before Ron called the Magic Child by name, but this awakening started him searching for the one who had called out. His experience was very similar to what May Sarton described in her poetry collection called *Halfway to Silence*. The poet portrays the soul's yearning to find the source of the voice that beckons.

The Voice

Blurred as though it has been woken
From an underground secret river,
This voice itself and not the language spoken
Has made the air around me shiver.

Seductive sound, mysterious chord
That speaks its message in the very timbre
And not in a to be deciphered word
That I might hunt down or remember.

It wanders through my dreams and there I learn
I have to make the journey, have to go,
Whatever I must change or overturn
To reach the source, so strong this undertow.

Like a tapped glass the shivered air
Echoes and echoes a single poignant note.
That voice, where does it live? I must go there,
Comfort, entreat, and bless the magic throat.

Ron's life soon took a very different course. The biggest change he made was learning to make choices which took his needs into account. Most past decisions had been based on "doing the right thing," as defined by society's expectations rather than his own inner voice. He began addressing long-buried emotional issues from childhood and exploring an ongoing spiritual relationship with that resonant Divine voice. Ron and his wife finally acknowledged the differences between their life visions and parted ways. His business problems were resolved. He made a commitment to follow his passion for creating music and started writing songs again and sharing them publicly. Ron and I met shortly after all of that and began creating the kind of relationship we both had been imagining.

Before surrendering, Ron didn't see any way out of the business difficulties or out of his unhappy marriage. He had no meaningful belief in God or spiritual practices. Music, so dear to his soul, was voiced only in solitude when sorrow demanded expression. In surrendering, he felt he had nothing to lose. Ron was too depressed to ask, or even hope, for a particular outcome. He simply could no longer carry his burdens.

We don't have to wait for life to get us in a headlock before surrendering, but even if we do wait that long, Ron's story shows the power of God to make miracles in any situation. God's power is unlimited. The only restrictions God experiences are the ones we put in place through the limited imagination of our conscious minds.

One of my clients, a schoolteacher, was ending a twenty-five-year marriage. Leanne, already stressed over juggling her career as a schoolteacher and her parenting duties, was panicking over unexpected complications in her move to a smaller home. She kept focusing on how unlikely it was that the move would occur smoothly. She dismissed all options and suggestions I offered, claiming that, in her difficult situation, none would work. When I mentioned the idea of surrendering to God, she told me, "That's not His job. All He's concerned with is that I live a good life. He doesn't get involved in changing light bulbs." This was true, in Leanne's case, because she was not allowing that option. However, if we invite help, the Divine can create an unlimited number of miracles in even the most mundane of situations.

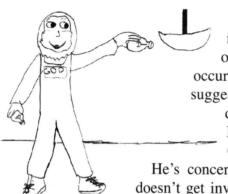

Ron and I experienced God's competence with the "nitty-gritty" in a most unlikely spot. In 1995, we spent the month of August honeymooning in a motor home Ron borrowed from his brother in Seattle. Ron said he knew before picking up the vehicle that we would have trouble with it "because it was a Dodge," a brand he distrusted. As he left Seattle, the RV, which his brother claimed would cruise at seventy miles per hour, wouldn't even do sixty miles per hour.

Trouble traveled along, lurking quietly in Ron's mental attic, until we reached the Great Divide between Provo, Utah and the Colorado border. Crawling up that long, lonely ascent late one cold, drizzly afternoon, the motor home acted like it was out of gas, even though the tank was full. Tensely, we limped along in the breakdown lane, hoping to eke out another mile, until the RV stalled. Like a great beast, it squatted on the side of the road and refused to budge. Ron got out and lifted the hood, mentally cursing this Dodge for acting exactly as he had predicted. All the mechanical tricks he knew failed to get it started again. He felt angry, frustrated, and stuck. Just as he had known the RV would break down, Ron knew what would happen next. After spending a soggy hour or more hitchhiking in the rain to a phone to call a tow truck, and losing a day of travel time, we'd have to pay hundreds of dollars to fix the RV. Clearly this was going to be a miserable part of the trip.

I was having a different experience. While trouble had been climbing out of Ron's attic and sabotaging the engine, I had been listening to "The Power of the Mind to Heal," a tape about the power of prayer, by mind/body pioneer Dr. Joan Borysenko. She was talking about the miracles that ensue when we turn situations over to God in prayer. While I was wondering if prayer could really have such dramatic results, even for an ordinary person like me, the RV broke down. Instead of worrying, I accepted the situation as an exercise to try out the power of prayer.

I shared this idea with Ron and suggested that instead of imagining dismal, expensive outcomes, we imagine positive scenarios, like a good Samaritan showing up to help us. Ron nodded, keeping his skeptical reaction to himself. Later on he shared what he had been thinking: "Oh great. Look what I married. We run into trouble and she gets mystical. Let's get real." Ignoring my suggestion, he headed into the wind and rain to deal with the situation like a real man: seriously.

Sitting in the RV, I prayed, surrendering the outcome to God. Although asking that the RV start back up, I didn't put any conditions on how it would happen. I asked only that the solution be friendly to us. While waiting to see what would happen, I sent love to the motor home, to the metals from the earth that had gone into its creation and to Ron, who was standing in the gray drizzle with his thumb out.

Several cars heading uphill passed Ron, but nobody stopped. As he glanced toward the cars heading downhill, a four-wheel-drive Chevy truck made a U-turn and pulled up behind us. Ambling over, the driver asked, "What's the problem?"

Ron wanted to say "I've got a Dodge," but instead replied, "I can't get it going."

"Mind if I take a look?" asked the stranger.

Ron was suspicious. "What does this guy really want?" he wondered. "People always want something." Still, he accepted the offer of help.

In minutes, they were both bringing out wrenches and the stranger was underneath the RV. "Here's the problem," he called out, "you're not getting any fuel. You need a new fuel pump."

"Great," thought Ron. His gloom was interrupted by the man's voice.

"I just happen to have an extra fuel pump in my rig. I just bought it. Would you like me to put it in for you?"

By then the forces of gloom marching around in Ron's head had been seriously routed and were scrambling in confusion. "Sure," said Ron, thinking the stranger would probably soak him for lots of money.

When the pump was in place and the RV was humming again, Ron offered to pay the man. "Well, I have the receipt here, so you can take it back if you have any more problems," he said. "It cost me fifty-five dollars. Would you be willing to pay that?" Ron was astounded. He offered to pay him a hundred dollars besides.

"No," said the man. "I just want you to be able to get on your way and have a good trip." Taking the check for fifty-five dollars, the good Samaritan headed off, maybe right back to heaven.

Ron got into the RV, his mouth hanging open. With this one incident, his whole framework for "the way life has to be" had been blown apart. I was equally impressed by this demonstration of prayer's power. Although having visualized the general possibility of a good Samaritan, I never dreamed up such details. To imagine someone with the skill and willingness to fix the RV, who had all the right tools and even the specific part we needed, and who didn't want money for his time, had not been in my field of possibilities.

This was an amazing lesson for us in the power of surrender—ask for help, turn over the reins and let God, who is highly qualified to devise and materialize perfect solutions, handle the details. The limited ego self who runs the "Quick Fix" department of our brains is no match for Divine creativity. The Magic Child, that Divine part of us, can make miracles out of thin air. The field of creative possibilities is infinite. Through surrender, we gain access to the whole field and to the concrete knowing that we are not alone.

Susie was a new client of mine seeking relief from stress, depression and a life in disarray. Intensely lonely and terrified of being alone, she kept gravitating toward unhealthy people who reinforced her low self-esteem. We were exploring her beliefs about spiritual connections, and Susie was considering, for the first time, the possibility that she was not alone, when a migraine headache drove her to reschedule a session.

Distraught about the physical pain and the general pain in her life, Susie reached a point of surrender on both the physical and emotional plane. She asked God to take over and show her clearly what to do. The response was an inner voice suggesting she face and disclose the full extent of her addiction to pain medication, something she had hidden from me. Susie made an appointment to be evaluated for a drug treatment program. The counselor seemed to speak for God, telling Susie, "Don't try to do this on your own. You don't have to do it alone."

After that appointment, Susie stopped at a video store and spontaneously chose a movie called *Safe,* which she'd never heard of but couldn't walk away from. The main character turned out to be just like her, suffering with an addiction and the same patterns of needing to please. The movie character checked into a treatment center and sent a message to her best friend, who just happened to have the same name as my client. "Tell Susie I love her," said the character. By the end of the movie, the main character could look herself in the mirror and say "I love you." Susie got the message. She was not alone. The loving and powerful presence of God felt very real. She checked into the treatment center and let God work through that environment to help her.

Despite tales of miracle healings, I think surrendering when in physical pain is very difficult to do. The pain increases our desperation, but instead of surrendering, most of us cling tighter to the desire to control the outcome. We insist on feeling better right now, growing increasingly tense as God fails to deliver instantly or completely. Most of us doubt that miracles can even happen and wait impatiently for God to heed our "request." Winning the lottery seems more likely. Maybe since our physical senses issue from the body, the greatest challenge is to imagine bodily possibilities outside the limits of what we know with those senses. This lack of trust clogs any cracks where God's healing energy might have slipped through.

When Ron and I came home from our honeymoon RV trip, I went through a string of health problems including an extremely itchy, spreading rash contracted while camping, a bout with the flu, and a debilitating congestion that moved into my lungs and refused to leave, ignoring the pile of eviction notices I was sending. During almost three months of illness, I slowed down and rested, saw the doctor, took herbs and pills, drank water and exercised, journaled and prayed, and even "loved" the blasted illness for at least twenty-four hours! I knew I was somehow involved in creating this illness, but couldn't intuit any information to make it go away. Nothing made a difference. I felt like a large cat in a small cage, pacing around and roaring loudly. I didn't understand why nothing was working. Why couldn't I heal this? Why couldn't I make my body behave the way I wanted it to behave? This miserable sickness was preventing me from writing my book, from working, from dancing, from doing everything that required any energy. I'd had enough!

Ron helped me out of the cage I'd put myself in. He said he felt sad to see me beating myself up for not knowing how to heal and shared that only the act of surrender had ever made a difference for him. His words had a calming effect, and I gradually let go, surrendering to God's mystery. I didn't get better immediately after that, but I was able to stop dwelling on my angry frustration. A peace descended, and a few days later I was feeling much better physically. Although I was happy about the change, it didn't matter so much anymore. I was flowing with whatever was happening. "How would it be if you let your life flow? You would glow; you would glow."

It is essential to eliminate blame from the concept of creating our reality. We certainly are responsible on some level for everything that happens in our lives but, more often than not, we can't understand why we create pain in our lives. This is part of the mystery of being a spirit expressing in a body dominated by limited conscious thought. The only part we can absolutely control is our response to whatever is happening. We can choose to argue and fight to fit experience into the "correct" form or we can choose to surrender. Only one of those options leads to peace.

My friend Marlie believes surrender takes real bravery. She says, "Every time I surrender I know I'd better hang on because my life is going to get intense." She shared the story of her child custody battle, a time of great fear because the outcome was very uncertain. Although the children's father, in her opinion, was not emotionally stable, he had the greater financial stability. Marlie was afraid to surrender, imagining that would be like letting go of her children's hands and watching helplessly while they were sucked away into a stormy emotional sea. Eventually Marlie realized clutching onto them emotionally would not protect them. She had already taken all the possible legal steps; the outcome was out of her hands. So Marlie walked straight into her valley of fear and loss and surrendered the people she loved most, trusting that God was present in every situation and that the outcome would be for the highest good of all. Surrendering did not take away her pain. Instead, she had to face it fully. Surrendering did not relieve her of her responsibilities. She still had to pay an attorney and compile documents. What did change is that Marlie felt stronger and more deeply peaceful while riding this tempest-tossed sea. Also, through surrendering, Marlie admitted to herself that these precious children were not hers. They were merely entrusted to her care.

Letting go of those we love seems to be the most difficult act of surrender. I often work with clients who are facing divorce and most people don't let go of a partner easily. This is especially true when one partner wants the divorce and the other doesn't. Divorce tosses partners into a swirling cauldron of guilt, confusion, grief and anger. The process of being severed from a life partner feels like death. We sink into the hopelessness of winter, when spring seems to be only a faraway dream. Words of encouragement can't penetrate the hard ground of misery where we lie trapped. Our only hope is surrender to the God within who knows how to create spring from winter. It usually doesn't change the circumstances, but it helps us find a layer of peace under the surface of our pain.

When I went through divorce, I felt as though there was a raging emotional storm around my heart. Through surrender, I found a sense of deep peace, which felt like the calm of the ocean bottom, centered in my belly. This peace is the first gift of surrender. Seldom can we imagine the gifts still to come while the storm is raging.

Yet, after a divorce, people often discover important aspects of themselves they couldn't access within the limitations of a painful marriage. And like the first shoots of a bulb in spring, those unexpressed parts can begin to grow into something beautiful.

Why don't we just do it: surrender? Sometimes the payoffs of remaining stuck are too high. At one point, Ron was going through a difficult time at his job. For him, anything work related was automatically "real serious." He had been hired as a Chief Financial Officer to take the company in a more profitable direction. His first step had been to introduce a computerized accounting system and supervise the transition process, which was prerequisite to the visioning and strategy work he enjoys. There were the typical problems with a new computer system, compounded with the difficulty of finding and keeping competent book-keepers in an isolated small town. Added to that, the top management was not always in agreement about the best course of action. Ron felt overwhelmed by the chaos and was struggling with "unreasonable" feelings of guilt and shame for not fixing everything fast enough. Most of all, he was not having fun.

One day while he was complaining about his situation I suggested it might be time for him to apply the lesson of the good Samaritan to the workplace and just let go, to surrender his problems. I imagined he would reply, "Oh right! I forgot about surrender. Thanks for reminding me."

Instead he challenged me angrily. "Then what am I supposed to do—just sit around and wait for it to change all by itself? I don't think so!" We had several more discussions about this issue. I kept asking if he would be willing to surrender, and he accused me of trying to fix him. Through every discussion, I noticed he kept gripping his struggle like a little boy who was afraid someone would take away his toy.

We talked about why he was resisting surrender. First he claimed he didn't know how, but then he admitted that he didn't want to let go. He liked being angry. I wondered what he was getting out of it. Pondering that, he realized that this situation was so big, he could justify acting like a victim, staying buried underneath his difficult life. Being so overwhelmed gave him the right to sit immobilized watching television all night, eating greasy French fries with lots of extra ketchup. He could act as irresponsibly as he wanted, and nobody could blame him. That's a pretty big payoff!

Even when he recognized this desire to be an irresponsible victim, Ron didn't surrender immediately to God. Instead, he surrendered to resistance. He allowed all those stubborn "dog thoughts" of his limited mind to climb up on a mental couch, share the fries, and make their case. He loved himself, complete with a couch full of sprawling "dog thoughts," until he was finally able to tell those thoughts, "Down, boys! God needs to sit on the couch now." Not surprisingly, once he did that, the job experience shifted, and he started having fun with it again.

Surrendering Ideas and Beliefs

Though hesitant to surrender our imaginary control over situations, other people and even our own bodies, most of us will eventually, as exhaustion and despair set in, wave the white flag and let go of all pretense of control. Compared to the physical plane, the mental plane is a subtle area. Instead of trying to exercise our will over the material world, we cling to intangible thoughts about how life is, or should be. Because ideas have no solid form, we often have more difficulty recognizing that we're even holding onto anything. The ideas seem like the air around us. They just exist as pure unquestioned truth. Someone with a different way of thinking seems peculiar, wrong or even invisible. The problem is clearly with the other person, since the familiar way of thinking is simply "the way it is." Dogmatic teachers, dictatorial leaders and militant bigots all share a belief that they know the way life should be. But even if you or I don't fall into one of those harsh categories, we probably all have blind spots—beliefs we have never stopped to question, that we assume are rules for life.

Some beliefs are very personal. Usually both subconscious and limited, these ideas are formed in early childhood. Typical beliefs are: "I'm stupid and can never do anything right; Adults always know better; Boys have more opportunities; Never say anything that isn't nice; Quitters never win; My needs don't matter." The list is endless and unquestioned. We go through life acting as if these ideas are absolute. For example, someone who can't say anything that isn't nice may never set firm boundaries because there is no "nice" way to do that. This person will be forced, by internal beliefs, to spend a lifetime being a doormat for everyone else.

Many of our more conscious beliefs are a cultural inheritance. We adopt the mental framework parents, teachers or society at large taught. We might believe mothers should stay home and raise their children, boys should take out the trash, companies should promote from within the ranks, governments should provide for poor people, grown men should never cry, minority groups should get special treatment, homosexuality is unnatural, or religious leaders have the inside track on God's will. Or we might believe exactly the opposite, just to prove we're not like our parents. Whatever the belief, chances are it's so strong that we have never stopped to wonder if somebody's opposing opinion could be right.

Because conscious beliefs seem as essential as air to breathe, most of us are highly insulted when someone suggests we may be narrow-minded or bossy. After all, we're only stating the obvious!

I started adult life as a schoolteacher. Even now, as a counselor, writer and speaker, I find much of my work feels like teaching. For me, one of the greatest challenges is to communicate beliefs passionately without bullying audiences through an attitude that says "I'm telling you how it is. I know, and you don't."

Ron has helped raise my awareness about my tendency to speak from a position of "the truth." Acutely sensitive to any hint of bossiness, he has a listening filter that often transforms questions into demands. For example, he can hear "Are you going to soak in the hot tub this morning?" as "I'm telling you to go soak in the hot tub, and you'd better do what I say because I'm in charge." So anytime I'm actually being dogmatic and bossy, he notices right away. Initially, whenever he pointed out my dogmatic tendency, I dismissed his comments as hypersensitivity to authority. Clearly, he wouldn't have any idea of "the way it really is," I thought. Letting go of that tight grip on the rightness of my ideas was very threatening. My ideas seemed as integral as my skeleton, and they were just as rigid.

The way I finally understood what Ron was saying was through my own childish reaction to being told what to do. When Ron suggested I was telling everybody "the way it is," I angrily challenged him to name a speaker who didn't do that. He mentioned several, including Mary Manin Morrissey, the minister of the Living Enrichment Center in Wilsonville, Oregon. Mary is a charismatic speaker who expanded an apostolic congregation of twelve into a community of three thousand people. I've heard Mary speak and really admire her style.

Mary's name was also being bandied about by leaders of the spiritual community Ron and I were involved in. People looked up to her as some kind of guru and wanted to model our center after hers. When Ron mentioned Mary's name, I felt jealous, like I could never measure up to her. That made me feel resentful. "What's so great about her?" I sulked. "Ron makes it sound like her style is the only right way!" OOPS! Suddenly I got what he was talking about. I don't like being told there's only one right way either. I realized that instead of just sharing my experience and inviting listeners to consider whether it was true for them, I was generalizing my experience into pronouncements on "the way it is."

In thinking about why I did that, I realized it was all about control! If I have the answer, "the way it is," then I'm in control. I have the big picture and can't be surprised by life because I understand how it works. An added satisfaction is having other people perceive me as having my life together—in control!

I realized this is the attitude of anyone who wants to impose ideas on others. Maybe I'm not as visible or fanatical as those who knock on doors with pamphlets, bribe politicians, or burn clinics and homes of people with the "wrong" beliefs, but I'm still "holding back the waters of chaos." Like Moses at the Red Sea, I'm holding the staff called "the way it is" and hoping it will save me from drowning in uncertainty.

For a long time I was really irritated by people who belonged to fundamentalist religious groups. I resented their attitudes of having a corner on spiritual truth. Their sense of conviction didn't bother me, but I was repulsed by their militant insistence that everybody else sign up for the same beliefs or go to hell. When they moved those beliefs into the political arena, I got even more indignant.

Recognizing my own tendency to expound on "the way it is" has given me more humility and compassion in thinking about other people who cling to their ideas. I recognize organized religion offers order in a world that seems wildly chaotic to many people. Beliefs presented as unchanging and unchangeable provide reassuring guidelines and safety nets.

In recommending a willingness to surrender on the mental plane, I'm not suggesting we toss out all our beliefs. I have discovered in surrendering, inviting the breath of Spirit to blow through my mind, that I am more at ease. Positions that once filled my mind like cement now have space inside them. Even if I still cherish the same ideas, I now recognize them as opinions.

When I cling to ideas, separating myself from people over the issue of religious beliefs, even if they did it first, I am forgetting my Divine connection. Insistence on being right prevents me from remembering we are all love because, beyond the five-sensory realm, love is all that exists. In surrendering to love, I feel peaceful. Individual ideas don't seem threatening anymore or even, ultimately, consequential. I once wrote a prayer poem invoking this mental freedom.

Winter Solstice

Falling
I am falling
deep into your arms
Oh, Mother Earth
Hold me close
Press me to your heart
Squeeze me tightly
Prune away the excess,
the dead skin I have mistaken
for my soul.

I surrender to you,
Oh, my mother,
you who are my finest self
my creator being,
Spider Woman,
who dwells within me
within the earth of all peoples
who weaves anew
the web of my soul.

I surrender to you the illusions
I cling to with such serious resolve
Breathe new life into the dark places
I have stuffed with the cobwebs
of unconsciousness
Prepare me during this sleeping hour
Prepare me to glitter and shine
with my true greatness
in the breaking day.

Surrendering Emotional Ties

Whereas the mental plane is connected with the element of air, the emotional plane is associated with the element of water. Our ideas seem as essential as the air we breathe. Our emotions seem as integral as blood. How can we surrender the way we feel?

One day I was working with my friend Dr. Patrick Eleam. We had a commitment to coach, prod and encourage each other to open to greater possibility and move beyond our limitations. As a chiropractor, Patrick helped me loosen emotions and energy patterns locked in my body. On this occasion, he helped me find a place in my body where I could hold a greater vision of myself. We talked about the possibility of my work having world-wide influence.

Later, I revised my personal mission statement to include global impact. At first, the possibility of positively affecting the whole planet excited me. Then I got vertigo. This big idea of myself conflicted with a subconscious emotional commitment to being little. Metaphorically speaking, I was used to taking up only a small piece of earth. In imagining myself as bigger, I ran out of ground to stand on and feared falling off the edge of my world. Like Alice in Wonderland, who grew too big for the house, I needed a way to get myself comfortably small again. Naturally, this was a totally unconscious process. Only later did I realize what I'd done.

I got smaller by sharing the new vision with Ron, unconsciously depending on his fear to yank me back inside the comfort zone. When he heard the mission statement, he started arguing that this was not my vision, but Patrick's vision of me. Didn't I know who I was? I retorted aloud that this was definitely me but I didn't really believe my own words. I retreated into the smaller, safer emotional space that was so familiar.

Because the mind and body are integrally connected, my emotional retreat showed up in my body. The next time I saw Patrick, I was tight all over. He noticed that the muscles holding me upright were particularly locked up. I hurt all over but didn't know how to let go. I only knew I wanted to. He worked on me as much as my body would tolerate for one day.

The next morning I awoke early with the first line of a poem floating in my head. The poem that emerged was full of longing to be free of tension and pain.

Salty Mother, Take Me Home

Out beyond the mountains that lead my eyes upward
but hem them in at the horizon
is a sea that rocks on into moonlight and morn.

Past the solid structures of these rocky mountains
that stand tall and rigid
is the fluid floating sea, rich with mystery in her underbelly.

The sea calls me with her salty smell
"Come home to me. Remember the rhythm of the waves
that do not have to be wound up tight to make a motion."

The waves rock me while I float upon them, as in my
childhood days,
singing to me "All is well,"
rocking gently on and on.

The beautiful sea, where the sunlight dances and the moon
prays
full of rich mystery and fluid songs
holds no tension.

She lacks the skeleton and muscle of the mountain
that paralyzes me with struggle and effort
to stand tall and be seen as majestic and pure.
She is so free.

Salty, singing mother, call me home, take me home.
I long for your lullabies.
My body is hurting and my soul is wandering, stiff and
lost.

Your salty water rushes out my eyes, crying for you,
flowing towards you.
Mother, where are you?

Let me rock through my life like a song
sweet and gentle on the winds of mystery.
Salty mother take me home.

I read the poem aloud to Ron, sobbing all the way through, surprised by the intensity of my desire to be free. I realized the pain came from a conflict between my longing for freedom of spirit and my emotional tie to being small. I still didn't know what to do differently.

Then I remembered an earlier experience of feeling tight and stuck. I had been so resentful of my pre-teen daughter's attitudes that my heart was completely closed to her. Our relationship, and my chest, had felt tense, angry and stuck. My strong attachment to my feelings had blocked me from perceiving any way out that time, too. When I finally surrendered, trusting it would lead somehow to a reconnection with my child, the relationship completely transformed in just two days. The love and respect started flowing strongly again between us.

If I could release my attachment to being angry and righteous and all the physical tension that accompanied those emotions, through surrender, I realized

I could release my attachment to being little and the cramping of my body into a smaller form along with it. So, trusting the Magic Child to know how to do what I couldn't do, I surrendered. After that, each time Patrick worked on my body, more of the tightness let go. Meanwhile, I just loved myself for being exactly where I was in the process and trusted that all the unwinding would happen in perfect time, layer by layer if necessary.

As we let go of emotional ties tangling up our bodies, we can expect to feel physical resistance to the process. We do not easily let our precious feelings bleed away. Bodies subconsciously hold onto emotions. We insist on staying angry or sad or fearful, and our tightened muscles accentuate our insistence.

It is not our job to know how to untangle these emotional ties. All we can do is intend to be free, make a prayer of surrender, and take whatever steps we feel guided to take. For me, right now, continuing to work with unwinding my body is important. At another time, I was intensively releasing emotions through therapy work. Maybe next steps for you might involve some physical release, or possibly communication work. The means are not intrinsically important. All that matters is whether you are listening to the inner directives of the Magic Child. If you surrender, listen and act, you will feel more truly alive, in the way that your being craves to experience life.

The Surrendered Ones

Surrender is a lifelong process. Bit by bit we learn to let go, like an onion being slowly peeled, finally revealing the heart. In her poetry collection called *A Grain of Mustard Seed,* May Sarton describes the grace yielded up by a lifetime of surrendering.

The Great Transparencies

Lately I have been thinking much of those,
The open ones, the great transparencies,
Through whom life—is it wind or water?—flows
Unstinted, who have learned the sovereign ease.

They are not young: they are not ever young.
Youth is much too vulnerable to bear the tide,
And let it rise, and never hold it back,
Then let it ebb, not suffering from pride,
Nor thinking it must ebb from private lack.
The elders yield because they are so strong—

Seized by the great wind like a ripening field,
All rippled over in a sensuous sweep,
Wave after wave, lifted and glad to yield,
But whether wind or water, never keep
The tide from flowing or hold it back for long.

Lately I have been thinking much of these,
The unafraid although still vulnerable,
Through whom life flows, the great transparencies,
The old and open, brave and beautiful…
They are not young: they are not ever young.

That image is so beautiful: "The unafraid although still vulnerable, through whom life flows." How would it be if you let your life flow? You would glow: you would glow. Our shining essence, the Magic Child, gets covered over by the mud of our fears, but if we would only surrender, our beautiful inner light would shine, illuminating both our faces and our world. Surrender is not a lofty goal. It is a path that leads straight to love. Set forth upon it with trust. It will take you home.

Wondersparks

1. Do you trust your God with your life? Why or why not?
2. Do you feel that your God betrayed your trust? If so, how? What were you expecting?
3. What areas of life do you clutch protectively?

4. What areas of life are steeped in struggle? Are you committed to the experience of struggle? Do you believe that's just the way it is in the real world?

5. Have you ever experienced a miracle? Had you surrendered first? Were you at a point of despair before the miracle happened?

6. How would it be for you if you let life flow?

Elixir for the Mind

The Path to Love, by Deepak Chopra, M.D. Chapter 4 of this beautiful book is devoted to the subject of surrender. I discovered Chopra's book after writing this chapter and enjoyed the way he expressed a similar message.

Chapter Five

Dancing in this world of form
we need darkness to appreciate light;
death to reveal life's sensual edges.
Shadows focus our attention
on what is most precious.

Magic Wand

Approach the banquet of life like a lover,
savoring the whole feast!

Cosmic Circle Dance

A willing act of surrender requires complete trust. Many people lose confidence in God's capacity for love when someone they deeply love dies. Unconsciously divorcing the treacherous God responsible for death, people unwittingly closet the Magic Child, who has the ability to love both self and others without limits.

When I suggested to Keith, a thirty-five-year-old client, that he ask for God's help, while struggling to feel more love for his wife and to move past his inner critic, he could not do it. He had stopped believing in a personal God at age ten. In that year, his dog Sparky, the only one who gave him unconditional love, had been senselessly poisoned by neighbors. Six months later, a favorite aunt died of lung cancer, despite Keith's prayerful pleas that she be spared. After that, Keith dismissed the teachings of his church as irrelevant drivel. He professed a belief in the life force, an energy permeating all that exists, but staunchly maintained it was indifferent to needs or desires of the individual, intending us neither good nor harm. However, when I asked him what, then, was the source of the love he felt for his small son, or the source of Sparky's love, Keith couldn't answer. Pondering this question, his tears began to flow. He realized he had been afraid to love or be loved since those childhood traumas.

Although his wife's faults had seemed to be the main obstacle to marital harmony, now he admitted being afraid to let himself love someone he might lose. Instead, he protected himself from hurt by being critical. Keith realized that unless he resolved this fear, the unconditional love he had for his son would be threatened when the boy grew old enough to recognize Keith's limitations and potentially reject an imperfect father. The loving Magic Child, imprisoned behind a protective mechanism of criticism, could only be freed through surrender to the power of God's healing love. To do that, Keith had to make peace with the mystery of death. The peacemaking process seems to require a time when grief lies buried in a fallow field of the subconscious mind. That was certainly my experience.

I remember when my mother was taken away in an ambulance. It happened one Sunday in late October. The sky was overcast, Miami was chilly, and I was seven years old. I was playing down the street from our house and was unaware that she was being taken to the hospital. When I was older, my father explained how my mother had been washing dishes that morning and noticed she couldn't feel the scalding water on her hands. Eight months pregnant with a fifth child, she called the obstetrician, who advised rest. By late afternoon, the unexplained numbness had spread and she was rushed to the emergency room.

I remember that Aunt Joan, my mother's younger sister, flew down from New Jersey. She and my grandparents, who already lived in Miami, converged at our house every evening for four days to join my father for a hospital visit. One evening, as they were leaving, I asked Aunt Joan, "Is Mommy going to die?"

"Oh, honey, of course not!" she replied.

The next morning we were called into my parents' bedroom. Daddy was sitting at the edge of the thick-satin-covered bed. Flanking him, at the sides of the bed, stood my aunt and grandparents. As the four children approached, he gathered us like chicks into his arms. Holding us close, he wept, lost for words. Ever the responsible one, or perhaps just the one gifted with words, I spoke the unspeakable. "Mommy died, didn't she." It was a statement, not a question. All my father could do was nod. Nobody mentioned the stillborn fate of the baby whose birth we had all been anticipating. Her life lost all importance to us in the wake of this greater loss.

The events that followed are a surrealistic blur. I remember skipping out to meet the school bus, wearing new white sandals, my voice ringing out with that childish quality that carries loudly across silent rooms. "We're not going to school today," I announced, "because our mother died." I've always wondered what the bus driver thought as she drove off. At the time, I don't remember thinking anything was odd.

I hazily recall seeing my mother in her coffin. She did not look like someone sleeping, though everyone was saying that. My wide, childish eyes saw only what was not there: her life force. Though lacking words to say why this stiff, pasty corpse was not my mother, I knew it wasn't. What I didn't know was where she had gone. Heaven was not real for me. Somewhere tucked beside my mother was the lifeless body of my baby sister, who had been christened Tara, but I forgot to look at her.

A big Catholic funeral followed, but I've forgotten what it was like. Instead, I remember: being given beautiful holy cards of Mother Mary smiling gently, getting to spend time after school being cared for by the nuns who taught us, and discovering that the secret world of nuns was full of ordinary pastimes like vacuuming carpets and grocery shopping.

For years my family went to the cemetery pretty often, always stopping at the nearby florist for carnations. Eventually, though, I wrapped my grief in tissue and stored it in a drawer of my subconscious mind, right on top of the Magic Child. Believing that grief was permanently out of the way, in the ensuing years I focused instead on trying to make friends, never realizing my social difficulties were connected to both the stuffed grief and the smothered Magic Child. Fifteen years later, while preparing to make final vows as a nun, I suddenly remembered a letter written the summer after my mother's death. Sitting on the front porch at a cousin's house, I had written the words, "I hate God." Then I'd scratched out the sentence, burying the forbidden feeling under many layers of pencil lead.

> *Dear Daddy,*
> *I hate God.*
> *Cross that out.*
> *Cross it out good and dark.*
> *Hide those words.*
> *Bury them deep*
> *so nobody will know you said them.*
> *Nobody hates God.*
> *God is good.*
> *God loves us all.*
> *God gives life.*
> *God killed Mommy.*
> *I'll scratch out my sentence*
> *but I'll still hate God.*

The truth was in the open now. I didn't trust the God to whom I was about to dedicate my life. I had cut the connecting thread when God betrayed me by taking my mother away.

Making Peace with the Past

Healing tears flooded out with that memory and washed away my anger toward God. The Magic Child inherited some breathing space, but the grief didn't go away. I still had to make peace with death.

Over the years, in therapy, there were many occasions when I cried the pain and screamed the rage that had lain fallow. Each time, peace followed, but somehow the grief continued to cling to the shadows of my heart. In unguarded moments, the pain of that loss still overwhelms me, and the tears start falling once again. I sob at death scenes in movies but also often cry at little things like my husband or children leaving on a trip, because saying good-bye feels like I'll never see them again. For many years, I struggled to hold onto form: loved ones, work, possessions, reputation. I kept thinking some form of therapy, prayer or grace would take away the pain once and for all, but I never seemed to find it. I reminded myself, bitterly, that it had only been forty years since her death; maybe it takes eighty years to finish grieving.

Finally, I realized grief is not a defect to purge and I found peace by celebrating my ability to feel both grief and the resulting gift of compassion. Now, it's as if that chamber of my heart is a well-furnished, comfortable room, where the Magic Child feels free to sprawl on the furniture.

In making peace with death, I had to surrender my insistence on a logical explanation. When I released that demand, the Magic Child shared with me the meaning of death through the mysterious poetry of sensation. As I stood alone on a cold winter night, the Magic Child shivered inside me, full of awe at stars shimmering in a black sky, shining bright and miraculous on a canvas of utter darkness. In this stark and sacred space, the Magic Child bestowed not words of explanation, but the hush of life, pulsing and precious in the silence.

By relinquishing a need for the security of form, I experienced the deeper reassurance of the Magic Child. In therapy, reliving the feeling of being all alone at my mother's death, I acknowledged that although my father, overwhelmed by his own grief, as well as by the needs of my three younger siblings, had neither the presence, power, nor devotion to fill the holes in my heart, that's exactly what I wanted. His failure to meet all my needs left me feeling emotionally abandoned. Now, the full depth of that loss resonated in my body, and I felt as if I were free-falling through dark and empty air. My muscles stiffened in fear of the unknown space all around, while my abandoned heart bled its juice into the wild night. I kept plummeting, in imagination, breathing through the grief and fear. That breath-filled fall yielded a miracle as the imaginary sky I fell through seemed to change. The air, no longer terrifying, felt like a warm gel: yielding and cradling.

With that bodily sensation, I recognized myself as a Magic Child suspended in the amniotic fluid of God's love, moving in slow motion, propelled by grace. All sense of separation between self and God dissolved in that moment. At the same time, death lost its fatal power because I could feel life and death dancing through each other in that thick, mystical sea of love.

In experiencing myself as Magic Child, I draw comfort in unguarded moments when the kiss of death challenges my sense of safety. Like the night Ron and I were sitting in his car, listening once again to the first song he'd produced for his first CD. We were both feeling soft and open, having just come from a very moving concert by Chris Williamson and Tret Fure. Listening to the music, I looked into Ron's eyes, appreciating the way he meets my gaze with fearless openness. As we kept looking at each other, I admired him for letting out the music that had been locked inside for so long. I felt proud of myself too, because I was finally writing my book. Relishing the love that was lifting us higher, appreciating the power and sweetness of this man, I felt radiance pouring out through my smile, my mother's big smile, that lives on in my face. In that moment, death brushed its lips against my cheek and whispered, "You can't keep Ron forever in this form."

Eventually, all the forms we treasure disappear, through the changes of time or the transformation of death. Now I sensed Ron's form shifting from my sight, even as I tried to hold him with my love, memorizing the beauty of his eyes that cry so freely, the gentle, open sweetness of his face. "Stay in the present!" I urged myself. "He isn't dead yet." But, as life and death hovered side by side, I felt my awareness expand, as the Magic Child spoke the words of meaning I'd sought for so long. Death is the shadow of night, enveloping the starlight of life. Without that shadow, we wouldn't realize how precious the light of life is. We couldn't see it clearly.

Ultimately, life is seamless. We go on and on and on, an inseparable part of the one Divine energy field. But here, dancing in this world of form, we need the darkness to appreciate the light; we need death to articulate the sensual edges of life. To pick clean the bones of this earthly experience, we need to taste every moment of life, inhale all its smells, touch every strand, hear every note, look at all its colors. This world is a sensuous banquet. If we approach it as lovers, savoring the whole feast presented, we discover the gift of true life and experience the radiant essence of life streaming through each seemingly separate morsel, connecting all in one.

But we cannot do that with hands clenched tight, holding onto treasures. Clenched hands can't caress or receive anything new. We have to open our hands, open our souls, to the energy streaming all around us, including the energy of death.

To be truly alive, we have to dance with death, whose power focuses attention and appreciation on the form life is dancing through. When someone dies, we instinctively reflect on the love we had for that person, and how much more we wish we'd let them know. Thoughts naturally turn to other loved ones and, for awhile, we remember to treasure them more consciously. Often we begin looking at our own lives more closely, examining them for meaning, sometimes charting new directions. It may take us years before we have this response to death. In the moment, often the grief, the anguish of loss, is all-consuming and paralyzing. We seem to die ourselves for awhile. Our bodies go through the motions of living while our spirits keep at a distance until we decide whether to walk with death or return to the arms of life. But those who return find gifts of increased appreciation for loved ones and more conscious choice about use of the time we have in form. Though death takes a loved one from the physical world, it also bestows the gift of life on those who have eyes to see and ears to hear. It can open our eyes to appreciation for the sensuous beauty that surrounds us, love manifesting in diverse forms, the bounty of possibilities that life offers.

The human ability to focus is both a gift and a liability. In concentrating on one aspect of life, we ignore all other possibilities. Focus is a helpful tool because it leads to accomplishments, but in the realm of thinking it can be a trap. We all too easily get stuck believing that life must unfold in a certain limited way or repeating reactive patterns based on beliefs in personal limitations. When that happens we fail to notice all the possibilities that life offers.

In *The Republic,* the Greek philosopher Plato relates Socrates's allegorical story about a group of cave dwellers. These people were chained up, facing the back wall of the cave. The sun behind them cast shadows on the cave wall of people and animals passing along a road outside the cave. They assumed these shadows were reality because the chains prevented them from seeing anything else. After a very long time, one person managed to break free of the chains and discover the world outside the cave. Although he had to struggle to adjust to this new brighter world, eventually he made the transition and then returned to the cave, bursting with excitement to tell the others how colorful and substantial the earth really was. They were unable to fit his new world into the narrow confines of their world and, rather than tolerate the chaos of uncertainty, they decided he was insane and refused to listen further to his message.

We can be just like those cave dwellers when we not only settle for, but even defend as real, a pale version of ourselves. The Magic Child within each of us is a more complete and magical version of ourselves than we dream possible yet we hide that genius and argue instead for our limitations. We avoid spirituality, don't do art, can't sing, are just not mechanical, don't understand finances, dislike exercise, or hate computers. Certainly we all have different talents and passions, but unless we have some physical limitation, there is very little we cannot do, if we choose to learn. However, early on we often discover natural abilities in certain areas. We get approval for those abilities but also get stamped with a label. This child is the artistic one; that child is the athlete; this other is the brain. As a result, we may never try or else are never allowed to do anything else. The gift becomes a prison as desires for non-approved activities get cordoned off inside our minds behind bright yellow police tape. Because the desires that we place off limits also belong to the Magic Child, we have to sacrifice total connection with that shining spirit and settle for only the part that fits our perceived mold. One day when I was doing my non-dominant journaling practice, a poem tumbled out that describes the fullness available to us.

Canticle of Wholeness

I am Sea Goddess,
moon-leafed queen of flow,
heavenly motion
dancing on a ribbon of grassy stars.

I am shy green first buds of spring,.
wild-nectared rosy summer,
autumn-pomegranate peace,
chill-wintered soft flakes at dawn.

I am all the seasons, all the moments,
all the feelings, in any moment.
You want to make me bad or good,
the way you do to yourself,
but I will not be diced up and evaluated.

I taste it all, devour it all, sing it all.
love it all, am it all.
I am life's lavish love song.
Learn from me.
Celebrate your whole self.
Put your whole self in!

The Menu of Life

None of us seem able to express our wholeness completely. The molds of other people's attitudes, which we have internalized, keep us from stretching out and tasting all that life has to offer. A client named Paula had a very rigid mold prescribed by her father. As she reflected upon his influence, she remembered a long and detailed list of proper ways to behave. For example, she was never to wear slacks; must always rise before her husband to fix her hair and then his breakfast; could not joke around or make loud noises; was always to put others' needs before her own; and was to thoroughly clean her house before doing anything else.

As an adult, Paula had stopped following most of his rules, but she realized she was just as trapped as those cave dwellers, by her unrecognized need to break the rules. We joked about "Saint Paula the Proper" who had to live in a straight and narrow way in order to remain on the pedestal of fatherly (and worldly) approval. Paula didn't know how to get off the pedestal gracefully. In a sense, she had knocked it over and smashed the statue-self. If her husband said she looked nice, she would tell him that she didn't. If somebody admired her fine character, she reminded them of what she was like on a bad day. Instead of a closet full of dresses, she now owned mostly pants. She had been unaware that her rebel posture was no more liberated than the saintly role. Paula admitted that, although being trapped on the pedestal was no fun, "Saint Paula the Proper" had some qualities that she liked. She preferred the elegance and ease of dresses. She was a good woman who took pleasure in helping others. There were even times when she actually enjoyed cleaning. Suddenly Paula saw that she had a choice.

Life is a banquet, full of possibilities. We can think of the Menu of Life as divided into two sections: house specials and an extensive à la carte listing. On Paula's menu, the house specials included the Daddy's Girl Special and Rebel's Delight. In selecting the first special, she was ordering her father's recipe for her happiness exactly as he served it up. If she chose the second special, she was guaranteed exactly the opposite. Paula had been living like someone who never opened the menu to see what else was offered besides the house specials.

Death opened her eyes to the full menu because when she considered the possibility that her earthly life could end at any time, Paula realized more clearly the importance of choosing à la carte experiences that were important to her, while she still had the chance. Not only was she unwilling to settle any longer for someone else's recipe for happiness, she was actively excited by the rich banquet of possibilities spread before her.

The Magic Child is nourished by a varied diet. There are many options on Life's Menu that will serve this hunger for variety. The choice is entirely ours. However, like minimum daily requirements, each of us have certain nutritional needs that are not optional. Some of these may be unique to us, dependent on the true gifts that we carry, while others are dietary demands for most people. If we ignore these basic needs, we will suffer malnutrition. To feel vibrantly alive and whole, we need a balanced diet! We have to nourish our whole magical selves so that we may bring forth everything within us and experience the fullness of life.

Think about whether your being is hungering for something new from Life's Menu. It may be something you've been daydreaming about doing recently, or it may be something you have always categorically been told or assumed you could not possibly do. Your excuses are illusions. The urge to express something more is a sign that the Magic Child's stomach is rumbling. Satisfy that urge. Call the waiter to your table and place a new order. Don't wait until you're dying to realize you didn't taste enough of life.

The Other Side of the Veil

Death calls our attention to the precious gift of life in form, but it does even more. Since death ends not life but only life in form, many first experience the world of spirit when a loved one who has passed through the veil of illusion returns to visit. People often describe seeing apparitions, hearing voices, sensing a presence, even smelling a familiar scent and knowing the person who died is there with them. Through such an experience, the Magic Child is able to expose the frightened ego-self to the reality beyond the world of form. This initiation opens some people to accept the beloved being no longer in earthly form as a guiding spirit in their lives. It may also lead an individual to sense the presence of angels and other loving entities who, though not in bodies, hover as close as our awareness, ready to help us move with grace through the world of form.

Besides revealing the possibility of guides from the spirit world, the person given the grace to die consciously can also share glimpses of the world beyond and reassure those being left behind. Recently Brian, a young man in my spiritual community, made his transition to the dimension beyond earthly form.

Brian was a handsome, fit, fun-loving man in his forties. Trained as a therapist, Brian had helped many people heal childhood pain. When suddenly diagnosed with an inoperable brain tumor, he began a radical and intense healing of his own pain. During that time, this man, who acknowledged that he had habitually retreated from emotional experiences to the safety of his intellect, opened his heart and transformed his life.

Brian became clear that feelings must be embraced. His heart overflowed with love and mercy in those last weeks as, like a child, he accepted whatever was happening with curiosity.

A friend and I sat with Brian one afternoon, discussing death for several hours. He shared quotes from a favorite text called *Emmanuel's Book*. One quote has stayed with me. "Dying is like taking off a tight pair of shoes." Brian was interested in knowing what we each felt about dying or if we had any experiences of the other world. He received our impressions with wonder. He laughed easily, even as he spilled food on himself, having lost motor control, just accepting the experience with an "Oh well!" Though letting go, he was incredibly present, savoring every nuance of earthly experience to the end. There was no fear in him. Being with Brian that afternoon gave me a much deeper knowing that physical life can be safely released. When I remember Brian now, I think about how eagerly I yank tight shoes off my feet. I have a comforting sense of him releasing into a larger and freer experience of being. Brian was a model at embracing both life and death fully and fearlessly. He died seven months after the original diagnosis, but in that time he gave a precious gift to those of us who were privileged to call him friend. He demonstrated a graceful way to do the cosmic dance of life and death.

The Changing Face of Death

Death isn't always a literal transition from the physical plane. Sometimes it is expressed as the loss of a job, an ability, a relationship, or a role in life. These transitions can leave us mourning and confused, not knowing how to reinvent ourselves. These are the winters of life, when we lie curled inside the dark earth, grieving the loss of a familiar identity, not yet daring to dream a new one.

Growth makes the protective shell, encasing the seed of our future potential, crack open. We have to find the courage to send out new tendrils, to envision them wending their way through the darkness, with only the instinct of the Magic Child to guide them, until finally they emerge from the earth's womb and feel the kiss of the sun. Only then can we experience resurrection, the joy of life recreated.

The process of rebirth doesn't hinge on whether the new life or the previous one is better, though often the new life is more comfortable and enjoyable. Like the caterpillar, who loses his ability to crawl upon the earth, whose body disintegrates leaving only imaginal cells to carry the visionary blueprint of a butterfly, we let go of a familiar form in order to be recreated, often in a more magical form than we could have imagined. The old forms are not bad, though sometimes they are painful, but they are always limiting. Through rebirth, more of the Magic Child bursts free, revealing new facets of our essence. The old selves are not destroyed. Instead they give texture to the masterpiece of art we are ever becoming.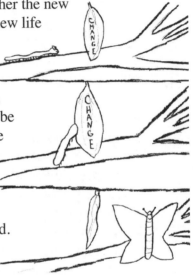

Although Western society has typically viewed death only as destroyer, this is an incomplete picture. Many religious beliefs incorporate the concept of death being a rebirth rather than just a destruction. The Hindus, for example, revere the goddess Kali as both the Destroyer and the Mother, birthing life from the ashes of destruction. Kali reminds us life and death are inseparable. The Hindus know what the Magic Child wants to teach us all. By accepting all facets of life, including the parts we'd rather eliminate; by accepting all of death and letting go of what we'd prefer to keep; by celebrating the whole experience; we will finally feel truly alive.

Life and death, together, create a cosmic circle dance. We are privileged to join this dance while glistening in this world of form. I don't yet know how to walk through this precious world constantly aware of the mystery of each

moment, but my prayerful intention is to learn. The Magic Child can teach me to embrace it all, to suck all the juices from the bones of form. Trembling and shining, the Magic Child in me is dancing with death, dancing with life. She is truly and fully alive.

Wondersparks

1. Who, or what, has died that was an integral part of your life?

2. Have you recognized some gift of life, some strength or quality or opportunity that you have now, because of your experience with this death?

3. How open are you to new ideas? To new ways of expression? Are you willing to sing? To dance? To make art? Can you let yourself be theatrical? Even silly?

4. Do you ever let yourself play without having to do it right or be the winner?

5. Are there certain subjects you will not even explore, maybe computers or cooking, poetry or mechanics?

6. When was the last time you let yourself learn something totally new?

7. Why do you avoid such subjects? What are the payoffs? The costs?

8. If you knew you were going to die in a year, how would you adjust your life?

9. What stops you from making those adjustments now?

10. Do you know for a fact you'll live more than one more year?

Elixirs for the Mind

The Grief Recovery Handbook, by John James and Frank Cherry. This helpful book outlines the process of grief and some of the dysfunctional ways we attempt to deal with it. Most importantly, there are many guidelines for healthy recovery.

On Death and Dying, by Elizabeth Kübler-Ross, M.D. This book, published in 1969, brought death out of the closet in the western world. Kübler-Ross helped society face the emotional stages of dying.

Life after Life, by Raymond Moody, M.D., This was the pioneering book about the experience of leaving the body, based on interviews with numerous people who had near-death experiences.

After Death: Mapping the Journey, by Sukie Miller. Cross-cultural exploration of beliefs and experiences beyond the moment of death are highlighted here. Miller presents death as a threshold rather than an ending.

A Year to Live, by Stephen Levine. The author decided to live as though he only had one year to live, hoping to reap the lessons that are usually reserved for the critically ill. Life became simpler and more precious to him.

Emmanuel's Book, Pat Rodegast and Judith Stanton, editors. This book is full of insights to ponder that transcend the reasoning of the logical mind. Chapter 11 deals with the subject of death.

Living Your Life Out Loud, by Salli Rasberry and Padi Selwyn. The authors teach and encourage readers to unleash joy through unlocking the hidden, creative aspects of self that are longing to be expressed.

The Possible Human, by Jean Houston, Ph.D. This long-time pioneer in the expansion-of-human-consciousness movement condenses an intensive workshop on mind expansion and conscious creativity into this book. These strategies expand a person's ability to use the native gifts we all possess.

Chapter Six

Love frees the very pains
that hatred ties to our backs.
Know the truth;
love the truth;
and it will set you free!

Magic Wand
Kiss the past good-bye!

Ancient Shadows

Life goes on and on despite the illusion that it ends with death. However, the form in which life continues is a subject of great controversy. Because the five senses do not pass with our consciousness through the veil of death, there is no way to establish a definitive answer based on physical evidence and logical proof. Nevertheless, what we choose to believe in affects the quality of our life experience.

If we believe each soul is only allowed one life on earth, the inequities, tragedies and unrealized dreams of this "vale of sorrows" can appear to be serious defects and limitations during the human experience. The temptation is strong to fix our attention only on the promised treasures awaiting in heaven and to undervalue the physical, earthly experience. But if our eyes are directed away from an earth we are simply enduring, we risk missing the gifts of physicality we came here to unwrap and enjoy. If we believe everyone has multiple lifetimes, we can more readily savor whatever experience life is actually presenting, instead of mourning the opportunities we, or others, are missing.

When I reflect on a child like Laura whose life was snuffed out before she got to be the ballerina of her dreams, I find more comfort in believing her soul came for a different lesson, and has many more incarnations to explore other life experiences.

However, reincarnation is not just a convenient theory devised to soften the reality of death. It is an ancient mainstream belief accepted not only by Eastern religions but, up until the Middle Ages, embraced by both Christians and Jews. According to Dr. Brian Weiss, author of *Many Lives, Many Masters* and *Through Time into Healing*, political powers suppressed this doctrine in the West because people who know this lifetime is not the only earthly opportunity are less easily dominated. During the repressive period of the Middle Ages, the belief was suppressed but not eliminated. Writing in the early nineteenth century, the poet William Wordsworth beautifully described the cycle of reincarnation:

Intimations of Immortality

Our birth is but a sleep and a forgetting:
The soul that rises with us, our life's star,
Hath had elsewhere its setting
And cometh from afar;
Not in entire forgetfulness, and not in utter nakedness,
But trailing clouds of glory do we come
From God who is our home.

There is strong supportive evidence for the idea of reincarnation. Weiss is just one expert who shares well-documented stories of subjects who, during hypnosis, recalled other lifetimes, giving detailed accounts of cultural and geographical information they had never been exposed to in present life.

While I don't have Weiss's extensive background on the subject, the experience I do have convinces me past lives can have powerful influences on the present. However, this influence does not absolve us of responsibility for our present lives. If we look to the distant past to explain everything in the present, life will be as stale, tasteless and unnourishing as month-old bread. This backward focus is just as distracting as explaining life as a mere preparation for heaven. Whether waiting for a heavenly banquet or rehashing feasts from lifetimes long past, we miss the fine meal life has spread before us in the present.

When the concept of past lives reemerged in the mainstream of Western consciousness in the 1960s, it enjoyed the celebrity status of a visiting dignitary from an exotic country. People were eager to learn who they had been and what they had done in former lives. "Come as you were" costume parties became the rage. Those looking for excuses for present behavior found a new scapegoat in their past miscreant selves. Certainly many people were using this idea to gain authentic freedom, but the popular image of reincarnation fostered by the media was sensationalist rather than spiritual.

Despite Biblical verses where Jesus asks his followers, "Who do people say I am?" and they reply, "Some say John the Baptist, some say Moses or one of the prophets," all of whom were known to be dead at the time, many Christians rejected the idea of reincarnation, perhaps because it threatened their belief in heaven and hell. The question of past lives became one more criterion for separating people as believers or non-believers.

Past-life information is nothing more than an interesting story unless it impacts a person's life in a positive way. We all love stories, and tales of past lives are perhaps the most dramatic and romantic variety. I believe we have done it all at some point and so the only lives that need to be explored are ones still causing us problems.

I also believe that past-life exploration stemming from idle curiosity is unproductive at best and can divert people from addressing difficulties in the here and now. For example, a couple having problems may well be repeating the energetic dance of many lifetimes ago, but they still need to learn basic tools of communication and recognize the unconscious aspects of self being reflected by the troublesome partner.

Simply hearing the story of a past-life drama doesn't solve relationship issues. I once recalled a past life as a man who forced my young daughter to marry a wealthy older man she despised. The marriage was an unhappy one. She treated the husband with defiance and scorn and he in turn tried to beat her into subservience. One day, lost in wrath, he killed her. I took charge of her young daughter after that. My remorse over her death awakened the memory of ancient teachings I had once known. I raised my granddaughter with an independent spirit and knowledge of the ancient wisdom, but died still blaming myself for my daughter's death.

After remembering this life, the extreme fear I felt when my former husband yelled at my oldest daughter made more sense. She was the daughter from that lifetime and he was her husband. They seemed to be caught in the same dance of defiance and control. Releasing the memory helped to ease my fear. My husband was certainly not going to kill or even beat her. However, their communication problems still remained. He still seemed to want to control my daughter; she still seemed determined not to let him, and I continued to feel responsible for protecting her yet powerless to fix the problem. These issues would have to be faced in the present before healing could take place, but recalling this past life helped me both to understand the strength of my feelings and to see how much responsibility I was taking for their relationship.

Healing Parables

Sometimes I think of past-life material as a parable or a dream. The point is not whether we physically lived through these stories. We are given the stories to help us discover and understand the feelings we have currently, which are difficult for us to sort out while enmeshed in present dramas.

For example, in an ancient Roman lifetime, I was a young man named Lucius, the lord of a city state. I relied upon my trusted friend, Claudius, for advice in ruling the state. That dependency increased as my opium addiction worsened. Only at death did I realize I had missed out on life, essentially giving it away to Claudius. This memory was liberating in the present, because I was overly involved with a friend whose intuition seemed more valid than my own. The story demonstrated, in a personal and convincing way, the importance of living fully for myself and trusting that my intuition held the right answers for my life.

Many of my clients have benefited from lessons conveyed through past-life stories, like Anna, who had a gift for creating systems. This skill had served her well in many organizations. Highly intuitive and sensitive, she was acutely aware of injustice and had a passion for uncovering history's untold chapters. Anna was having problems because she always felt on the outside despite a potential for making important contributions to the organizations she joined. Repeatedly, she felt politically ostracized and the contributions she offered were rejected. Anna was aware enough to recognize a responsibility for this pattern, but she couldn't figure out how to change it. As we explored the origins of her distress through hypnosis, the journey led to a couple of past lives that clarified the pattern.

The first life she revisited was set in the 1800s, during the struggles between cattle ranchers and railroaders in the United States. Anna was a man in that lifetime, who knew that a group of dishonest men were plotting to cheat the ranchers out of their land. He alerted the ranchers and convinced them that they could save their ranches by joining together and refusing to sell. Unfortunately the resistance backfired violently. Homes were burned; ranches were devastated; landowners were left with nothing; and everybody was angry at him. He spent the rest of his life alone in a cave, filled with remorse.

When Anna recalled this story, I asked what lesson she needed to learn from it. She identified the man's arrogant insistence that everything happen according to plan, which prevented other people from experiencing their own lessons. She acknowledged having the same attitude in the present. She realized that she had always tried to force organizations into alignment with her vision instead of seeking groups whose goals already resonated with hers and that desired the skills she wanted to offer.

The next lifetime Anna remembered was set in World War II, in the trenches. This time she was a Nazi soldier, discouraged because the Germans were losing the war. But even more, this young man was disillusioned. He had believed passionately in the ideals and promises of the Third Reich, but was so filled with shame for being associated with the atrocities of Hitler and the Nazi extremists that he gave up his spirit and died on the battlefield.

The lesson Anna derived from this story was not to take responsibility for other people's actions and attitudes. She realized she needed to let go of both the shame from that lifetime and shame in the present over failing to correct injustice in the organizations she worked for.

Anna moved on from those sessions with more freedom to trust her intuition and feel her emotions without taking responsibility for other people's experiences. She could see that she was hanging onto situations, still hoping to influence other people and she realized that efforts to change others kept her separate, on the outside. When she decided to let go of the people and situations she had been so desperate to fix, she was surprised at how easily change could come about.

Many clairvoyants have the ability to intuit past-life memories clinging to another person's aura. Readings from such psychics have been helpful to me, but never as powerful as the revelations of my own subconscious. When the memories come from the inside out, in my experience, the emotional connections always come, too. Whenever the story comes to me from outside, like a psychic reading, I have mostly been engaged on an intellectual level. Occasionally the reading sparks an emotional response and then the story feels truer to me. I believe changes require emotional energy to be lasting. No matter how long or often a person thinks positive thoughts, without the fuel of desire, the emotional drive to change, nothing significant seems to happen.

If your emotions are engaged but you're not changing, a past life may be influencing you, keeping you stuck. Past-life feelings may be holding you back, but hidden from view. It always seems to be easier to understand somebody else's problems, including somebody you used to be. Investigating past-life influences is a way to gain understanding and to liberate yourself in the present.

Guilt Survives Death

Donald, a client I described in chapter 2 who was plagued by desires for sex with prostitutes, discovered a past-life element to his addiction. Through the journey of hypnosis, this man looked into the eyes of a sad and frightened young woman, whom he knew during the Middle Ages or perhaps the Renaissance, and whom he eventually recognized as his sister in that lifetime.

He and this woman, Celeste, had been teenage lovers in that distant time period. She had been raped by her uncle/guardian, perhaps, in part, because she had a lover. Donald seemed unsure why she was raped, but felt very guilty because he had witnessed the rape but had made no attempt to prevent it. He went into denial about the impact of the rape on Celeste, preferring to think about how the two of them would be able to escape together afterwards. All he thought about was how he wanted to be with her. That never happened because Celeste dealt with her pain by committing suicide. Now, at least a lifetime later, Donald was still torn with guilt and was punishing himself sexually. Through the past-life regression he discovered an unconscious belief that if he had sex with someone he loved, that person would get hurt. Donald realized prostitutes were safe because he didn't get emotionally involved with them. I asked him to write Celeste a letter because his feelings were still raw at the end of the session. A few hours later he dropped by my office with this letter.

Dear Celeste,

I can't believe I saw you again today. I've missed you so much. I love you so much. I'm so sorry. I thought if I just let it happen we could get away together. I didn't know it would hurt you so bad. I was being selfish. I just thought you could ignore it. I know now; I knew as soon as I saw your eyes that you feel I betrayed you. I could have stopped him. I did betray you. I wanted us to be together forever. I just thought we could get away after. How could I be so selfish, so stupid?

I know that you killed yourself because your one true love stood by and let you be raped. You felt you had nothing to live for. I don't blame you. I do love you. I did then and I still do. I should have killed him. I could have tried. I know you don't come back because you feel there is no point and also that you think you can't because you killed yourself. What happens to you is based on what you believe. We believed that suicide was the last and final sin. But it's not true. You were so young. How could you not kill yourself after that? You should not be punished forever.

I've gone through my lives half-heartedly because somewhere inside me I knew that the only thing that mattered was you and you weren't here. I've felt like I was looking for an answer—the way to get you back—or, barring that, not caring what happened to me because without you it was all meaningless. If there was no hope of meeting you, then what was the point?

I have a wife and beautiful baby girl in this life. They deserve my full being, my love. My daughter deserves a daddy her whole life. Since I haven't killed myself already, I need to stop trying. Celeste, I will love you through eternity. I will not stop. If we get a chance to be together again, I have to be a whole person. Let me, help me, love my wife and child in this life. I can't offer a good reason why you should. I only ask it. Please know that my soul will always love you. Come back to earth, please. I want to be fully in this life. I know I do not deserve your forgiveness, but my daughter deserves the best daddy she could have. Help me be whole now, please.

All my love…
Paulo/Donald

This was a powerful experience for Donald and an important step in his healing. By confessing this long dormant guilt, Donald was able to voice the desire for intimacy that had been buried underneath it.

Yankee Lonely Heart

Adrienne was a client struggling with loneliness and excess weight. She thought she had difficulty attracting a partner because she was so heavy. When we explored the issue through regression, her subconscious returned to a life in Connecticut in 1829. Adrienne's memories were very detailed, and she spoke with a pronounced British accent. She reviewed that whole life in several segments.

I share this story in the sequence in which her mind revealed it, to illustrate the storytelling style of the subconscious mind. Notice how important emotional details of a scene are recalled and then the mind jumps ahead to the next scene, often years later, that holds emotional power for the soul. The connection between the scenes only becomes apparent at the end, when the soul reflects on the meaning of the life. While the story is unfolding, the perspective is the same limited view the character had in life. Only after the life has been relived as it was understood at the time, is the soul free to draw from a more enlightened mind and discover the life lessons that it can then apply to the present life.

Adrienne remembered being a five-year-old girl named Rebecca, one of "many, many, too many children." She had short, curly black hair and was wearing a maroon velvet dress, white shoes, and a white petticoat. The little girl pointed out a large tree in the front yard that she loved and believed was hers because her father had carved her name in it. Rebecca, speaking in a chirpy, childlike voice, flitted around in her story, the way children often do, sharing important information in the order it popped to mind. She revealed that her father had been killed in a fight and was buried in the back yard, and so she was afraid to go back there. Next she claimed her mother didn't love her.

I have often found that a person will be able to get inside the consciousness of other characters in the revisited lifetime, which certainly supports the idea that the mind is not localized. So in this case, I asked Adrienne to connect with Rebecca's mother, whose name was Mary, to explore, from another angle, the belief that the child was unloved.

As Adrienne tuned in to Mary's mind, not only the perspective but the accent changed. Mary, who said she came from Yorkshire, spoke with a clipped British accent. Before I could even ask a question, Mary plunged into the story, sharing parts that mattered to her. At the age of forty-four, this woman sounded exhausted as she complained of her responsibilities: so many children and no way to make ends meet. She despised America and kept hoping her wealthy sister would send money for passage so she could return with her family to England.

Mary referred to the same tree Rebecca claimed to own, revealing her intention to cut it down for firewood. She knew the child would have a fit but argued that they were all cold and the wood from the tree would last a long time. She didn't sound pleased that the child was making a fuss about the tree. Tenderness was noticeably missing from Mary's narration, and she openly confirmed her dislike of Rebecca. Mary believed her relationship with her husband had changed for the worse after that child was born.

The scene jumped ahead seven years to a point just after Mary's death. Rebecca, now twelve, sounded older and had a more noticeable British accent. She began by announcing her success in preventing the tree's destruction and then shared the doctor's diagnosis that Mary died of a heart attack. Rebecca seemed to be examining whether, for having thwarted her mother's will to chop down the tree, she might be responsible for Mary's death, revealing her suspicions that the cold house hastened the death. "Nobody else died of cold," she snapped, somewhat defensively, curtly dismissing her charges against herself. There was no hint of sorrow or remorse in her tone. Scornfully noting that the aunt in England never did send money, Rebecca related that a younger sister went to live with people from the church after Mary's death, but that she refused to go there, planning instead to go to the saloon and hire out as a dancer. She was determined to take control of her own survival.

As we again moved ahead in time, Adrienne's body began to writhe as if she were giving birth. A heartbroken Rebecca said her baby was born dead and taken away. Rebecca had been saving money to escape saloon life but had spent most of it buying things for the baby. Now she had nothing. The scene ended and we moved forward to the next important memory.

Rebecca was fifty-four and lying in a bed, being nursed by the parson's wife. The illness wasn't terminal, and the only comment Rebecca made was to brag that she looked better than her mother had at fifty. Evidently she hadn't yet let go of resentment toward her mother.

Finally we moved to the death scene. She was now sixty-four and dying of venereal disease. The other saloon women came to visit her. Unaware that she was still conscious, they remarked cattily that she'd got what she deserved. Rebecca was incensed that they had the gall to judge her when their lives were no different, and they were headed for the same fate.

In leaving her body, she felt pity for the ugly old woman lying there. When I asked about a light, she said she saw light everywhere and felt completely safe. Her face looked very joyful. I asked Rebecca what she had learned in that lifetime. The answer indicated that her soul had not yet stretched into its expanded awareness. "To survive. I never got what I wanted, which was to be loved," she complained. At that point her higher self seemed to burst through and interject a message. "Love your own soul, your own self. Don't wait for someone else to love you first."

Returning to consciousness, Adrienne reflected on the lessons of this lifetime and the message about self-love. She realized her weight wasn't holding her back from finding love. She used to purge food until she was so skinny she was getting sick, but when, in her opinion, she looked her best ever (i.e., the skinniest), nobody even wanted to take her picture. Adrienne understood on a deep level that love wasn't dependent on looks, and she wasn't going to get love in this lifetime or any other by waiting for it to show up from outside. The gift of this past-life review was to focus Adrienne in the present on the importance of self-love.

Still Angry after All These Years

Bruce, a client in his fifties, was depressed because he couldn't make lasting connections with people, particularly a life partner. Discontented with many aspects of his personal life, he also felt depressed by the sorry state of modern society. Bruce was keenly in tune with the earth and animals, and he decried the way people's unconscious lifestyles were threatening the life of the planet. He felt disgruntled but impotent, with no form of activism to match his beliefs. He was so totally cut off from anger that complaining was all he could muster.

During a regression, Bruce saw himself as a Native American, standing alone, looking over a pristine valley graced by a ribbon of river glistening in the sun. The rest of his tribe were making preparations to leave for a reservation. This lone Indian was angry that the white man was forcing his people off the land. He protested the loss of connection with the earth, convinced this rapport was unavailable on a reservation. His plan was to live as a hermit. He would not succumb to the white man, even if the price was disconnection from the tribe.

Clearly, Bruce had carried this resentment forward into this lifetime. He still related more readily to animals and nature than to other humans, even though now he desperately wanted human connection. To change the present, Bruce had to surrender—first in the past—not to the white man, but to the Great Spirit. He had to accept that, for whatever mysterious reason, this experience was the right one, and stop fighting it. Perhaps he was being challenged to find connection with the earth even in the restrictive atmosphere of the reservation. Perhaps the challenge was to perceive the connection with the oppressing white settlers. If everything is part of the web of life, then by definition, no person, place or experience can be outside it. This shift was hard for Bruce to make. During the regression, he was not able to surrender. He left my office pondering the possibility.

Mental Transplant Surgery

Chloe, another client struggling with weight issues, was anorexic. Using hypnosis, we examined the past for clues to her present problems. Like Donald, she first recalled a prenatal experience. Identifying with her young mother's fears, Chloe was afraid to be born, concerned that there would not be enough of whatever she might need.

From that memory, Chloe moved back through time to a life as a little boy in China, an only child with many relatives. Although it was a peasant family, there was always plenty of love and plenty of rice. His happy life ended abruptly when a band of marauders arrived and killed everybody. The last impression Chloe recalled, as this little boy, was the look in the eyes of his murderer. The boy seemed to have merged with the killer's mind through that gaze because Chloe began recounting the killer's story, which was one of starvation. He had never had enough to eat in childhood, and now, as a marauder, spent his life plundering, believing he still didn't have enough. Chloe reflected these ancient feelings in the present by starving herself.

I have found that some clients respond well to the healing power of story. After they face the original trauma, I weave a new story for them while they are in that receptive subconscious place. It's as if I'm performing mental transplant surgery. Perhaps the Magic Child has the power to change the fearful mind, once the traumatic truth has been released. I helped Chloe imagine a uterine environment without fear, and supportive of great curiosity and a belief in plenty. Upon returning to alertness, she acted playfully. I brought her a variety of sensuous foods to taste, and she experienced, perhaps for the first time, delight in eating. Chloe moved away shortly after this session, so I don't know the long-term results, but this past-life healing seemed promising.

Betty was another client who benefited from "mental transplant surgery." Betty started smoking as a teenager and now, in her fifties, wanted to stop. In hypnosis she recalled a lifetime in the United States during the nineteenth century as David, a young half-breed who followed his white father's ways. David worked as a ranch hand, herding other people's horses, but his heart hurt. He longed to follow his mother's Indian ways but saw the white men ruling the land and believed the only way to survive was to be like them.

Then one day David was falsely accused of stealing horses and sentenced to hang. Dangling from the noose, in the last moments of life, gasping for air, he bitterly regretted his choice to ignore the call of his heart and follow white men's ways just to survive. Now the white men were killing him anyway. Betty lay in the chair choking while recalling this painful end. As she grew more peaceful, I suggested a different story.

A young half-breed named David, who was also known as Crow Boy, grew up living in two worlds. From his father he learned to tame wild horses and whittle wood. On his mother's lap he learned stories of the Indian ways. His father taught the attitudes of white men, but Crow Boy didn't listen. His heart belonged to the Indian ways.

When the boy reached the proper age, his father allowed the mother to take Crow Boy to her people for initiation. During the ceremony, he began to sing the songs of the Indian people. When he sang, they felt the light of the stars and the heat of the earth in his music. The people were deeply moved; even the Chief began to cry. They gave him a new name: Singing Crow.

Singing Crow and his mother returned to the ranch. Several years later, the father died. Singing Crow sold the property and brought his mother back to the land of her people, where they both made a new home. Singing Crow continued to heal and inspire his people through song. When his mother lay dying, he sang her across to the other side; she went with a smile of rapture on her face. Singing Crow lived a long and satisfied life.

Betty never smoked another cigarette.

Ancient Roots of Physical Pain

Sometimes we are led to past-life memories while searching for the roots of emotional pain in the present. Other times memories are retrieved when we seek healing for physical pain. One time when I was suffering with a severe cold I couldn't shake, I explored its origin with a fellow hypnotherapist. As we began the session, I suddenly remembered the sneezing had begun just after skinny-dipping with a friend in the chilly waters of a secluded wood. I hadn't been skinny-dipping in years and this had been quite a spur-of-the-moment idea. In hypnosis, I pictured myself as a young girl dressed in turn-of-the-century clothes, leaning over the back of a couch, gazing out at the moonlit ocean. I recalled wanting to go swimming but my mother forbidding it because young ladies didn't do that kind of thing, and besides I would catch my death of cold. Later that night, I snuck out, peeled off my clothes and went for a moonlight swim. In the next scene, I was in bed with pneumonia, feeling guilty for disobeying my mother. I died from this cold, just as my mother had predicted. The guilt that had slumbered for a century had to be released before I could recover my health in the present. After that session my cold vanished quickly.

Past-life memories don't automatically eradicate physical problems. First of all, not all physical pain and disease stems from unresolved past-life issues. This is only one angle to consider. In some cases there may be one or more past-life experiences layered inside a particular place in the body where we experience chronic pain or recurring injury. It's as if these body areas are collector points, storing so much trauma that it can only be released in stages. In those cases, untangling a past-life connection will only yield temporary relief from the physical pain.

A place in the back of my neck, at the base of the occipital bone, is a collector point for me. One day, while I was journaling, a story emerged from the shadows of ancient memory. In this lifetime, set in the early 1800s, I was a soldier in charge of a band of men and was leading them through the jungles of Africa on a treasure hunting venture. The men were afraid to go any deeper into the jungle because the indigenous tribes had a violent reputation. Fixated on potential gold and treasures, I pushed my men on, ignoring their concerns until, one night as I slept, they mutinied. One soldier drove a fatal spike into the back of my head, right at my collector point. The soldiers ended up being killed by the natives as they tried to escape. The assassin died full of anger at me, not only for leading him to his own death, but for putting him in a position where he had to kill me. That soldier was my first husband, David.

I told David the story and we did a forgiveness ceremony with each other. I thought that would be enough to heal my neck. I did experience temporary relief, but there seems to be more tied up in there. Also, at the time, I didn't realize that past-life information has to be connected to present attitudes and behaviors before the release is complete. Had David and I known that, we might have been able to explore the relationship dynamics between us that this lifetime illustrated. I have definitely been known to push, he has certainly felt like a victim, but we failed to address those tendencies openly.

Another collector point for me has been the middle back. Years ago, amidst the chaos of leaving a home in Texas to move to Oregon, I experienced some middle back pain that did not respond well to chiropractic treatment. I took an inner journey, with another healer, to the nineteenth century in the western United States.

I was a rancher with a wife and child. One day three men came to the door and offered to buy my land, but I wouldn't sell. A few days later my family and I were ambushed by these same men as we drove home from market. They shot my wife and son and beat me nearly to death with the butt of a rifle. The pain and rage I experienced while recalling this episode were intense.

After the beating, I awoke in an abbey. Having lost everything that mattered to me, I stayed on and became a monk. It was my job to tend the garden. The back pain never went away. Eventually I lay dying in a little room near the front entrance. Three men came to the door carrying a wounded man. The abbot took the body and handed them an envelope. Suddenly a buried memory flashed back to consciousness. Those were the same three men who had ambushed me years earlier, and the same abbot who had paid them off for their villainy. I realized the abbot had wanted my land for the church and had hired these men to steal it when I refused to sell. All these years I had taken comfort from this church and served this abbot. I began screaming and choking with impotent rage.

Although the woman who guided my journey led me to construct a new story, I wasn't through yet. The next morning when I woke, my back was so sore I could barely drive. I felt every bump in the road and I couldn't turn my neck enough to merge safely on the busy freeways. My chiropractor couldn't find anything physically wrong with my body, but a psychic energy worker, without even hearing the story, detected massive past-life issues flooding through me. After several hours of intensive energy work, the pain in my back was all gone.

I believe this experience was precipitated by the victim part of me feeling forced to give up my home in Texas. I couldn't effectively deal with my grief in the present until I had released unexpressed grief and rage from the past. Or maybe since I couldn't express rage about leaving in the present, I had to do it through a story. There is mystery here. I only know that the intensity of emotion and increased back pain came up with the story and were ultimately released on the energetic plane. My back remained pain free for some time, but the pain continues to reoccur. Sometimes I am aware of physical causes and chiropractic treatment eliminates the pain. Other times new stories emerge from the past, bringing relief for awhile.

Buried Treasures

Past-life retrieval is not always about pain relief. During our many lifetimes, we have been gifted with a wide assortment of talents. One of the most interesting applications of past-life regression is to help clients retrieve those talents. One woman, who recalled a lifetime as a mathematician, went on to become a successful mortgage loan agent, despite having been a D student in math all through school.

Another client, whose career was at a dead end, recalled a lifetime as a doll maker who instilled magic into her creations. This woman was presently making dolls, but just as a hobby. After the regression she decided to find a way to make a living as a doll maker. I'm guessing her subsequent dolls sparkled with extra magic, too!

A third client recalled a lifetime as a harpist. Shortly after that session my client bought a harp and learned to play beautifully and easily.

After being reminded of a lifetime in Indonesia as a playwright and mask maker, I started using mask making as a healing art with clients.

For many people, the value of regression to a previous life is not remembering the details of the lifetime, but recalling the process of dying and the memories on the other side of death's veil. Sara, a client with a history of depression and sexual abuse, was full of fears that kept her stuck in unhappy situations. Recalling one lifetime after another, she repeatedly focused on the death scene. As each life ended to be replaced by another, Sara learned at a much deeper level that life goes on. She had a vivid vision of life on the other side and imagined a peaceful grove that smelled of citrus, filled with souls who radiated love and peace. A staircase stretched from the grove to the earth plane and a steady stream of souls traveled up and down the stairs. This work helped Sara release the fear preventing her from living fully in the present. She felt like she had a broader perspective on her troubles and was able to start taking practical steps to create a more positive life for herself and her child.

The experience I related in chapter 1, of being buried in the funeral mound, utterly conscious of connection with the earth, filled me with peace. The mind cannot simultaneously hold a positive experience of peace through death and the fear of death.

The Greatest Gift

In going through the pain of past-life memories, there is always a release of stuck energy that leads to greater freedom, peace and joy. For me, the greatest gift came through remembering the greatest misery. As the writing of this book drew to a close and the time when I would speak to audiences about it grew closer, my throat shut down in pain.

The conversation with my throat emerged in chapters. First, thoughts of sexual abuse floated to mind, but my throat spoke of abuse from another life, when I was just a baby. Although I was invited to release the memory and step into freedom, I couldn't do that. A sense that I was undeserving nagged at me. This feeling led me beneath the comforting blanket of victimhood to karmic responsibility.

The lifetime begging for recall, set in the early 1600s, was more grisly than any I have personally recalled before. I hesitate to share this memory for fear that some people may read the account and infer that I am somehow sanctioning this kind of behavior. I am not. I believe that I sank as deeply into evil as a human being can descend. As the details slowly came back, I felt like vomiting with disgust. In that life, I was the leader of a cult involved in black magic and ritual abuse of children. How fitting that I am now dedicating my life to end the abuse of children! At any rate, during that lifetime, we sexually abused small children and slit their throats. Most horrible of all, we ate their hearts. I was in terrible pain as I remembered this, and then an even more violent memory returned. I had eaten the heart of my own baby. My abhorrence was softened as insight followed about why I had made such destructive choices. Terrified, in that life, of being soft, I could not afford the vulnerability of motherhood. Later I realized that, as a small child in that life, I had witnessed the slaughter of other little children, and had been determined to protect myself by being harder and crueler than anyone else.

As my body released the long-hidden revulsion and pain, my consciousness left the earth plane. Suddenly I was beyond physicality, beyond time and space. My whole body hummed with warm energy and well-being. The understanding that came to me was difficult to translate. I had an awareness that this life had been an exploration into the darkness as a means of hollowing out that darkness and leaving more space for light. The eating of a heart was a primitive attempt to put heart energy into my throat center, and indeed into my whole body. My conscious mind could never have invented such meaning, but in this place of pure being it was so clear.

I now felt love energy radiating from the heart center throughout my entire being. It was the most exquisite feeling I have ever experienced in my life, pure and total love. In that moment, which seemed eternal, I surrendered my destiny completely to love. I imagine this is what death feels like. No wonder people who have near-death experiences are reluctant to return. I didn't want this experience to end, yet mundane matters like the demands of a bladder reminded me that I wasn't ready to live full time in this state of bliss yet. Even as I drew back into earthly awareness, I took with me a knowing that this state of love is what is real, regardless of whether I'm paying attention to it in a given moment. I know it will change my life dramatically, although I don't yet know how.

This incredible gift was only possible because I was willing to face a dark inner shadow. If you avoid the darkness within, you may be able to find comfort in a sense of being good, but you will miss the ecstasy of wholeness, of being inseparable from all life. Separation is caused by dividing experience into good and bad, instead of taking the eternal perspective that nothing on the earth plane has lasting significance because all is part of the soul's learning. Peace comes from transcending the illusion of good and bad and resting in love as the only reality. We transcend evil, not by avoiding it, but by facing the evil within and unmasking it.

Our ability to live as the Magic Children we are, expressing our love essence, depends on a willingness to face all that is within us with truth and compassion. If you remember episodes and emotions from an earlier time, I believe you can find freedom in your present life as a result, as long as you remember one thing: You must kiss the past good-bye! I use the word kiss intentionally, because we kiss those we love. Just as I have encour-

aged you to love all the parts of yourself and all your past and present situations, I ask you now to lovingly accept the way it was for you in lives long past. All that you have experienced has contributed to making you the exact and precious person you are. Even as you choose to move forward, to let go of the traumas of days gone by, release those memories with a kiss. Love frees the very pains that hatred ties to our backs. Know the truth, love the truth, and it will set you free!

Wondersparks

1. Is there someone in your life with whom difficulties persist despite all the consciousness and communication skills you apply?
2. Are there places that hold an allure for you that seems unusually strong?
3. Do you have talents that seemed unusually well developed from an early age, or which you accessed without any training? Yes to any of these questions may indicate past-life connections.

Elixirs for the Mind

Through Time Into Healing and *Many Lives, Many Masters*, by Brian Weiss, M.D. Weiss provides the most thorough and interesting study of past lives I have found. *Many Lives, Many Masters* records detailed regressions done with a single woman, the client with whom Weiss first encountered the mystery of past lives. *Through Time Into Healing*, written later, is based on thousands of regressions with varied clients.

Past Lives, Present Dreams, by Denise Linn. This past-life therapist travels internationally, conducting regressions with hundreds of people, as well as helping individuals privately. This book is full of healing stories of her own as well as from her many clients. Linn also shares techniques for the reader to use independently, including a helpful chapter on dreams and another on spirit guides and angels.

After Death: Mapping the Journey, by Sukie Miller. "That one reincarnates is a basic premise of cultures ranging from Tibetan Buddhism to that of the Yongu Aborigines of Australia and the Krenar Indian tribe of Brazil, to the ancient Vedic tradition of India," writes Miller in this cross-cultural study of beliefs and experiences of afterlife.

Children's Past Lives, by Carol Bowman. Filled with stories of past-life memories recalled by children, this book provides a useful guide for parents about how to deal with the emergence of past-life information, how to distinguish it from fantasy, and circumstances that may trigger such recall.

Chapter Seven

The truth of the feelings and memories
wrapped inside the facts
is what has to be told
before love can be restored.

Magic Wand
Admit your true feelings!

W hen I reflect back on my life, I am struck by one lesson more than any other, the importance of telling myself the truth about what I am feeling. As a child, telling the truth meant admitting if I had done something that wasn't allowed, or—very righteously—reporting if one of my siblings had done something wrong. I had a courtroom approach to the truth: "Just the facts, Ma'am."

Now when I reflect upon truth, I realize that facts are only the outer covering of a situation. Underlying the skin of facts are layers of memory and feelings, which form the flesh and blood of the experience. I could tell you my former husband has never thanked me for any gifts I have sent him since we've been divorced and use that fact to support an accusation that he is an ungrateful person. But neither this statement of blame or the supporting fact would tell you anything of importance. The truth lies in layers beneath the surface of the fact. The truth is I felt angry and full of judgment about the way he has dealt with his feelings about me. An even deeper truth is I long to have a friendship with the father of my children and I am sad this doesn't exist yet. Another deep truth I'd prefer not to admit is some of his anger toward me is justified and I feel guilt for that. I feel sad because there is such a gulf between us. I cannot imagine having an honest conversation with him, in which we both accept responsibility for all that happened in our marriage.

Whether counseling couples professionally or just listening to family and friends talk about their lives, I notice this pattern over and over. People get stuck pointing fingers and arguing about the facts of who did what to whom. Ultimately none of this matters, because the truth of the feelings and memories wrapped inside the facts is what has to be told before love can be restored to the situation.

Why don't we tell the deeper truths? I am aware of several answers. Love seems to be our most basic need. We have scientifically proven, through observing babies whose basic needs for food and shelter were met while their needs for love and touch were not, that a human being does not develop normally, and in many cases does not even survive, without love and touch. Love is so important, we will not risk losing it. I think, despite a basic impulse to be truthful, often we do not tell the truth because we fear the truth will cost us love. We will deny any feeling rather than express it and risk disapproval and rejection.

On the other hand, some people have given up on the possibility of getting love, which often leads to despair or love starvation. When love is devoid of physical affection, laced with constant criticism, or punctuated with physical abuse, it is equivalent to love malnutrition, a condition often seen in children.

To compensate for lack of love, children protect themselves by taking responsibility for the situation. On a deep level, they assume the lack of love stems from their inherent inadequacy. They cover this assumption with the illusion that they have the power to control another's love through their behavior. The sense of control masks their underlying pain.

For example, an obese client once discovered that he was hiding, underneath layers of fat, from the "fact" that his mother didn't love him. By imagining that her disapproval was based on his overweight, he could pretend that her love was attainable if he lost those extra pounds. Of course, diets inevitably failed because a deeper part of him realized that her love wasn't under his control, and wanted to protect him from the pain of knowing he was unloved.

A highly criticized child, conditioned to believe that love hinges on achieving some impossible standard, often hides from the futility of earning love by pretending to be acceptable. Such individuals absolutely need to be right all the time, or their "cover" will be shattered. The argumentative and critical nature of such a person is really a desperate attempt to feel in control of the supply of love. To admit feelings is very threatening because that opens the door to exposing the carefully hidden "truth" that the person is unlovable.

Whether we conceal our true feelings for fear of losing love or losing control, we all share another problem. Often we don't even realize what we are feeling. The three feelings most difficult for people to recognize are sadness, anger and fear. We all know we're feeling sad while crying, angry while screaming, afraid while trembling. But until we get to those dramatic expressions, the feelings are often hidden from conscious awareness. People may be able to recognize one feeling but consistently ignore another. For example, some people know they are sad. They may become depressed over constant sadness, but be unaware of their underlying anger and so never express that emotion. Feelings are rarely pristine. They swirl inside us in layers. Seldom is the surface emotion the whole truth.

Why are we so disconnected from our own feelings? We are taught, from a very early age, that some feelings are not okay to reveal in the family, or even in the culture. As children, if we express those particular feelings, some form of punishment follows. We may be beaten, ostracized, verbally shamed or made responsible for somebody else's feelings. We are told that by daring to express a certain taboo feeling we have hurt someone we love. Certainly there are both hurtful and healthy ways to share feelings, but we get the message a particular feeling is bad and any expression of it is always hurtful and wrong. For example, a child expressing sorrow may be mocked as a crybaby or threatened with, "Stop that crying or I'll give you something to cry about!" An angry child may be accused of being ugly, slapped for uttering a rude expression, or sent out of the room until "fit" to be around. The child may also be burdened with responsibility for someone else's reaction and told, for instance, that such angry behavior has "made" Mommy sad or angry. Many a child has been shamed by parents or siblings for showing fear. The child is called a scaredy-cat, and the fear is discounted or ridiculed. Sometimes family members take advantage of knowing that a child is afraid and try to frighten the child even more. The youngster soon learns to keep fears hidden.

Sometimes, instead of punishing us for certain feelings, parents teach us the art of denial. A crying child is told, "Stop crying, there's nothing wrong with you. You're okay." Those are the people who can sit in my office and tell me they're fine, ignoring the inner turbulence that brought them to see me in the first place. Or the parent may simply ignore the child's feelings and distract the child's attention. The child is crying and the parent says, "Would you like a cookie?" I wonder how many overweight people learned to eat instead of cry as children.

Parents who have trouble expressing a particular feeling usually have little tolerance when their children express that same feeling, so that fear of expression gets passed down to another generation. In order to keep getting our parents' love, which seems conditional on stuffing "wrong" feelings, we learn to ignore the emotional signals our bodies are sending. By adulthood, adept at ignoring the signals and oblivious to the presence of the taboo feelings, we are incapable of admitting those feelings to self or others. The emotional communication lines have been cut.

Then, suppressing emotional honesty, most of us become polite people. Otherwise, we may be judged and avoided by others. I heard a story of a girl who had been told an old lady in her neighborhood was a witch. She had to go to the woman's house and was scared the stories might be true. "You have a question," the woman stated when the little girl came inside. "Yes, ma'am, I do," admitted the child, "but it's a rude one." Undaunted, the woman replied, "All children's questions are rude if they've really thought about them!" When children are absorbed in curiosity, they don't think to censor questions that may make adults uncomfortable. After repeated episodes of scolding or shaming, most of us learn to subordinate our curiosity.

We sacrifice honest expression on the altar of politeness. I'm not suggesting we march forth indiscriminately hurting people by using truth in obnoxious ways. We do need to be aware of people's feelings and treat each other with kindness. There are gentle ways and cruel ways to say the same thing. The cruel ways are usually dripping with blame, while the gentle ways involve taking responsibility for our own feelings.

Emotional truth-telling has always been difficult for me. Although for several years I had been absolutely committed to telling the truth, and had already written several drafts of this chapter, one evening I was unable to tell a guest in my home that I was too tired to entertain her any longer and ask her to leave. Constrained by a need to be polite, I couldn't even acknowledge to myself that I was failing to tell the truth. Politeness prevented me from insulting her in a cruel and irresponsible way, by accusing her of being rude and insensitive to my not-so-subtle yawns. But it also prevented me from taking care of my own need for rest. A small and helpless inner voice whispered "How come nobody's taking care of me?" An angry voice masked the plea, deciding somebody else should have been taking care of my needs, such as the guest! I felt righteous about mentally convicting her of insensitivity and bad manners, deftly letting myself off the hook for the situation. What could I do? I had to be polite. That was clearly a "solid excuse" for not taking responsibility for my needs.

At the time, this unconscious internal debate was hidden under a conscious awareness of being weary, annoyed and trapped—a victim. What I could have done instead was tell the truth. I could have owned my feelings of exhaustion and simply asked her to leave. She might have felt embarrassed or disappointed or even angry. That would be her problem.

A desire to be polite can lead us to the mistaken belief that others' feelings are our responsibility. This idea inhibits truth-telling when we attempt "saving" people from having the emotional reaction we anticipate. While striving to be polite, we can easily deny a deeper agenda. Our interest is usually not just to prevent hurting someone's feelings but to avoid being sprayed with the "shrapnel" of the person's reaction.

Ron says he hesitates to tell me something if he suspects I will cry. Crying women push his rescue button and "force" him to solve their problems. I hesitate to say things when I suspect someone will get mad. A subconscious part of me fears their anger will destroy me. Fear of emotional consequences holds our true feelings hostage.

Sometimes that fear is justified. If you live with an abusive spouse, you might endanger yourself by sharing truths about your needs. For example, it may be true that you get angry when your husband watches TV in bed past midnight because it disturbs your sleep. But telling him this and asking him to turn off the television could be enough to instigate a beating. People in abusive situations need to be honest with themselves, not their violent partners, and then seek professional help to learn how to change or leave that unsafe environment.

In more stable situations, although you may feel as though you will die if you express a particular emotion or admit something that is true for you, this is an irrational feeling, not a realistic possibility. In moving bravely forward and telling your true feelings, you will most surely experience a sense of aliveness brought about by the other side of truth-telling.

Your fear that truth-telling will destroy another person in some way is an equally irrational fear. Most people are not that fragile. Co-dependent relationships are based on the belief that one person has to be responsible for another's life because that other is incapable and will fall apart unless rescued. Sometimes the truth will, however, plunge a person into strong emotional reactions. We have to give others the freedom to feel, and trust that they have the inner strength to deal with their own feelings. Our role is to communicate our true emotions, not just the surface ones, and take responsibility for those emotions. You do not cause my anger or my sadness or my fear, regardless of what you do. I choose my reactions, even if I choose them for very complex and unconscious reasons.

Whole families can work in concert to inhibit uncomfortable feelings. One morning at a restaurant, my daughter Rachel became indignant over the taxidermy specimens on the wall. "People who hunt are stupid," she said. I don't like hunting either but I felt a need to broaden her judgmental mind. I started sharing a historical perspective about our culture's consciousness regarding the rights of various groups, including animals. Rachel was less than receptive, mentally barricading herself from the perceived attempt to change her opinion. I got mad because she wasn't listening to me. Ron hesitantly pointed out that no one present was interested in my comments on that subject.

What an emotional slap that felt like! Shocked, indignant and hurt, I began to cry. He had anticipated my reaction, but he lovingly held his ground. Meanwhile the girls scrambled to staunch the flow of my tears. Rachel started hugging me, telling me not to cry and blaming Ron for hurting me. Holly started babbling like a tour guide about all the interesting decorations on the wall, energetically attempting to distract me. I told Ron how hurt I felt that nobody was interested in a more intellectual conversation. I felt victimized and righteous and had to struggle to listen to his patient explanation.

Ron helped me recognize that anger about Rachel's narrow opinion had fueled my discourse, and that the rest of the family felt like they were attending a lecture instead of sharing a conversation. Being less than perfect feels the same as being a terrible person to me, even though I know perfection is an irrational expectation. So I needed to shed many tears before I was able to accept Ron's point of view. It would have been more comfortable for the whole family if he'd hoarded that insight, but we would all have missed the chance to grow our communication skills and learn that feelings are not deadly.

Because we fear the power of our feelings, a common reaction when we are plunged unexpectedly into a strong emotion is to blame the one who seems to have caused the feeling. But laying blame does not help us discover truth. If a desire to blame is the primary emotion you feel, assume there is a truth you are overlooking. This doesn't mean you have to keep quiet until you know what that truth is, though.

One time I was angry at Ron, who had promised to help me make a hypnosis tape, a project that required his recording equipment and expertise. The promise wasn't kept because he spent most of the scheduled Saturday in bed with a headache, only rousing himself to watch a video in the evening. I awoke

Monday feeling very separate, judgmental and angry. I was having trouble expressing my feelings because I knew that blame reveals lack of consciousness; his schedule was very busy, and I understood the emotional issues behind his headache. I didn't want to be insensitive and selfish but also wasn't ready to absolve him as a helpless victim.

Now that I understand my body's communication style, stuffing emotions isn't acceptable anymore. My body grew tense and hostile to touch, clearly illustrating the angry thoughts rumbling round and round, like a hamster on a wheel, and after a while I did express my anger, first presenting all the disclaimers about understanding his problems. Ron made my job easier by playing the dramatic role of an unconscious blamer, pretending to be me criticizing him. He exaggerated how awful he was in such a way that I was convulsed with laughter, even while recognizing that his words reflected my true feelings, much to my shame. In the end, all the feelings had been expressed, Ron knew what I wanted, no commitments or plans of action had been made, and we both felt completely connected. I felt buoyant and alive, just to know I could express all my feelings, even when they weren't all neat and tidy and fully conscious. For the rest of the day, whenever I thought about Ron, I felt connected and happy. That's the payoff for telling the whole truth about your feelings, whatever they are (eventually we even got the tape made!).

Some people avoid feelings, especially anger, out of spiritual opposition. They quote the Buddhist teaching that all is illusion, including feelings. In my opinion, this is a misreading of the teaching. During peaceful meditation, we can experience the illusion of the dramas that preoccupy us. We can choose to let go of the victim attitude that underlies so many of our feelings. However, we can only let go of something if we know we are holding it in the first place. I can choose peace instead of anger, oneness instead of separation, only if I recognize my tendency to perceive myself as separate and angry. The Dalai Lama, the spiritual leader of Tibetan Buddhists quoted in *The Essential Mystic,* described the importance of moving toward that which we experience in order to discover its illusory nature:

A form seen in the distance
Becomes clearer the closer we get to it.
If a mirage were water,
Why would it vanish when we draw near?

The farther we are from the world,
The more real it appears to us;
The nearer we draw to it, the less visible it becomes,
And, like a mirage, becomes signless.

I clearly remember Bill, a client in his late forties who was depressed and listless. Bill was philosophically opposed to being angry, but during our sessions he appeared to be a very angry man. He thought he was being a good person by keeping those feelings private. He hid them from his conscious mind completely and so had no awareness of the anger he was carrying around. By starting to acknowledge his anger and take responsibility for his own needs, he started feeling more alive and in control. Then he could begin to let go of the anger consciously, knowing others were not responsible for his happiness anyway.

Jim, a successful man in his sixties, came to me for help with relationship issues. Although he had always met all his business goals with ease, his relationships with women had all been unhappy. Jim started to realize that his dissatisfaction stemmed from hiding feelings and needs from his partners, and even from himself. By going along with whatever his partner asked, thinking he was being a cooperative, nice guy, he was consistently ignoring his inner self. In making a connection with the innocent young boy he had once been, Jim began to release his tears. He remembered how little his feelings had mattered to the adults in his young life. Jim had kept those feelings secret ever since. Jim started dating someone new, the kind of woman he had always wanted for a partner, but had never let himself pursue. He began taking chances and expressing feelings to her and was surprised at how well the relationship developed. He felt happier than he could ever remember.

The primary human emotions are sadness, anger, fear, excitement, joy, sexual attraction and love. Other feelings are variations of these. I haven't met many people who survive childhood still able to express all of these feelings in healthy ways. The situation isn't terminal, and many adults learn to be comfortable expressing the full range of feelings, but usually only after much courageous emotional recovery work.

Because everyone seems to have a weak spot on the emotional continuum, I intend to focus on each of the primary emotions, to examine the healthy and unhealthy expressions of each one.

Sadness

Most women I know are comfortable expressing sorrow because this culture allows girls to cry. That fits what has been, until recently, a culturally accepted model of the "helpless female." Men, in contrast, eke out tears only on rare occasions, with a guardedness befitting the most precious elixir. Even two-year-old babies are admonished to repress tears in manly fashion. "Big boys don't cry," they are warned. Many men have sat in my office shedding tears for the first time since childhood. The tears always seem to surprise them and open forgotten emotional places.

Though tears are culturally acceptable for females, many women judge themselves harshly for crying, or actively resist expressing sadness. Some take pride in not being crybabies, as if being tear-free is a badge of courage. For fifty years my friend Evelyn has lived by her mother's injunction not to cry in public. If tears threaten to flow, she even chases her husband and children out of the room, demanding privacy.

Before starting primal therapy, I too was afraid to cry. Sensing a well of uncried tears inside, I feared that once the tears started flowing, the "faucet" would get stuck, permanently, in the "on" position. I soon realized that was not the case.

Repressed sadness is self-destructive, with unshed tears eating away at internal organs like battery acid. Emotions facilitate a chemical release in our bodies which can become toxic over time unless dissipated through a healthy expression such as tears. When those tears are stuffed, the results can be deep depression, relationship difficulties, physical illness, or even a shortened lifespan.

By avoiding the sadness inside, we also end up limiting our experience of joy. Linda, a woman in her fifties, began therapy because she never felt joyful. As a young child, Linda had been suddenly abandoned, first by her mother, and later by her father. She felt sad and lost for a very long time. As an adult, Linda was determined to avoid sadness if possible. When I suggested connecting with the sad child inside her, Linda recoiled, afraid that any contact with the old pain would spill into present life. When she did approach the child, in hypnosis, she moved slowly and was surprised that nothing bad happened. Eventually Linda was able to imagine holding and comforting the child. Following hypnotherapy, Linda used the non-dominant journaling technique I described in chapter 2. Through this process, the child requested that Linda paint pictures of her, over and over, "until you can see my beauty." This was a transforming process for Linda, who, in time, learned to love the terrible beauty of her sadness. Her life did not revert to unending grief but instead was more joyful. Now, if a wave of sadness comes along, she simply feels it. Sadness is no longer her jailer. Is it yours?

Anger

While tears are culturally off limits to men, anger is acceptable. Our society expects boys to settle fights with their fists. We line up to watch movies of violent men expressing anger and solving problems with guns and bombs. While this anger seems natural in a man, for women the standard is different. An angry woman is called a bitch or worse. A saying I first heard when I lived in Texas appalled me. "Don't be ugly," was the message to any woman or girl who was angry. With one comment, girls were both forbidden expression of anger and required to focus on their looks.

Anger is a frightening emotion for many—men as well as women—because of traumatic memories of parents livid with anger and out of control. The emotional, and sometimes physical, abuse directed at children because someone was angry, has caused many people in our society to avoid other people's anger at any cost and to view their own anger as something dangerous. This is understandable, but unfortunate. Anger is an important tool, when expressed appropriately.

Brad was a client in his early forties whose wife of fifteen years had just demanded a divorce. Heartbroken and paralyzed by sadness, this devoted father was desperate to soften the experience for the children and so he carefully hid any anger toward his wife. His childhood home had been a place of rage, and he was determined to protect his children from that experience. The wife, meanwhile, was treating him with scorn, making unreasonable demands, ignoring his efforts, and ridiculing him in front of the children. Brad's only reaction was to cry.

Once Brad started to recognize feelings of anger, he was still terrified to express them, even in the privacy of my office. Just the thought of expressing anger stopped his breathing. He felt as if there were a padlock on his throat. Then he remembered how his childish requests had usually been answered with a slap in the face. No wonder it was so hard to be assertive now. Finally, Brad was able to let the anger out. The release of all that pent-up anger was very powerful. Afterwards, he seemed more alive and surprised to feel so good. He began making intuitive connections. Reflecting on his wife's repeated infidelity and other violations of integrity, he realized the importance of protecting his own interests and setting boundaries. Although Brad would still have preferred to spare the children from witnessing anger, he now realized that modeling an inability to set boundaries was also harmful.

Like Brad, some people find courage to take steps that otherwise seem impossible, when the incentive of setting a positive example for their children is present. I believe in using any motivation that inspires us to take the steps necessary to make positive life changes.

Most people spend a lifetime stuffing their angry feelings, the way Brad did, trying to be nice. They keep tossing more and more unspoken anger into the boiling pot inside them. Periodically the pot boils over and scalds the people standing closest. It doesn't have to be that way. If you empty the pot by facing the painful memories and expressing your stuffed anger in a safe environment, then you can begin to express anger in the present that is mainly about what is happening in the present. This anger is not encrusted with all the unexpressed anger of a lifetime. It's instinctual. A mother bear doesn't need to think about whether or how to protect her cubs when danger approaches. She strikes. My experience of expressing healthy anger feels like setting or defending a firm boundary. It's that mother bear energy. I don't need to scream. I feel powerful, focused and connected.

I often feel good about expressing anger now and am less afraid of other people's anger. I've worked hard to get to this point. In chapter 2 I described learning how to recognize anger, like a lump in my throat, before I could begin to express it. One difficulty I experienced in giving myself permission to be angry was feeling as though I needed a briefcase full of legally certified documents clearly establishing justification for being angry. Anger never seemed to make it through such a rigorous trial process. That was the stumbling block when I was telling Ron how I felt about his broken promise to help me make the tape.

I've also learned anger is usually about something else, something older, that is being triggered by the present situation. Sometimes the thread of anger can be traced to a pivotal incident from the past. Often it's a broader anger, referring back to the way we usually felt in childhood.

Jean was experiencing depression. We had worked through many different layers, and she was well aware of angry feelings toward her parents. The part she was unable to get past was expressing that anger. Her husband's job often took him away, triggering abandonment issues, which we had already addressed. However, his homecoming brought on depression, and that puzzled Jean. As we explored this, she realized that any time other people intruded into her life with their needs and expectations, she had to go away, get smaller, focus on them and explain herself endlessly. The husband's homecoming was a signal to put herself aside once again. Staying in the process, Jean discovered she was intensely angry for never being allowed to be herself but was terrified of expressing that anger. Using guided imagery, Jean took a journey that finally empowered her to give voice to anger.

Jean imagined wandering inside a room of shadows, filled with the voices of other people's expectations and needs. One door led out of the room. Approaching the door, Jean felt a deep chill. She knew that if she went through that door she would die. On the other side of the door she sensed great energy. This door of life could only be opened by a magical sound: a terrible shriek, a release, from the depths of the great anger she'd been holding. Facing the door, tightening her jaw to stifle the shriek, Jean imagined a goddess figure standing near the door. The goddess's hands were raised above her head in a posture of invocation, calling Jean's soul home. Jean realized the need for approval prevented her from expressing anger about having to live according to someone else's rules. She had become her own captor, walling herself inside this room of the living dead. The part of her unwilling to risk disapproval had to die in order to free her voice and open the door of life. Paradoxically, life and death shared the same doorway.

Jean struggled desperately. Fear-based tears ran down her cheeks. Then the anger began to rumble deep inside. As it built up strength, she gathered anger from the earth: for all the women who had been burned at the stake for being healers; for all the children whose spirits had been locked away; for all the people who are not allowed to be free because they are judged to be somehow wrong the way they are. The anger churned deep inside her womb like hot lava bubbling in the base of a volcano and it traveled into her belly where it expanded and grew hotter. The anger traveled through her heart where she loved it and gave it greater strength, and then it seared through the lumps of fear clogging her throat and came pouring out of her mouth.

As Jean shrieked on and on and on, her face seemed to shapeshift. Her eyes were empty red sockets, and her mouth was contorted like a gargoyle mask. I was witnessing the ancient presence of one of the Furies. I knew now firsthand why those who had been wronged—the Furies, Medusa, the Gorgon, the witches—had been immortalized in legends as the evil ones. The power of a Fury is terrifying. It also seems incredibly beautiful to me. When her shriek was done, Jean's face seemed to shift again, first into the visage of an ancient Seneca Indian woman, then to that of an old Appalachian woman. Both faces registered incredible hardship, but also something much stronger. It wasn't simply the will to survive, but an unalterable, intrinsic knowing: *I Am*. There were no explanations, no apologies, just total acceptance: Life knowing itself and knowing itself to be good. As Jean's shriek of anger led her soul back home, I understood what the poet Keats meant when he said "Truth is Beauty." In expressing the truth that terrifies us, we claim our right to exist in all our terrible beauty and fullness.

Fear

Fear of catastrophe seems to be culturally acceptable. I haven't noticed any shame attached to fear of nuclear holocaust, terrorist attack, violent crime or natural disaster. These threats hang like smog over our collective social awareness. Because they seem so real, so deadly, and so outside our personal control, I think most people walk around with a free-floating sense of unease that depresses our energy level.

Beyond this general fear, most of us have more personal fears. Everyone I know seems to be afraid of something: failure, success, being wrong, confrontation, chaos, intimacy, commitment, abandonment, loneliness, old age or death. Does your worst nightmare show up on that list? Most people don't think about these types of fears actively all the time, but I think they influence our behavior and shape our conversations, and we don't even realize it. The next time you notice yourself righteously attacking someone for the "terrible" thing they've done, ask yourself if that person's actions stirred up fear inside of you.

I passed a house, one wintry day, where a young mother stood on the porch, harshly screaming at two small boys. They had been prancing around, heading home with their puppy and sleds. Her voice was full of angry authority as she shamed them for joining the other children sledding on the street. The boys looked confused by the interruption of their joyful play. As a mother, I understood her fear that they would be hit by a car while sledding on the street, but she never communicated that fear to them, only her demand for control. Fear is often hiding in the underlining of life experiences.

Ron used to get very agitated when our home grew thick with clutter. He would get angry and judgmental, and I would react defensively. In sharing the truth about our feelings, we discovered deeper issues. Ron grew up with an abusive alcoholic father. Neither he nor his parents knew how to control those alcoholic rages. The only part of life that seemed to be controllable was order. The house, even with six children, was always neat and tidy. His father's logging truck was always shiny and in good repair. For Ron, order kept the chaos at bay. Clutter in our home set off a deep-seated fear, for him, that the last line of defense had been crossed, and the deadly enemy "chaos" was about to invade. Underneath my conscious sense of help-lessness, I discovered angry defiance. Nobody was ever going to tell me what to do. Below anger, was fear of being powerless. We were both surprised to find these deeper layers of emotion. After telling the truth to ourselves and to each other, we had the opportunity to make free choices about clutter.

Excitement

You might expect that, of the primary feelings, excitement would be comfortable for everyone. Yet this is not so. "Settle down," parents and teachers say over and over. My friend Bernie remembers how excited he would get, as a small boy, when his father pulled into the driveway each evening. He and his brothers would be jumping up and down, unable to contain their joy. Inevitably, before his father came inside, his mother would walk into the room with the same message each night. "Settle down," she'd scold them. "Your father has had a hard day. He's tired and needs some peace and quiet." If the boys didn't settle down, they would be sent to their room.

A client named Nate, now in his fifties, couldn't seem to maintain enthu-siasm for projects he started. In exploring that pattern, he recalled one of his parents' pet phrases: "Put a lid on it!" Nate reflected sadly, "I could never be a kid around my family."

Childish, unbridled exuberance is threatening to people who have accepted a contained, low level of excitement in their own lives. Children are reminders of what adults have sacrificed. Unfortunately, instead of understanding and releasing their own buried pain, some parents attempt to restrict their children's enthusiasm, so the children will fit into society and be successful.

Children do need to settle down in certain settings, like school, so everyone can participate in the lessons. They need to learn to be considerate of other people's needs for quiet. But balance is also important. Children have high energy and they need plenty of opportunities to express it. Yet, I've noticed that most situations in our society require subdued behavior rather than exuberance. What does that say about our culture's tolerance for healthy excitement?

Joy

People are usually not afraid to express joy; most just don't often feel joyful. Ironically, the inability to feel joy stems from the unwillingness to express sadness and anger. Joy is weighed down by the painful feelings we have hidden away. Expressing all our emotions leaves us free to feel joy. When we refuse to express our true feelings, joy is the first casualty. How can we be genuinely happy when part of us, our feeling nature, is not okay?

Imagine sadness and anger as two big dogs sitting on a little sprite called Joy. If we would let the dogs outside to bark and run sometimes, then Joy could go out as well. But we keep those bad dogs in the cellar of our beings, afraid they might dig up our yard, afraid they'll disturb the neighbors. So the dogs stay locked inside, chewing on our emotional wiring to relieve boredom and even sitting on little Joy, squashing its attempts to find expression. Occasionally we wonder whatever happened to Joy, but don't get up and look for it. Instead we hoist another beer or buy a new dress, pretending that will bring Joy back. We never suspect that the dogs of stuffed emotions have it trapped. We don't even remember putting the dogs in the basement. Only when the chewed wiring causes malfunctions in our bodies do we start to wonder what's wrong inside us. If the wondering leads to making friends with the uncomfortable feelings, then we will finally find Joy again.

I experience joy as a deep delight in being alive that underlies the experiences of the moment, even when they are unpleasant. It feels like an always present bottom layer of my life. But until I learned to express all my feelings and accept life as "the right experience," regardless of how it was showing up, I did not experience joy in this way.

Sexual Attraction

Although feelings of sexual attraction are normal, most people carefully closet these feelings because of shame. Having sexual feelings does not require acting upon them, and yet many people behave as though they are guilty of inappropriate actions just because they have a feeling. At the first Hendricks training Ron and I attended, the opening activity involved telling small-group members something we felt about each other. Ron felt sexually attracted to Kay, another group member, but chose not to express that feeling because he judged it to be inappropriate, or "bad." Instead, he said she had nice eyes. He told me she withdrew, energetically, at that point and, for many days after, avoided eye contact with him. Ron was convinced this was because she had intuited, and condemned, his sexual attraction to her. His self-judgment was so strong, he started having daydreams that mixed sex and violence, fear and shame. Finally, he talked to Kay and discovered her "avoidance" was all in his mind. She seemed to be flattered by the compliment he had given her. The daydreams went away, and Ron felt as though he had learned an important lesson about the difference between a sexual feeling and a sexual action.

It is very natural to experience sexual attraction. The feeling does not force us into action. We can simply enjoy the pleasure of the feeling. If we act upon the feeling in a way that breaches our integrity, then we cause problems for ourselves and others, but this is never an unavoidable outcome of just having a sexual feeling.

We need to control sexual behavior, but if we attempt to repress sexual

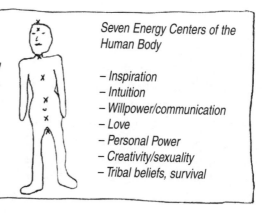

Seven Energy Centers of the Human Body

– Inspiration
– Intuition
– Willpower/communication
– Love
– Personal Power
– Creativity/sexuality
– Tribal beliefs, survival

feelings, fearing their power to control us, we give them more power. Moreover, we repress all the energy connected to the sexual center. The human body has seven major energy centers, called chakras in the Hindu tradition. The second chakra is located in the genital area. Both sexual pro-creativity and general creativity emanate from this chakra. So fearful attitudes toward healthy sexual feelings lead to diminishment of overall creativity.

In addition to feelings of sexual attraction, most people have some shame about sexuality. Shame is a mixture of fear, anger and sadness. We feel ashamed of our sexuality because we are given both subtle and blatant messages that the sexual parts of our bodies are bad. We are shamed for touching and pleasuring our sexual organs. Many people have an added layer of shame because, as children, they were sexually used by someone, usually an older person, who did not respect their innocence or powerlessness.

Gabe was a client of mine who was viciously abused as a boy. For a couple of years, after abuse memories surfaced, he was stuck in feelings of grief and shame. His marriage began to fall apart, yet he remained stuck, unable to change. In hypnosis, arrows of shame came toward him. Despite fearing them, he embraced the arrows and, after doing so, imagined himself dancing in a circle with them. Gabe's face was transformed with rapture, as he accepted himself, through this dance, complete with the feelings of shame.

The acceptance of our sexual selves, even with all the messages of shame we have been given, is a liberating step. With that acceptance, we can find the courage to tell our truths even if we still feel shame. If we don't make this move of acceptance, shame will inhibit us from telling the truth about any feelings in the sexual arena and from asking for what we want sexually.

I have discovered, both by hiding my sexual feelings in earlier relationships out of shame, and by sharing them in my present relationship despite shame, that mixing sex and truth is a powerful aphrodisiac. When Ron and I first got together, we made a commitment to be truthful to each other. It wasn't very long before we were challenged to be truthful in the bedroom.

The Catholic Church, whose doctrines I was raised to believe in, is not known for fostering sexual ecstasy. Bodies and sexuality have been problematic for Catholics, and really, for most devout Christians, ever since the Garden of

Eden, so sexual shame was deeply ingrained in me. In time I was able to overcome most physical inhibitions and thoroughly enjoy lovemaking. However, my sexual freedom was non-verbal. Sex was too shameful for words! Too shy to share fantasies and too skilled at discounting my needs to ask for anything sexually, I had always kept quiet when I made love. If sharing my feelings in everyday situations had been difficult, using words and speaking my whole truth sexually seemed more dangerous than carrying a bottle of nitroglycerin across a high wire!

Ron was also loaded with sexual shame stemming from boyhood sexual abuse, which he brought along into marriage. Ron felt ashamed to kiss his first wife unless the living room blinds were shut. He relaxed with time, but he doesn't feel they ever had a fulfilling sexual relationship together. Because neither of them knew how to ask for pleasure and because they were withholding so many feelings from each other, he believes their sexual energy was sapped of strength. As a result, Ron relied mainly on fantasy and masturbation for sexual satisfaction.

Soon after becoming sexually active, Ron and I were enjoying making love one morning. Shortly before Ron reached orgasm, I got a vague, uncomfortable sense that he had gone away. Feeling abandoned and sad, I had to force my voice out over the lump that had suddenly appeared in my throat and past the logic guard telling me Ron was right here so I must be imagining things. Despite all those deterrents, I stayed true to my inner voice and told him what I was feeling. His reaction surprised me.

Instead of discounting my feelings, Ron said he had something to share about this, but had to work up to it. We headed downtown for breakfast, but he kept turning down side roads. After about twenty minutes of driving around, Ron finally found enough courage to share his side of the morning's experience. He admitted turning, out of habit, to a fantasy of a former girlfriend in order to reach orgasm. That was why I felt him leave.

This was a difficult truth for Ron to share because he wanted to be present mentally, and was ashamed of needing sexual fantasies. He also expected me to react with disgust to his confession. I was not thrilled to be sharing mental space with the old girlfriend, but I was relieved to have my intuition validated. His willingness to share, despite feeling scared and ashamed, drew me closer. Fantasies didn't make him bad in my mind. I just acknowledged that, over time, we could both practice being more present during lovemaking.

Another time, Ron and I were having a "quickie." He was stimulating me, hoping to deliver a quick orgasm, but the intensity of his touch was uncomfortable and I told him so. I didn't think of mentioning what I wanted, just what I didn't want. Ron immediately stopped doing what I didn't want but failed to read my mind about what I did want. He penetrated me quickly and had an orgasm himself. I lay there, feeling neglected, used and angry, wondering whether to share those feelings with him.

Guilt and shame fought for the front seat of my mind. The critical voice was loud. "You knew there was only a short time. How could you expect slow stimulation?" I chided myself (failing to notice that I hadn't asked for it). "If you knew how to come to orgasm more quickly (i.e. do it better/right), you would not be having this problem!" nagged the critic. I wanted to crawl under the covers and go numb. Instead, I honored my pledge to the truth and told Ron what I was feeling.

Ron didn't get caught up in establishing blame but he told me that when I squirmed, the strain of keeping his fingers in place hurt his hand and he felt angry. He was surprised when I explained that the squirming was an attempt to regulate the stimulation at a pleasurable level. By using words, we traded in our "victim chips" for a payoff in new information that would increase our skill at pleasuring one another. Although we might eventually have discovered similar techniques through some sex expert's book, it makes more sense for lovers to be their own sexual authorities, simply by sharing with each other the truth of what they're enjoying or needing in the moment.

Love

Only when we can accept all of our feelings, all the aspects of ourselves, can we really love ourselves. Until we do that, we can't love anybody else. True love of self is very difficult. We all have traits and feelings that we have decided are bad and should be eliminated. We can certainly decide to change habits and behaviors, but we need to be able to love ourselves. Most people are looking for unconditional love, yet nobody seems to get enough of it. I think it's because we're looking in the wrong places. Love is not outside of us. It is the light of our shining essence, the light we see when we take away the filter of judgment and look at ourselves with the accepting eyes of the Magic Child. Once we can do that, self-love will shine outward to others, and we will find it reflected everywhere.

Love that is rooted in healthy self-appreciation has the beloved's welfare at heart. This respectful, generous affection creates space in which the beloved can grow and learn lessons, even difficult ones. This love is patient, realizing we are all works in progress. Such love does not lie down under the angry feet of the beloved, twist its shape to please the beloved, or try to possess and control the beloved. It can walk away from the beloved or be left behind, without resentment. This love is centered and peaceful and knows there is no private good because we are all connected. Love can look at any weakness without hatred and discern the threads of good hidden in the folds of any situation. Love is both the path to, and the payoff for, accepting all your feelings. Love is the most transformative and creative power there is. No wonder so many religions describe their deities as love. The Magic Child, your essence, is love, so this love is natural to you. It resides within you. Look there first, instead of expecting love to show up from an outside source. And when you find the love inside, give it to yourself first.

Accepting my feelings and telling the truth about them has been a major lesson of my life. In the past, I've caused misery for myself and others by hiding the truth, but I'm living in a new way now. I am absolutely committed to acknowledging my feelings, especially to myself, and I strive to be honest with other people as well. Even when uncertain about the full range of what I'm feeling, I tell the truth about what I do know. Then sometimes the deeper truths come creeping out like small children peeking from behind their mother's skirt. The truth I know leads to the truth that is hidden. I may still stumble, but now I'm walking in truth most of the time, and I feel so much more alive.

My husband and I have a more vibrant relationship than I ever knew was on life's menu, because we keep telling the truth. When we slip, and walk around projecting unspoken feelings onto someone else or just feel heavy with the weight of stuffed feelings, before long we realize what we're doing and then speak the truth. This works. Issues and feelings arise regularly, but because we tell the truth as we feel it, we never have blow-ups or periods of long, stony silence. Every act of sharing brings us closer together and keeps us moving in harmony down the road of life.

Telling the truth about your feelings is powerful medicine for life's pains. If you are feeling depressed, if your marriage is stale, if you're stuck in resentment, if you feel good but want to feel better, tune in to your body and start telling the truth about what you're feeling. I am convinced that if you do this the Magic Child will start juicing up your life!

Wondersparks

1. Are there certain emotions you avoid feeling and expressing or which you judge yourself harshly for expressing?
2. Think about a current problem in your life, especially one that seems to be somebody else's fault. What feelings do you have about that situation that you have not expressed?
3. What percentage of life do you rope off in order to avoid certain feelings?

Elixirs for the Mind

Conscious Heart and *Conscious Loving*, by Gay Hendricks, Ph.D., and Kathlyn Hendricks, Ph.D. This couple practice what they preach about truth-telling, and their books are loaded with illuminating personal experiences and client stories.

Hot Monogamy, by Pat Love, Ph.D., and Jo Robinson. This book gives good tips on clear sexual communication, perhaps one of the most challenging truth-telling areas in our culture.

Chapter Eight

*Through playful acceptance,
we can move past self-judgment
and unconscious creation
to loving empowerment.*

Magic Wand
Study the roles you're playing.

Playful Compassion

I once had a dream set in an ancient society, or perhaps in another world, where embedded in everyone's hand there was a red stone. The vibrant color of the stone began to fade as the person's allotted lifetime reached its end. This was the signal for the individual to complete worldly affairs and say good-bye to loved ones. In this dream, I was a woman with many children and a loving husband. While I was still relatively young, my stone lost its color, and I began the process of leave-taking. According to custom, I went into a cave, without food or water, to await death.

Quite some time later, one of my children came to the cave to pay respects to my remains. To her surprise, I was still alive, despite having had nothing to eat or drink in all that time. The only difference was I could no longer speak. My daughter shared all that was happening in her life, all that she was feeling, and I listened. Word soon spread, and my husband and other children began stopping by for visits. No matter what they shared, I listened and loved them. I awoke from the dream in tears, realizing the cave woman represented an energy inside of me, the Magic Child, that has compassionate acceptance for me, too, exactly as I am.

I have so often denied myself that acceptance. I can mentally harass myself for days if I think I have made a bad decision, especially if someone gets angry at me as a result. There are parts of my body, aspects of my personality and limitations of talent that I have long treated like "the wrong experience." I am finally learning the lesson of the merciful cave woman, but it has taken me nearly fifty years to be able to welcome my entire self.

My clients have shown me that self-judgment is a common trait. We all seem to have parts that are harder for us to love than other parts. So many clients make the same request, it almost sounds like a mantra. "I just want to get rid of this part of me," they plead. I think humanity has subconsciously taken all the qualities we find unlovable in our species and collectively agreed that these traits really belong to a monster we call The Devil.

Luanne, a self-critical woman raised in Mississippi and heavily Bible-belted, could find no more to love in humanity than she could in herself. "I can't believe I deserve to be alive," she told me. "There are too many people, and we're ruining our planet. We're all so bad." Luanne could quote lengthy Bible passages but she couldn't imagine a loving God. Having been taught that the devil was rampant in society and responsible for her sinful nature, she turned not to hopes of redemption by God, but rather to despair.

Perhaps Divine qualities of love and forgiveness had been part of her upbringing, but the wrath of Divine judgment was indelibly written into her heart. This negative religious indoctrination was reinforced by parents who focused on their children's shortcomings. Luanne's sister, equally insecure, has attempted suicide repeatedly. Luanne stated once that she understood the relief from pressure that her sister experienced by slashing her wrists. "It's like there's a huge pressure to be perfect pushing from inside me," she said. "Sometimes I think I'll just explode." Luanne's experience may be more extreme than the average person's, but I imagine most of us have felt enough internal criticism to relate to Luanne's feelings on some level.

I once wrote a poem for a friend who couldn't stop focusing on her faults and seemed to attract criticism from those around her instead of appreciation. The intent of the poem was to turn her focus onto her positive qualities, initiating a cycle of self-love.

Winter Rose

So conscious, little rose,
of the thorns that cry your pain.
You fear their sound is all that's visible.
But what of your lavish, pillowing flower
that warm-nestles tired dew,
deep-treasures honeyed gold,
and soft-whispers fragrant music—
all without a touch of thorn?
Those spears are only felt by despoilers.
Your lovers, too gladdened by your gifts,
have no fear of thorns.

For too long, we as a society have been imbibing self-judgment like morning orange juice. We have to learn new ways of thinking and relating if we are ever going to experience peace and joy. I have a vision of transforming the way we look at ourselves. I believe there are no unlovable parts anywhere inside us. Even though some of our attitudes and actions may range from inconsiderate to atrocious, we, as human beings, are still lovable. The tendency to withhold love from ourselves, because our darker parts seem unacceptable, perpetuates a self-hatred that ripples out as negative judgment of others, resentment, and even violence.

The Magic Child's loving light, shining in our hearts, has the power to transform the way we view ourselves and others. A heart full of light is not only totally accepting but also playful. We would all choose to be conscious of our light-filled hearts all the time if we could, but self-judgment blinds us to that inner love light. I have found an alternate route to that loving space which works really well for me. If a light heart is playful, then play can slip us into the light heart. My route is through persona play.

The Masks We Wear

Persona is a term I learned from Gay and Kathlyn Hendricks, but many teachers use this concept. Persona comes from the Latin word for mask. Literally, it means to sound through. In the early days of Greek theater, actors wore huge masks with mouthpieces designed to magnify their voices to the top rows of the theater. Audiences identified the characters by the masks they wore. Like those actors, we go through life hiding our essence behind masks, showing the world the selves we think they will accept, the parts of ourselves we have voted most likely to succeed. We also show the world masks that don't succeed, that cause trouble, that keep people at a "safe" distance. The masks all reveal some of our essence, usually in distorted form, and they all protect us from the pain of rejection. Rainer Maria Rilke has two beautiful poems about our masked lives, contained in his collection called *Book of Hours*.

1.

No one lives his life.
Disguised since childhood,
haphazardly assembled
from voices and fears and little pleasures,
we come of age as masks.
Our true face never speaks.

Somewhere there must be storehouses
where all these lives are laid away
like suits of armor or old carriages
or clothes hanging limply on the walls.

Maybe all paths lead there,
to the repository of unlived things.

2.

And yet, though we strain
against the deadening grip
of daily necessity,
I sense there is this mystery:
All life is being lived.

Who is living it, then?
Is it the things themselves,
or something waiting inside them,
like an unplayed melody in a flute?

Is it the winds blowing over the waters?
Is it the branches that signal to each other?

Is it flowers
interweaving their fragrances
or streets, as they wind through time?
Is it the animals, warmly moving,
or the birds, that suddenly rise up?

Who lives it, then? God, are you the one
who is living life?

We typically adopt these personas at an early age because something about us is unacceptable to those whose love we need. We disown the unacceptable parts and, as poet Robert Bly writes, we stuff them into "the long bag we drag behind us." We then refashion ourselves in what we interpret as a more acceptable form, becoming The Pleaser, The Smart Guy, The Quiet Gentle Soul or The Clown. We might adopt unpleasant personas like The Rebel, The Loner or Raging Bull, that attract negative attention and keep us in control of how close others get. Sometimes we use masks to diminish ourselves, becoming The Dumb Blonde, The Klutz or The Helpless One. We might manipulate others to get them to care for us because we're so incompetent. Sometimes we compensate, through these inferior personas, for the audacity of having other talents. We think the people who matter to us will accept our physical beauty if we're also dumb, or our intelligence if we agree to appear as the absent-minded professor, walking around in a fog. We make deals and don masks to survive in our families and to get whatever love is available. These personas work; we do survive. Unfortunately, over time, we confuse the now familiar personas with essence.

Also, while we are wearing a mask, our view of the world and other people is distorted. Smart Guy sees a world full of dumb people. Super-Competent lives in a world where people are uncooperative or bungling. Righteous, God-Fearing Man is surrounded by sinners. Each persona lives in a world fashioned after its own requirements.

We maintain personas out of unconscious habit and because we get to keep on being right. Everywhere we look our world view is confirmed. "Most people would rather be right than happy," the Hendrickses kept saying during training sessions. They explained that people cling to being right because it gives them a sense of control over their world. The Scholar, for example, may not be happy about being rejected and misunderstood by a world full of shallow people who don't appreciate academic fine points, but he can find comfort in being right. Every interaction with a less intelligent person confirms the accuracy of his world view and reinforces a conviction that his own approach to life is superior. The Scholar, like all our persona parts, longs wistfully for happiness, while clinging to the life preserver of being right that maintains the illusion of control.

The best way to ferret out these personas is to look at the people we're pointing at. Anytime we absolutely know the other person is at fault and we have documentation to prove it, we are in persona. By asking ourselves what we are afraid of because of the terrible things these people are doing, we can unveil the fears that govern our hidden personas and begin to sketch the personas out as fully developed characters.

The persona game gets really interesting within the context of relationships. Invariably, we will find partners with a complementary set of personas. These personas usually represent our disowned selves, the parts we didn't dare to bring forth in the world we grew up in. Relationship expert Dr. Hal Stone believes this process of being attracted to the qualities we have hidden from ourselves is inevitable. He says, "Every disowned self becomes one of God's little heat-seeking missiles." These missiles, of course, like Cupid's arrows, land in the heart of someone who will put "flesh and bones" on the energy we're afraid to express. So, for example, a woman who needs to keep everyone at a distance sees a world full of people wanting to trample on her boundaries. Inevitably she'll partner with someone awash in abandonment issues and accustomed to chasing the aloof individuals who fill the world. This person will require intense closeness. Soon they'll both be working to purge the unacceptable energy from the other while resisting making any changes of their own. The power struggle will continue until they either separate or apply consciousness.

Conscious partners can help each other become whole as they learn to accept the disowned energy being reflected by the partner and also find relief from the tyrannical rule of their own dominant personas. This view of relationship as persona dance applies to all relationships but it shows up most intensely in intimate, committed relationships from which there is no easy escape.

Playing with personas is a wonderfully healing path to wholeness, and it's also fun. Personal growth requires the rich soil of loving acceptance. If we hate the person we are, wallowing in shame over our personas and all the terrible ways they make us act, we will be very unhappy. We'll also remain quite stuck. The persona was put in place to keep us safe, and, like a loyal nursemaid, it will not abandon its post just because we are angry at it. In fact, rejecting an offensive part seems to make it cling more tightly. Only love can get the persona's attention and show it a new way of being. The same is true of the disowned parts that haunt our lives unrelentingly in the form of other people. Dr. Sidra Stone, author of *The Shadow King*, says, "Our disowned selves are like the tar babies that stick to us." Attacking a tar baby imprisons us more strongly. Only love and acceptance can set us free.

As we learn to accept our personas and view them with gentle, indulgent humor, we can move past shame and habitual, fear-based reactions, into choice. Under the radiant sun of love, the persona relaxes and unfolds to reveal its shining essence. This creates a hospitable climate of self-respect for growing new, positive behaviors.

The Secret Lives of Ron and Jane

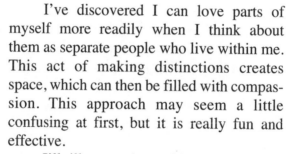

I've discovered I can love parts of myself more readily when I think about them as separate people who live within me. This act of making distinctions creates space, which can then be filled with compassion. This approach may seem a little confusing at first, but it is really fun and effective.

I'll illustrate how this can work by sharing some of the personas Ron and I have identified and how they interact in our lives. I invite you to be curious about your own personas while reading these stories. Certain ones, like the scared child, seem universal, but the nuances vary. Some personas are readily evident to us, while others are carefully hidden.

Resist, if you can, the tendency to see only the personas of your partner in these pages. We are all quick to notice the

weakness of others. One friend read an early version of this chapter, underlined all the parts his wife needed to notice about herself and handed the chapter to her. He was more interested in being right than in investigating the limits to his freedom. The personas of a partner are easier to detect than one's own, so it helps if partners cooperate in the game of persona discovery. However, I encourage you to remember that people's gentle curiosity about themselves is more conducive to change than sharp judgment by another, which usually creates resistance to change.

Please use gentle eyes to examine the aspects of Ron and me that are fearful, unenlightened, politically incorrect victims. We have plenty of foibles you could judge, if you wanted to feel superior. Ron and I certainly used to spend plenty of time condemning ourselves. The purpose of getting to know personas is to have the choice of acting consciously. This is not a choice when unrecognized personas begin exercising control, and the individual doesn't know it's happening. Situations filtered through persona eyes seem very serious, and finger-pointing feels righteous and necessary. Persona awareness gives us tolerance for ourselves and others. In realizing that the persona is not the true self and the persona's world view is subject to debate, we all gain the freedom to laugh compassionately at the caricatures who want to be in control of our lives, and we get clues to the whereabouts of the buried treasures of our disowned selves.

I imagine my personas as a bunch of children, who are funny and frustrating. They get to ride in the car and sometimes sit in the front seat, but they are not allowed to drive. The driver's seat is my conscious mind. The more I'm aware of who is riding in the car and trying to slip into the front seat, the more I am able to keep my hands on the steering wheel of conscious behavior.

Ron and I find that giving the personas individual names helps us to remember they are not our essential selves, and we treat them with the compassion we accord to others. I invite you to enjoy the persona descriptions of Frank, Clyde, Edna, Mildred and the rest.

Frank

When Ron and I first came together, sparks of passion were flying, and sex was great. At the same time that Ron was enjoying himself, shame was crowding him from behind. I explained in the previous chapter how his upbringing primed him to mistrust sexual passion. As a result, Ron had trouble believing that I actually liked sex. His confusion alerted Frank, Ron's persona who works for the FBI. Frank keeps detailed files on anyone who might hurt or betray Ron or those Ron holds dear. Frank suspected me of being a sex maniac, just biding time before the inevitable act of treachery and abandonment.

Frank's suspicions had been aroused early in our relationship by the scent of patchouli oil. I loved its wonderful, sensual fragrance and, not having been in the mainstream during the sixties, had no other associations with it. Frank, however, knew all about patchouli and the women who wore it. They were all drug users who slept with any man that came along. He tried to warn Ron not to get involved with me, but, like many a new lover, Ron ignored incriminating evidence and followed the passions of his heart.

Once Ron and I moved into the same house, Frank clocked quite a bit of overtime. In Frank's world, sex always leads to betrayal, so he hovered around me constantly, looking for proof of infidelity. No one, not even Ron, knew Frank was around.

Three months after moving in together, we did the first Conscious Loving training with the Hendrickses. At the time, Ron had a sore neck. In fact his neck had been sore since the move, but we attributed that to strain from lifting furniture, even though regular chiropractic treatment had provided little relief. During the training, Ron engaged his sore neck in conversation. Kathlyn Hendricks encouraged Ron to exaggerate the pain in his neck by stretching his neck forward and then listening intuitively to what his neck told him. When the neck "spoke," it uncovered agent Frank and revealed the secret mission. Ron realized his neck was stiff because Frank was constantly straining forward, watching for signs of treachery.

Once Frank was out in the open, we began to play with him. Instead of judging Ron for harboring a detective, we accepted Frank as an aspect of Ron who had emerged for healing. When we looked carefully, we saw Frank's essence, which was a beautiful guardian spirit with an intuitive gift of discernment. We also became aware of the open, trusting, sexually free self that Ron had disowned. Both the guardian spirit and the liberated sexual being gained a little elbow room and began to show up more openly in Ron's life, but for awhile, the agent persona continued to monitor my every move, especially those involving men, and turned in complete reports to Ron. Because we viewed Frank as somebody distinct from Ron, we didn't get caught in judgment about whether Ron was too suspicious. Instead, we enjoyed playing the game of having a compulsive FBI agent popping up out of every closet.

Daisy

During the training we also met Daisy, one of my personas. Daisy is the kind of person who sees the best in other people. Because she is so trusting and accepting, people like to be around her. They feel special and shower appreciation and admiration on Daisy in return. Daisy revels in this. She needs constant admiration to feel good about herself, because she doesn't realize that every being is inherently special.

When someone admires Daisy, she gets mesmerized and doesn't notice anything happening around her. She becomes a very poor judge of character, because the admirer's character doesn't matter to her in that moment. All that matters are the words of admiration. This causes problems at times because while loving, accepting Daisy basks in the sun of admiration, sometimes her male admirers misunderstand her reaction. Oftentimes, men interpret messages like "I accept you as you are" and "You make me feel special" to mean "I want you!" That has certainly happened to Daisy. But Daisy stays so busy feeling special that she misses any clues until a man begins to touch her. At that point she's trapped. It's too late to clear up the misunderstanding because then Daisy would risk hurting his feelings. If she did that, he might get angry and then she wouldn't be special anymore.

Daisy has been used and betrayed more than once, by both men and women. Her trusting nature, combined with her addiction to admiration, makes her easy prey for those who think they can benefit from associating with her. Frank had to keep constant watch on Daisy.

These two personas alone could have wrecked our relationship had they remained in the shadows. But in the light of consciousness, everything is different. Whenever Frank turned in a file, Ron told me about it. I reassured him, without resentment or ridicule, and both of us enjoyed a loving chuckle about Frank's paranoia. Ron has made a point of reassuring Daisy, in a very loving way, that she is special. Frank started coaching Daisy about how to pay attention to her environment and to clues people were giving. He even gave her a beeper that goes off whenever someone compliments her. As a result, Daisy has begun to learn how to enjoy appreciation without making her admirer the source of her worth. The enjoyment of positive strokes no longer prevents Daisy from noticing hidden motivations or boundary crossings. She began to discover the power of the disowned energy represented by Frank, and to be more discerning and set boundaries. With Daisy making such progress, Frank could relax considerably. After about six months, Frank couldn't find enough to do, and he left for a satellite office in Kansas. Occasionally we get a fax from him, or he flies home for a routine inspection, but we don't see him much these days.

Edna

So into Ron's persona vacuum came Edna. Ron gave this persona a female identity because it reminds him of his mother. I want to emphasize that Edna is not a carbon copy of Ron's mother. In part, she represents aspects of his mother that Ron has internalized and still has unresolved feelings about. In naming personas, each individual should choose names they personally associate with this energy. The names may be slightly stereotypical and I think that's okay. We're only playing. I recommend avoiding names of real people in your life. For example, if Ron had given Edna his mother's real name, we couldn't have played as easily because we'd be confusing Edna with his mother. This would also be a disservice to his wonderful mother who has many positive qualities in addition to her Edna aspects, which are all based on Ron's perceptions anyway.

Where Frank feeds off sexual energy, Edna uses it as a depressant. Edna tolerates sex because "it's just one of those things you have to put up with when you're married." But sex is really an unpleasant activity for her. Her attitude is "Men do it to you and you have no choice." Foreplay makes Edna very weary. When Edna is around, Ron is not interested in sex. Everything that's wrong in life comes complaining into his mind. If I'm persistent, he'll go through a few lifeless motions, designed to bore me into giving up. Or he'll act like a corpse: "Go ahead, get me excited. I dare you. I'll just lie here waiting and see if you can do it." His third choice is to call upon a third persona, Clyde, who enjoys dominance fantasies. When Clyde shows up, the sex act is brief; Clyde then feels like a real man, and Edna feels relieved because the unpleasantness of sex has ended quickly.

Since sexual energy is the life force, clearly Edna doesn't have much pep in any area. As a result, when Edna is around, work is a drudge and getting out of bed to go to work is an act of martyrdom. To Edna, the children are a noisy irritant and they drain heroic amounts of energy. If I suggest a family outing, I may have trouble communicating with Ron if Edna starts sighing and huffing. Edna prefers to sit on the couch watching TV. Eating isn't enjoyable; she just stuffs food without paying attention to it. Not surprisingly, Edna is overweight. She'd like to be thinner, but she can't seem to lose any weight. It's such hard work. If I suggest a walk and Ron agrees, I often end up dragging Edna along instead. Heavy sighs convey that she never wanted to go in the first place. Edna was more difficult to love than Frank was. Her energy is heavy and exhausting. Also, her anger is buried, so it's more potent.

Although neither of us liked being around Edna much, by accepting her presence and playing with that energy, we discovered that she was driven by shame. We also glimpsed her essence, which, surprisingly, is curiosity. Ron remembered a family outing at a lake when he was three. He wanted to get into the water and play, but his big brothers didn't want to watch him and his mother was busy with a baby, so she tied him to a tree to keep him safe. The family laughed as he struggled against the clutches of the rope. They didn't understand a toddler's need to explore freely. Ron stored this particular incident as a symbolic reminder that it was futile for him to follow his desires. Accordingly, he buried his dreams—angrily.

He recalled other incidents that contributed to the Edna mindset, like when his big brothers pinned him down so the younger brother could beat him up. Ron later got hold of his younger brother, the only safe target, and retaliated. His mother walked in on that scene, and Ron got in trouble for hurting his brother. Internalizing the message that his anger is deadly, he buried that, too.

Hiding his curiosity, dreams and anger, Edna actually is the persona safeguarding Ron's power. We imagine Edna stripping off bathrobe and curlers the way Clark Kent strips off the reporter suit, and underneath would be Ron's powerful essence, radiating light, ready to charge into life like a locomotive!

We're doing pretty well with Edna these days. I recognize her at the first sigh and usually greet her by name. That's almost always enough for Ron to recognize she's slipped in, then he can choose not to let Edna control his response. That freedom of choice is the payoff for playing with personas.

Lily

Before we learned to recognize Ron's Edna, she showed up unannounced and unnoticed. As soon as she arrived, Lily, one of my most tenacious personas, would start accusing Edna of terrorizing her. Only when Lily started crying would we realize something was wrong.

Lily is the helpless little girl inside me. There is very little Lily knows how to do herself, other than suck her thumb. She doesn't try new things because much of life is roped off in the "too scary" pasture. Her feelings are more fragile than dried butterfly wings. Lily doesn't feel very lovable, so even mildly critical comments upset her. "Mean" treatment makes her sob uncontrollably or curl into a fetal ball. If I make a suggestion, or attempt a sexual overture, and Edna is the one who responds, Lily's heart is broken. She quickly finds a corner where she can hide and cry unnoticed. Lily does not have the capacity to ask confidently for what she wants, to insist firmly, or to yell in anger. All she can do is curl up, cry, and hope life goes away soon. When Lily is running my life, I am not at full power and I am seldom able to imagine choices. I never ask for what I need. Lily is me at my most helpless.

Lily is Daisy's twin sister. While Daisy uses all her energy to find the people who think she's special, Lily is on guard against people who reject her and her ideas. Lily's essence is sensitivity, but because she uses that gift solely for self-protection, she's very unhappy. Lily is sure she's wrong, so any of Ron's personas that insist upon a "right" way of being inevitably conflict with her.

Clyde and Reggie

Clyde is Ron's "real man," who knows the one right way to do everything that needs to be done. In his essence, Clyde is an archer who knows how to hit

any mark exactly, but this gift is weakened by the need to control. There is no space or freedom inside Clyde. That receptive, trusting feminine side is disowned. Instead, Clyde is on a mission to save the day. He knows the only way to succeed is to focus all energy on the task at hand and push away diversions. If anyone wants to hang around Clyde, they'd better get with the program. He has no time to waste listening to other people, especially the ones off in "la-la land." He certainly doesn't want anybody, particularly a woman, telling him what to do or how to do it. He's not stupid, after all! If I ask Ron a question about something he's planning to do or make an actual suggestion, Clyde takes offense at my meddling. He hears most remarks as interference. For example, if Clyde is doing the bill paying and I ask a question about our finances or make a request, he will clearly communicate through his disgruntled facial expression, demeaning tone of voice, and irritable gestures that I have disrupted his important business with my "mindless" comment. Clyde uses these non-verbal signals to shame and intimidate me rather than to acknowledge his own anger or openly request what he needs. Clyde's intolerant, blaming attitude crushes poor little Lily, who knows she's wrong, and who cries whenever she's reminded of this "fact."

Reggie, Ron's yuppie persona, always dresses in stylish cotton shirts and polished shoes, and is obsessed with other people's opinions. In essence form, Reggie is a lover of beauty. His persona flaw is a focus on external approval. He was vastly relieved when we finally traded the dilapidated pickup for a BMW, a much more suitable car for someone like Reggie to be seen driving. My appearance, naturally, is also very important to Reggie. He

believes other people evaluate him by whether his wife is neat and attractive. If I dress carelessly, Reggie is displeased, and Lily, ever on guard, knows that once again she's done the wrong thing.

One Saturday, Ron and I were headed to his office to do some cleaning. There was a good chance his boss would show up to help, but I had still chosen clothes to withstand both cobwebs and cleansers. As we drove along, Lily noticed Reggie staring at her. She thought his lip was slightly curled. Because Lily is an excellent mind reader, she could tell Reggie was displeased with her clothing choice. When confronted by her, Reggie admitted the truth. He told her she embarrassed him and that he wanted his wife to look perfect all the time. Well, Lily couldn't handle the criticism and started to cry. She knew she could never be good enough for Reggie since her appearance was hopelessly flawed. Lily's sorrow and despair over shortcomings hide her anger. The anger is expressed through a different persona: Cynthia.

Mildred and Cynthia

Mildred and Cynthia are actually a split personality, and it's the two of them who end up doing all the work. The difference between them is in attitude. Mildred, who in her essence knows how to create a home, in persona gets stuck with all the drudgery, like housework, that nobody else wants to do. Mildred believes she has to be responsible if nobody else will, because the task has to be done. Like Cinderella, she has no time to rest and take care of her own needs. Her self-centered, self-nurturing aspects have been in exile for a long time. As a result, Mildred's work is joyless, and she constantly feels exhausted and unappreciated. Mildred represses anger and resentment. When she can no longer repress it, she flips into Cynthia who is angry most of the time.

Cynthia is super-competent and energetic, an asset to any organization. Unfortunately, her own competence overshadows the performance of everybody else, so she can't possibly delegate a single job. She's irritated that nobody offers to help, but doesn't wonder why. She knows other people are lazy and incompetent. Occasionally, she has had to supervise somebody else's work and always had to monitor it carefully and correct all the mistakes. Cynthia is very helpful, but seldom slows down to ask if anybody even wants help. What would they know anyhow? Cynthia is in charge.

Her anger is expressed the way a tennis player spikes the ball. Using her mental superiority, Cynthia verbally slams opponents into the ground with quick shaming retorts. They are left speechless. Cynthia knows how to put someone in their place! She reserves her most stunning slams for occasions when Ron's various personas criticize her choices or performance, which she perceives as insults to her intelligence and, therefore, attacks on her self-worth.

Persona Profile

Jane:

Daisy is trusting and sees the good in everyone; she looks for approval because she doesn't know she is innately special.

Lily has a beautiful, sensitive spirit, but uses her sensitivity to find rejection. Unable to ask for what she wants or voice anger, she can only cry.

Mildred creates a home, but because she doesn't consider her own needs or expect help, she does all the work and exhausts herself. She is a martyr.

Cynthia is a ball of fire who can do anything. Her weakness is believing that her skills and accomplishment are her only assets. She is angry because she tries too hard. If only she could relax and trust she could just shine.

Ron:

Frank is a guardian who detects dishonesty. Afraid of being hurt, he cannot trust anyone.

Edna is curiosity turned to despair. She has given up on life so everything seems too hard.

Reggie is a lover of beauty, but he gets caught up in seeking approval. His beauty making is compulsive. He is not free.

Clyde is the archer who knows how to hit any mark. He weakens his power by trying to control everything. He is afraid to trust life and surrender to the flow.

Waltzing Personas

It should be no surprise that Ron's Clyde and my Cynthia hate each other. Cynthia doesn't trust him. She knows he's going to mess up, no matter what he attempts. In her view, he's a brainless rooster strutting around the yard without a clue. Clyde thinks Cynthia is an interfering bitch who steps out of line just by walking through the door. When those two start fighting, it often ends in a persona free-for-all!

A good illustration of this conflict happened during our first year together, the night we decided to put up the Christmas tree. Clyde took over the job immediately. He knew the one right way it had to be done. Then Cynthia butted in, all worried he wouldn't do it right. He clammed up, ignored her suggestions, and started stomping around. Lily realized Clyde was not willing to treat her as an equal partner and that she'd never be good enough, so she started crying.

A few years later, wallpapering was another big challenge. Since I didn't have much experience applying wallpaper Cynthia stayed out of the way. Clyde insisted on being in charge and wouldn't let anybody else help. When Lily made the mistake of trying, he told her to stop. Poor Lily was in tears again.

You may wonder how a marriage can survive so many conflicting personas. If we were living unconsciously, then I think we'd be struggling by now. But awareness, and loving acceptance, is a miracle. We are not on a campaign to wipe out any of these personas. We are curious about how they show up in our lives and how they interact with one another. In the Christmas tree episode, we unmasked the personas by sharing our feelings, which led to laughter. By the time we were doing the wallpaper project, we'd been playing with personas for three years. As soon as Lily started crying, Ron called her by name and admitted Clyde was on the job. We play with our personas since they're around anyway because it defuses angry situations, and we can then have fun acting them out. It's like being in a play where you can improvise the script.

Simple awareness of the personas opens the mental door to choice, but theatrics rushes us through the door to the field of delight. When I catch myself being Lily or one of the others, I play with that by taking the persona on as a dramatic role, exaggerating the character's attitudes. Ron does the same with his personas. For example, I would take whatever Lily was crying about and pretend it was even more awful than she had imagined. I would openly bemoan the terrible, unfair situation. I easily imagine the scripts because I've done all this plenty of times before I learned to recognize Lily. The only difference is that I used to take it all very seriously.

When we caricature the personas they don't seem much more serious than any foolish character we encounter in the movies. We laugh at our excesses but also swaddle each persona in a blanket of love. We communicate to one another, and to ourselves, the message that we can show our whole selves and still be lovable. And once we finish dramatizing a particular scene, we are free to step out of persona and consciously choose our responses to any situation.

Who is That Masked Man?

I love watching the changes when I teach this approach to couples I counsel. So often they are caught in righteous blame of each other's behavior. One client, Elizabeth, complained that her husband was dishonest and ridiculously childish. "He claims he doesn't let the dog sleep on the bed, but whenever I'm not home he does. Then he actually admitted he doesn't want to let the dog sleep on the bed when I'm home because he's afraid the dog will like me better." She offered this accusation as just one more proof that living with this man was a hopeless prospect. But when we started exploring personas, we discovered that

Little Petey, an insecure child persona, was the one hogging the dog. Elizabeth had an easier time appreciating her husband when she realized Petey was just an aspect and not her husband's essence.

Another client, Vera, was outraged by her husband's craving for expensive "toys." She described a Reggie-like persona and was appalled to think her husband was really like that. Not only did this guy need a BMW, which she insisted she would never be seen riding in, he boasted that his Rolex watch could operate at 600 feet below sea level even though he didn't dive. Vera thought they had plenty of money, yet he spent long hours working to be able to leave their children a large inheritance, something Vera felt was unnecessary. She believed grown children should "pull themselves up by their own boot-straps." Vera was practically frothing with disapproval for this vain man she had married. When we explored why Vera thought his behavior was so horrible, she discovered a persona of her own.

Farmer Sue grew up on a Midwest farm. People there didn't have money for fancy things, except for a handful of rich folks who flaunted their extravagance and greed. Most folks didn't expect an inheritance because money was so tight. They made their own way and were proud of it. Farmer Sue brought the envy and judgment of her entire farm community down like a mallet on the head of her flashy husband. With this insight came laughter and the freedom to let her husband be. Vera realized her Midwest values were not mandatory guidelines for the whole world.

Ted and Amy were also trapped in the finger-pointing game. He was mean and unavailable; she was selfish and remote. In exploring personas, they encountered some interesting patterns. Whenever Amy asked Ted to show interest in a class she wanted them to take or to discuss certain issues, a persona named Bud butted in. He believed Amy had a secret agenda to entrap him. Feeling extremely pressured, Bud would get angry and start shouting to prevent any further intrusions by Amy into his safety zone.

When I watched Ted express his feelings about this, his movements reminded me of a baby struggling to move through the birth canal. His body suggested to me that he unconsciously interpreted his wife's requests as pressures that might kill him. As I explained in chapter 2, all our experiences are recorded in our bodies. People commonly reenact the trauma of their birth in unconscious ways, perceiving life threatening situations even in minor conflict.

At any rate, whenever Amy made a request, Ted would go into his Bud persona, shouting to cut off all threatening communication, while accusing his wife of being unreasonable and demanding. That would quickly invoke Little Katrina, Amy's Lily-like persona who feels as though she can never do anything right. Katrina is afraid to stand up to Bud because the shouting reminds her of her father's drunken behavior.

Katrina had learned that safety lay in hiding out, so her smoldering anger had to be expressed secretly. That was the job of a persona named Hank. As a teenager, Hank had driven Amy to act out in many rebellious, but sneaky, ways. As an adult, Amy was stuck in a pattern of defiance, behaving like a guerrilla fighter, always hidden, striking from the bushes.

Believing her husband was insensitive and unavailable, Amy avoided him, walling up behind her anger, which gave Ted the impression she was remote and cold. The tender touch and affection he craved seemed completely out of reach. Only when they began to unravel these patterns, did this couple have a real chance of relating to one another from their true essences.

Philip came for counseling because he felt angry all the time. In exploring the issues, we discovered a persona he nicknamed The Grinch. Because Philip was not given much encouragement to express ideas or talents as a boy, The Grinch adopted a belief that he was always being forced to behave in certain limited ways. Naturally, he resented that, but he didn't believe he had the choice of expressing anger. Instead, The Grinch used passive non-compliance instead of outright defiance. Philip carried this behavior to such extreme lengths that if someone said he should see a particular movie, he would definitely never get around to going. Ironically, he thought of himself as a non-conformist. He began to realize that he wasn't leading much of a parade, since he felt compelled to keep backing away from everyone else's insistent ideas into the safety of his quiet, angry, non-compliant corner.

Not surprisingly, Philip's partner, Gail, was someone who believed that nobody ever listened to her. A network marketing agent, she promoted health products with apostolic fervor, disdaining anyone who didn't want her products.

This infuriated The Grinch, who thought she was self-righteous. When Gail tried to share her ideas for healing with him, he retreated sullenly, and she felt even more rejected.

Ted and Amy, Philip and Gail, and any other individuals who are unconscious of their personas are trapped in reactive patterns, following a script written long ago that continues with only minor variations. Because the persona is desperate to be right, we can only be satisfied when the persona gets its way. There is no room for compromise or consciousness.

Persona Power

If we cultivate awareness, we can acknowledge the needs of each of our personas, which is often all we need to do, and then choose how to respond. We can also begin to discover what each persona needs to become whole. We experience a more complete sense of personal power as we learn to address those underlying needs and access the resources of our disowned selves.

I was working on my book at home one rainy day when Ron called and asked for help. Since the trunk of his car was full, he wanted me to pick up the winch from a truck we had recently sold. He asked me to bring a crescent wrench, and take this thing apart so it would fit in my car.

Now, I was warm, dry and comfortable at home, enjoying my writing and the soothing sound of the rain outside. If I have a disowned mechanical self, she has managed to lock herself up in the basement of my psyche, and throw away the key. She is not coming out during this lifetime, as far as I can tell, and so the idea of heading out into the rain to perform a feat of mechanical derring-do held no allure. Normally, Mildred would have sighed and shouldered the heavy load of responsibility. She would never have expressed any resentment. This time I played with the situation. "Oh, I suppose Mildred could do it," I sighed dramatically. "I can hear you're not craving it," Ron laughed. Because of all our practice, this shorthand communication was enough for us both to understand my feelings. With those feelings expressed, I felt free to choose a response. I ended the phone call without promising to get the winch.

I thought it over, feeling quite free to let Ron handle the job, and yet in the end, decided to do it as a loving act. So Mildred did do the job, but this time she did it with love and energy, instead of repressed resentment and weariness, which is what she needs to learn to be whole. Because I spoke up, Ron didn't take Mildred for granted, the way she expects people to. Instead, he was very appreciative and even showed up at the car lot to take care of the mechanics and the lifting. All I had to provide was the trunk.

Persona play is fun. One night, Ron and I were lying in bed talking. Edna managed to creep in, and Ron's thoughts turned to worry about work. As we explored his concerns, I noticed Edna wandering around in her bathrobe, bemoaning her failure to save the day, telling anyone who would listen just how hard this situation was. She rejected comments designed to offer perspective.

Once I realized wallowing was more important to Edna than feeling good, I started playing. Remember, in persona, situations are always very serious. So I mockingly took on a serious tone, and exaggerated just how terrible it all was, suggesting we needed to hold a wake. I had trouble keeping a straight face and kept laughing at Ron's Edna stance. He accepted the teasing and joined in the play. He stayed in character, intentionally playing Edna, who was relieved that I saw the situation clearly now and realized she was right. Ron laughed about how Edna wanted to be right more than she wanted to be happy. Once a persona is unmasked, the seriousness vanishes.

Our conversation then turned to a movie we had just seen, and Ron made a comment about a firm bottom being desirable in a woman. Since he had been teasing me earlier that evening about my own bottom being less firm than it used to be, Lily squeezed between us immediately and began to sob. She cried about how hard it was for her to lose weight even though she'd tried, and how unfair it is that our culture places such a premium on model's bodies, and how she might be stuck forever with a too-thick, middle-aged body. Ron held me comfortingly while Lily sobbed for at least two minutes. Then suddenly I realized we were attending another wake, and we both exploded with laughter. The terrible sadness of moments before was completely gone.

Persona awareness does not mean that someday the personas will all go away and we'll never again have unreasonable feelings. Feelings, by definition, have nothing to do with reason. Feelings will arise throughout our lives. What changes, with awareness, is the length of time we're stuck with the very serious persona's feelings.

With the freedom to feel, experience awareness, and let go of the feeling, comes delight-filled play and deep joy. From joy, we can more easily love ourselves, even with all those personas. In loving a persona, instead of shaming it, we can discover the jewel of essence hidden inside each one and have the freedom to act from that essence instead of from persona. Love unmasks essence. It is truly the greatest power.

Masks of Evil

How powerful is this playful love? Is it even stronger than evil? The battle between the good and evil within us has raged at least as long as there have been human beings, and perhaps longer. Greek mythology records the battle of the Titans, which predates humanity; the Norse gods, led by Odin, were destined to face destruction by the forces of evil led by the demon Loki; the Judeo-Christian tradition relates a struggle between good and evil angels. In modern times, we have movies like Star Wars where the Evil Empire threatens The Force. Why do our mythologies all record such battles? Evil has always been around. Though in every society it may be projected onto, or acted out, by only a few individuals or groups, the people on good behavior still suspect themselves of the same capacity.

We probably all fear that horrible aspects of ourselves lurk in the shadowy underworld of our deep unconscious, and if these evil aspects ever came skulking into the light, love would vanish. In fact, we all do have very destructive parts that usually remain hidden. In my opinion, these are the hateful, self-destructive demons, so appalling to the conscious mind they have been confined to the underworld and labeled by the collective unconscious as The Devil—evil incarnate. They are those aspects of ourselves too loathsome to be owned. Yet even they must be owned and accepted. As long as we hate and fear any part of ourselves, there will be war instead of peace. Despite the triumph and destruction portrayed in myth, we cannot destroy evil by fighting it. The Titans, for example, were not destroyed but only confined to Hades, the Underworld. The fallen angels, led by Lucifer, met the same fate. Love is the stronger force because it can encompass evil instead of rejecting it.

One of my clients, a young woman named Kiva, was troubled by a persona that could be violent when aroused. This part of her screamed hatefully at other people, and tore up her apartment in fits of rage. She described this part as a devil. When invited to speak, the persona identified itself as Lucifer. It would be easy to gasp and say Kiva was possessed, but love offers another possibility. Lucifer was enraged about the injustice in Kiva's life, all the heartless people she encountered. When I asked Lucifer what he wanted, he said peace. We discussed alternative ways to create peace. I told Kiva that the name Lucifer came from the Old English word for the morning star; the Latin word for light bringer; and suggested the anger Lucifer expressed was an unhealthy expression of her own power or fire. She realized fire was an integral part of her life force. As Kiva saw Lucifer in a new light, she decided to rename this part Lucy after Santa Lucia, who is honored with processions and crowns of candlelight near Winter Solstice, as a bearer of light. Kiva lost her fear of Lucifer and began to accept Lucy lovingly as an important part of her life. Getting to know our fears diminishes their power over us. Kiva's uncontrollable rages gave way to direct and appropriate expressions of anger.

In 1995, I did some powerful work with Anna Halpern, a seventy-year-old modern dancer who uses movement and art as shaman's tools. The work with Anna brought me face to face with my own inner demons of Vengeance and Self-Blame. We used a process combining art, journaling and dance to confront our monsters. Their faces were horrible to look upon. These are the messages mine spoke through non-dominant journaling.

Vengeance: "There is no end to me, I have no boundaries. You cannot contain me. Do not attempt it. I will kill you and then everyone will see they should have taken better care of you, should have seen who you were while they had the chance!"

Vengeance terrified and appalled me. I realized for the first time how destructive the victim aspect of myself could be. Self-Blame attacked after I realized I had passed the demon of Vengeance down to my daughter.

Self-Blame: "There is no room for error. This is all your fault. Your daughter will pay for your weakness, for your blindness, and there is nothing you can do but watch and feel her hatred, her contempt. She should never have suffered in this way. She is paying for your stupid, blind mistakes. You have no way out of this. It will always be."

I remember feeling shaken for two days after doing that work. But somehow, the facing of my inner demons and the difficult prayer of self-love brought me to a place of deeper peace. Knowing I could contain both the light and the dark and love the whole was a very powerful experience. I don't know if those demons will emerge again one day in the atmosphere of loving acceptance Ron and I have created. I do know if they pay another visit to the surface, we will welcome them.

Persona play allows us to accept even our darkest parts and learn to take back the power we have given them through denial of their existence. When we accept our less conscious parts, we create a hearth where all our personas can come to warm themselves, and perhaps even evolve more consciously. Love is more powerful than evil. Through love we can all grow and learn to accept ourselves as whole. Persona awareness can transform your intimate relationship with a partner, and it can affect every aspect of your life: attitudes at work, interactions with friends, social involvements, and most of all, child-rearing.

Personas: The Next Generation

Children have their own constellations of personas. As Ron and I grew more familiar with our own personas, we began to notice that our children had inherited some prize personas. My youngest daughter, Holly, has a strong dose of my Lily persona.

A sad little girl Holly named Juliet sobs when hurt, mourning everything that's wrong in life, as long as she's already crying. Holly has another Lilyish child she calls Mortimer who lacks confidence to try anything new. Mortimer's idea of risk is selecting an unfamiliar video or trying a new brand of canned pasta.

I think that my older daughter, Rachel, keeps her Lily in the basement because nobody is supposed to know this child cries. But her secret Lily is very needy and seems to motivate many of Rachel's other personas. For example, the persona that holds her anger, a loud-mouthed punk we named Tony, is out to punish the world for Lily's pain. That's why Self-Blame attacked me. Lily is a victim who, if left to fester in darkness long enough, turns into Vengeance. Tony's anger sometimes feels a bit like the hidden rage of Vengeance.

Rachel also has a Queen Mother persona I dubbed Victoria. Born in another age when everyone had servants, Victoria still expects everyone to wait on her. I've actually watched this girl walk through a door she has managed to open, turn to Holly, sitting nearby, and ask her to shut the door. When her sister refused, Victoria was shocked and angry. Perhaps Victoria thinks if she's properly attended to then Lily won't feel so bad. But Victoria never tells the rest of the family we're really being asked to help Lily. Instead she just raises her imperious royal voice and issues the command of the moment. If we dare say no, Tony shows up, the Queen Mother's first knight! We used to resent that part of Rachel and labeled her as a spoiled, demanding child. Now we laugh at the arrogant Queen Mother and acknowledge when she's stepping on the toes of our own personas, such as "Don't-tell-me-what-to-do Clyde," or "I-suppose-I'll-have-to-do-that-too Mildred."

One of the persona stories we've told so often it's become family legend involves Rachel's Little Mary, the drama queen. We had planned to go out to lunch and then to a movie one Sunday. When we were finally ready to go, there was only enough time to go to the one fast food restaurant close to the theater.

Rachel didn't like Bubbaloo's Burgers and Little Mary went into action. When we got to the restaurant, she stayed in the car, wailing. Inside, we ordered a milkshake for her, just in case she joined us. Close to the end of the meal she staggered in like a soggy tissue with feet. The milkshake, of course, was the wrong flavor, and she was not interested in anything else. Moments before we got up to leave, Little Mary decided she had to have some fries. There was no time left so we walked outside, trailed by Little Mary who was choking in dramatic protest.

Before I knew about personas, I would have lost control, gripped by irritation and embarrassment. This time, I enjoyed her show and calmly suggested that if she were going to vomit she do so over the sewer grate so we wouldn't have to clean it up. Then I got in the car and she sullenly followed. Two minutes later, as we passed through the theater's doors, Little Mary had vanished, replaced by a happy young girl eager to watch the movie! Rachel didn't appreciate our identification of Little Mary during her performance, but since then she has been able to refer to it with amusement. Not only has she been able to recognize her tendency to go into that persona (usually not while doing it), but she's spotted other people's Little Marys when they step onto the stage. I hope this playful tool will lead my daughters to consciousness sooner than I made it.

When we introduced the persona concept we didn't know if our children, who were nine and eleven years old, would understand it. Not only have they had fun playing with it, but Holly also shared the idea, in a very coherent way, with one of her friends and his mother! Including the children in persona play has lightened up our family dynamics. They most love to laugh at our foolish personas. On a good day, they'll laugh at their own. The personas the girls themselves have identified are the ones that have made the most impact on them. Holly named all of hers, but Rachel has only signed off on "Little Mary." She wouldn't necessarily agree that she has the other personas. They represent my idea of her more than her reality, but they help me to be more compassionate towards her.

Ultimately, I want to become the compassionate cave woman of my dreams, able to love and accept all the aspects of myself and the other people in my life. That is my wish for you readers as well. I love the feeling of freedom I have gained from persona awareness. I have fun playing in the theater of my own family. I offer this persona outlook to you as a playful tool for conscious living.

Wondersparks

If you want to ferret out your own personas and disowned selves, you need to look at two main areas: qualities you can't stand in others and qualities you long for. You can begin to make a list of these and start to identify your personas and disowned selves. Be patient with yourself if you don't immediately recognize them. They have been incognito for a long time. The following questions may also help illuminate personas.

1.   Is there something in your life you wish you could change but feel you cannot control? Describe your complaint.
2.   If the part of you that feels this way were a character in a novel, how would you describe it?
3.   Make a list of what upsets you when this part of you is in control.
4.   What beliefs does this part hold about the way life is?
5.   How does it require other people to behave in order to confirm this world view?
6.   Is there someone in your life who really irritates this part of you?
7.   Have you known other people like this?
8.   If you were counseling the person you have just described, could you spot any   thinking   limitations?   Are   there choices being overlooked by this person?
9.   What does this person need to be satisfied?
10.   What is the person getting instead of that satisfaction?
11.   Give this persona a name.
12.   What positive essence, quality or gift is at the root of this persona?

Here are sample answers to the questions that can help you to identify a persona:

1.   I wish I didn't have to work so hard all the time, but I don't have a real choice. After a long day at work I come home to a messy house. If I want it clean I either have to do it myself or keep after the kids until they do it.
2.   She's hardworking, considerate, very aware of what needs to be done, super-responsible and exhausted.
3.   Clutter on the kitchen counter; Ron's coffee cups; dirty dishes by the computer; piles of paper in the in-basket; lazy children; lack of appreciation.

4. There is no way to organize the household. It takes more effort to get help from kids than to do it myself. I have to do it all alone. The work must be done.

5. Other people have to be lazy, messy and unappreciative.

6. My kids always irritate this persona and sometimes Ron does, too.

7. No, I didn't have this problem when I lived alone. But I have had roommates who were messy and forced me to choose between cleaning up their mess and leaving it there as an eyesore.

8. I notice this person doesn't consider using anger but seems to be resigned to the way others are. The idea of hiring help also doesn't seem to be on the agenda. Neither does the possibility of ignoring the mess.

9. Appreciation; to know she can ask for help and get it; the ability to ignore a mess and relax.

10. She gets to be a martyr, who works harder than everyone else.

11. Mildred is her name.

12. She has a gift for creating a wonderful home.

This persona tracking can be tricky. Here's another set of questions. Try it from this angle now:

1. Think about a recent argument. What irritated you about the person you were arguing with? List everything you can think of.

2. How would you describe yourself, compared to the way the other person behaved? For example, if he was acting like a four-year-old, were you acting like a much more mature five-year-old? Or if she was acting like a know-it-all, were you acting dumb or maybe defiant?

3. Take these qualities and round them out into a fuller character sketch. Assuming this is a persona, how would you describe its behavior?
4. What irritates this persona?
5. What kind of irritating people show up repeatedly in your life?
6. What does this persona want?
7. If you didn't behave this way, what are you afraid would happen?

Elixirs for the Mind

Centering and the Art of Intimacy and *Conscious Loving*, by Gay Hendricks, Ph.D., and Kathlyn Hendricks, Ph.D. Learn how we project beliefs from our own past onto others, how we get stuck in repeating the past, and suggestions on how to change the pattern.

The Aware Ego, by Hal Stone, Ph.D., and Sidra Stone, Ph.D. This is an audio series: the authors present the idea that a personality may consist of many parts and explain the tool of voice dialogue as a way to communicate between the parts and increase our understanding and acceptance. The Stones offer an extensive collection of tapes and books, full of powerful images and gentle humor that can help you gain an in-depth understanding of this concept.

The Shadow King, by Sidra Stone, Ph.D. Dr. Stone exposes the hidden patriarch concept mothers unconsciously plant inside their daughters' psyches to keep them safe in a man's world. These patriarchs are the ones who keep women "in their place."

Walking Between the Worlds, The Science of Compassion, by Gregg Braden. Braden discusses the way the arrangement of matter (atoms, bacteria, viruses, climate and even other people) surrounding your body is directly linked to the feelings and emotions you experience. He connects the latest scientific research on emotion with ancient sacred texts that assert the critical need for humanity to develop compassion in order to live happily and to access the full extent of inner power.

Chapter Nine

Be quite still and solitary—
the world will freely offer itself up to you.
It has no choice but to roll in ecstasy at your feet.
—Franz Kafka

Magic Wand
If you would be rich, shine your light lavishly!

Living Richly from the Inside Out

King Midas was the character in Greek mythology who personified the human lust for riches. Obsessed with gold, Midas spent his days counting the piles of coin in his coffers. When granted his heart's desire and given the ability to turn everything he touched to gold, he experienced momentary delight before the terrible truth about his gift became clear. No longer could he enjoy the rich juice of a pear dribbling down his throat, for the pear turned to gold before the first bite. Refreshing, life-sustaining water became a memory as each cupful he reached for sparkled solidly in his hand. Worst of all, his precious daughter turned into a golden statue after she surprised him with a heartbreaking embrace.

Although Midas came to curse the gift he had been given, the story of that gift lives on. A person who seems to attract easy, abundant wealth is said to have the Midas touch. Our culture pays homage to such people because, like Midas, we are focused on how much money we have. Enough to pay the bills? Enough to send the children to college? Enough to fly around the world taking lavish vacations?

Many people struggle their whole lives to satisfy needs and desires, never feeling as though they have enough money to do so. Many people who have achieved financial prosperity keep struggling to get more, believing they could lose it all, believing "too much is never enough." This is not a new problem. In the Bible there are more passages referring to money than to any other topic, including love, prayer or heaven.

Prosperity involves much more than money. It is primarily about an attitude rather than possessions. In the United States, the majority of people seem to fear scarcity. The advertising industry encourages us to acquire "stuff" so we can be happy and fulfilled. The credit card industry allows us to live beyond our means, fostering an attitude that we need more than what we have. Besides that, there seems to be a widespread impression that only a small percentage of society is rich and that this will always be the unfair case. Resentment and envy seem more predominant than optimism. The fear-of-scarcity attitude influences more than our beliefs about money. Most of us, believing there is never enough time to do the things we need to do, never make time to do those "extras" that we really want to do, the things that feed our souls.

The fear-of-scarcity attitude applies to love and work as well. Fearing a shortage of love, we struggle to get attention and approval. Many of us believe we aren't lovable enough or worthy enough to have a loving partner, a satisfying job or anything else we want. The average person lacks willpower and fails to follow through on self-promises. Volunteer organizations all seem to be short of helpers as well as funds. We don't have the leisure to love life fully while coming from limitation and focusing on survival. We need to heal this attitude, individually, and ultimately, as a society.

I served on the Board of Trustees for a local spiritual community. During a retreat, Board members were asked to identify the major problem besetting the organization. We decided it was lack of follow-through. We had plenty of good ideas and even made decisions to carry them out, but somehow the implementation didn't happen. The situation felt hopeless because we didn't have enough volunteers to do all the work or enough money to fund our plans. The retreat facilitator asked an important question. She wanted to know how many had followed through on the personal commitments made at the previous retreat. Only a few people raised their hands. Suddenly we understood the connection between lack of personal follow-through and the problems of the organization we served. We also realized that a belief in scarcity and limitation was at the root of this problem.

A belief in the scarcity of time and love are often at the basis of conflicts in couples I counsel. Aja and Steve sat in my office complaining about each other's shortcomings as partners. Aja was angry because Steve left dishes lying around and because he expected her to do the bulk of the childcare. She felt he didn't respect her job because it was only part time. Steve was angry because Aja didn't keep the house as clean as his mother had and because she didn't understand the pressure he was under to meet his job deadlines. He thought Aja should do his share of the housework on all the frequent occasions when his job got hectic. Neither felt appreciated, and both withheld nurturing, each feeling more needy than the other and too deprived to meet the other's needs. They presented a dramatic example of the unhappiness that belief in scarcity causes.

I know firsthand the struggles that scarcity thinking produces. Regardless of how much money I had, I always felt as though there wasn't enough. I could usually pay bills, but I seldom had enough to pay for the goods or opportunities I craved. When I finally decided to heal my attitude toward money, I read many books on the subject and meditated and journaled about it. Through this process, I began to understand the secrets of prosperity. I discovered that these secrets apply to every area of scarcity thinking, not just money.

A Tale of Two Starfish

One spring morning in 1994, I walked along the seashore, thoughts rumbling with the surf, contemplating the likely ending of my first marriage. A beached starfish, about five inches in diameter, lay in my path. Placing it back in the water to see if it was still alive, I detected only the slightest movement. I knew it wouldn't survive and so accepted the starfish as a gift from the sea.

Back at the motel, I drew a picture of the starfish and began writing, listening for the meaning my intuition attributed to finding it.

"Even a little bit of life is so precious that we cling to it, unwilling to let go. But clinging to remnants of life is not the same as being alive. Open your body; open your soul, to life in its fullest expression!"

I was still seeking a way to reinvest my marriage with life and love, but sadly I also realized it was time to let go. From its new home on my meditation altar, the starfish became a graphic reminder, through the pain of the divorce, that I was committed to a life filled with love and passion and would not settle for less.

Two years later, on an early spring morning I was again walking along the seashore, this time meditating on the abundant nature of life and asking to be open to it more fully. Whole sand dollars seemed to line my path. I collected about a dozen; a typical find is two at most. Feeling rich and in sync with life, I turned to retrace the path home. Since this section of beach was already combed, I didn't expect to find any more treasures. Yet a whole starfish lay tossed way up on the beach, seemingly beyond reach of the water. It was the largest starfish I'd ever seen, measuring eleven inches in diameter. The earth seemed to be flinging treasures at me, ready to shower my life with riches if I would just open the door. When I placed the starfish on my altar, the size difference between the two starfish spoke louder than words, of the contrast between the life I had been desperately clinging to earlier and the possibilities available now.

Those two starfish, standing side by side, continue to remind me that life offers so much more than what the fearful parts of us can imagine. When the Magic Child directs our lives, we experience the magic of prosperity that fairy tales describe: the purse that never runs out of coins; the pot that overflows with rice cooked from a single grain; the goose that continues to lay golden eggs. Since the Magic Child is your truest self, you have the power to experience this richness in every aspect of life.

The following list of prosperity secrets may help you as they did me. For maximum value, spend a week meditating upon and practicing each secret and then start over, until the secrets are part of your life.

I have not invented the wisdom I share here. These ancient secrets are not new; they have been recorded throughout history and taught in varying forms. I am indebted to all those who have mastered these secrets and perpetuated the energy of prosperity so the rest of us may learn from them.

Seventeen Secrets of Prosperity

Prosperity Secret #1: Remember That You Are One with God.

We must realize who we are. Belief in separation keeps prosperity just out of our grasp. We are not separate. There is only one energy, which I call God, and it cannot be diced up into little God/big God. There is no measuring of which part or how much of God we, individually, are. God is a seamless energy, manifesting in an infinite diversity of forms: midnight skies crammed with stars; flocks of birds flying through the autumn air; dandelions poking through lawns; noisy children playing in a park. Abundance is an inherent quality of the life force. The evidence of this truth is everywhere in nature. Energy is unlimited and also timeless. Consider the time available to create the Grand Canyon or to develop the life forms we know. Life is not a process of "Quick! Slap it together!" On the other hand, creation can happen in an instant, as we are discovering through quantum physics. A particle suddenly appears where before there was none. The Creative Force is not limited by time. How, as an expression of this abundant, timeless energy, could we be anything less than plentiful?

When we realize that the source of prosperity is within, moving in and out of us as breath, indistinguishable from essence, we can never again believe in scarcity. We are inseparable from this God energy. Only by retreating into the limited self of five-sensory consciousness, can we possibly create the illusion of lack and inability. The physical evidence may suggest there is not enough of whatever we need, causing us to fear. In that moment, we have to discipline ourselves to remember that fear is an acronym for False Evidence Appearing Real. Fear reminds us of the veil of physical illusion obscuring the deeper reality. The shining truth of our indivisible Godness remains, waiting for the moment we choose to be transparent, to reveal ourselves for all the world to adore, to bring our light forth where it has the power to remind others of who they are.

This is a great thought—it is too great for the conscious mind with its positions about separateness to comprehend. We must contemplate this on a deeper level. When aware, through contemplation, of our radiant essence, we can experience life as a rich blessing. The beautiful smiles that light our faces are a manifestation of this radiance shining outward, blessing the world around us. This is the greatest secret of prosperity.

You may wonder, as I did, how this prosperity secret can be true when so many people in our world are starving and seem to have no hope of experiencing abundance. I now believe that these people can also experience abundance, but the group consciousness of impoverishment they have been born into may be too strong to overcome. However, even in that environment, a person can experience abundance. Money is only one expression of wealth. Unfettered by a cultural belief in scarcity, a person might feel rich—in love or beautiful natural surroundings or internal experiences of mystical union. We need to remember more is happening than what our five senses indicate, or we will be trapped, believing in lack instead of abundance.

The idea that we are one with God and therefore necessarily rich always seemed like a good, but unrealistic idea to me until I experienced a physical understanding of my connection with God. It happened while I was doing some breathwork in therapy. I began the session acutely aware of my limitations, especially with regard to money. As I focused on my breath, memories of birth returned to my conscious mind. I experienced the feeling of scarcity, but now the commodity I lacked was air. I had a sense of anesthesia dampening my ability to move forward or to make a connection with my mother. I felt alone, helpless and terrified. Death seemed to be waiting to suck me away. That wave of anguish passed and was replaced by a new sensation.

A warm energy began to swirl through me along with the deep realization that, although I was unable to be born on my own, I was born. I became conscious of the presence of God swirling around and within me. I no longer simply believed. Now I knew I was connected and provided for. The union I felt was too intimate to be separated into God and me. All powerful God was birthing Herself in a form my parents would call Jane.

Prosperity Secret #2: Know That, as All-Powerful God in Form, There Is Nothing You Cannot Create.

Regardless of the culture, creation myths all describe a God force that decides to create and does so. Wouldn't it be strange to imagine God having a desire, an inspired idea, and not knowing how to create it or wondering if it were even possible? There is no hesitation, no fear, no uncertainty about the process of creation. God thinks, "Let there be…" and it is so and it is good. We are inseparable from this God energy. When the Board of Trustees for that spiritual community I was serving began to become aligned individually with Divine creative power, instead of human belief in limitation, the results were dramatic. Personally, and as a group, we felt a powerful energy surging through us and we began making desired changes.

We create by focusing on what we want. Thought is absolutely creative. Unfortunately, unconscious thought is even more creative. We can focus on winning the lottery, but the unconscious thought that we are needy and dependent on the lottery to save us has greater power. We will continue to manifest the need we are unconsciously focusing upon. The pile of bills we focus on will, likewise, continue to expand.

Money is simply an expression of creative energy. We need to be focusing on what we want to create and then listening deep within for the whisperings and promptings of inspired action. We will know what steps we need to take to further our creation by listening with trust.

As we focus on creation we need to imagine ourselves in rich, graphic detail, already experiencing the creation in form. We have to act as if the creation has already been accomplished because, mentally, it has. Confident thoughts seed the material plane. When I plant bulbs and seeds in my garden, I don't worry about whether they will grow. I imagine the garden in spring with colorful flowers everywhere. Spring arrives, and I see the material expression of the seeds planted earlier.

Always, in the creative process, there is a time of faith before the physical manifestation of creative mental efforts is visible. While we heal attitudes about scarcity and deal with the issues we need to confront, we almost inevitably have a time of faith when we affirm abundance while experiencing lack. I remember when, after weeks of contemplating how my Divine connection assured abundance, I was staring at a checkbook register that showed $7.56. I had great difficulty feeling abundant and remembering that this checkbook was not the source or proof of my abundance.

When our faith is being tested by apparent reality, we have only three choices:

1. Accept physical evidence as reality and believe we truly do not have enough. In response, we can affirm scarcity and scale back our living to a "safe" level.

2. Make decisions based on a belief that God will generously provide, but keep worrying, as if the job of providing belonged to us. Worry sabotages God's prosperous intentions.

3. Trust the process completely. We have to proceed with creative plans and affirmations, trusting that whatever physical "juice" we need, like money or helpers, will be in place with perfect timing. We are the forms the Creator chooses to work through on this plane and all God's creations are flowing with juice!

Prosperity Secret #3: Decide to Create.

Often we tell ourselves we don't know what we want when we really mean we don't know if we can have what we want. We need to ignore our fear and decide what it is we really want. Then we need to make a decision to create exactly that. If we postpone deciding to create something like a new house, job, relationship or skill because we don't have the money, experience or confidence, we will surely never have what we want. When we decide we will have it, we begin moving forward, reassuring our fearful selves that it must happen because we are creators, and subconsciously we begin finding ways to bring our creation into form. While the creation is only a wish, there is no need for the resources to appear.

Prosperity Secret #4: Watch Coming Attractions Instead of Reruns.

As long as we focus on what we have already created and use that "physical evidence" of our abilities to predict our potential, our lives will be a long season of monotonous reruns. What we have already accomplished has nothing to do with what we may yet do. It only illustrates the quality of our imagination so far. We need to fashion new images for ourselves and then focus on those, imagining them as already accomplished. If we fix our attention in the new direction, soon, like eagerly awaited coming attractions at the movies, the good we desire will be showing up in our physical lives.

Prosperity Secret #5: If Not in the Flow, Check Who's Running the Show.

There is no need to struggle to achieve abundance because it is a natural attribute of life in all its forms, including the human expression. If efforts to gain life's goods and necessities start to feel painstaking, it's time to see who is making the effort. Struggle is the hallmark of the limited ego self. The ego has to conduct a big campaign so we can be or have whatever we want because the ego doesn't believe we deserve it. The ego believes in a limited universe that is indifferent at best and cruel at worst. Life is never easy for the ego. This doesn't mean we can dispense with effort. We still have to show up and do our part, but we don't have to experience our part as burdensome, unless the ego is controlling us. If the ego has taken charge, it's time to surrender. Let the Magic Child take over. Synchronicity and effortless manifestation are the fruits of surrender.

Prosperity Secret #6: Focus on the Outflow and the Inflow Will Be Automatic.

Instead of focusing all energy on how to get whatever seems to be lacking, the prosperous person meditates on the innate quality of abundance and then thinks about how to express it. When we know that our cup overflows we naturally want to share the gift of plenty. By focusing on our creative talents and looking for ways to make a contribution, we create a natural flow of abundance. As our riches pour forth freely and joyfully in material form, we create an inner space that magnetizes even more material expressions of abundance into our lives.

Prosperity Secret #7: Experience Life through a Grateful Heart.

Like attracts like. When focusing with joy on present good, we vibrate with an energy of overflowing richness and attract more of the same. When we engage in the act of creation, gratitude must follow our mental act of creation even before we see the physical results. Gratitude reinforces faith.

We need to fill our hearts with grateful thanks for all our blessings. Even if life seems to be littered with unpleasant people or experiences, we need to honor these "negatives" as powerful teachers. Gratitude for the lesson they bring, even before we figure out the lesson, not only fosters understanding but also keeps us vibrating with mellow appreciation. A bitter heart can't give heed to gratitude and abundance. We all choose, consciously or unconsciously, our focus, and our lives reflect that choice. If you want to be prosperous, savor and express gratitude for the richness of the time, money, talent and love you are already experiencing, instead of focusing on how it's not enough.

Prosperity Secret #8: Realize That Money Is Energy

Money is only energy, an expression of creative power. If money isn't flowing easily and fully, we probably have erroneous beliefs and attitudes that repel money, such as: Money is the root of all evil; Rich people are greedy and heartless and can't get into heaven; People with money never know who their true friends are; Money makes people sick.

At a lecture I attended, Bob Proctor, a man who has studied and taught the secrets of prosperity all over the world for twenty-five years, helped me put this type of thinking in perspective. "People always say money doesn't make you happy," he said. "That's like saying that you'll never be able to drive downtown in your refrigerator! Money wasn't intended to make people happy anymore than a refrigerator was designed for driving around town. People also say money isn't important to them, but I'd bet their creditors don't share that viewpoint." These negative attitudes about money prevent us from ever having any, so it's important that we recognize our subconscious erroneous ideas. You may think, as I did, that you don't have such negative ideas. However, by closely examining our reactions to experience, sometimes we discover mistaken beliefs at their root.

As I began to heal my money attitudes and attract more financial abundance, I started thinking about how to spend money. Simultaneously, I was outgrowing the compulsion to rescue people and embracing a desire to empower them instead. As I began thinking about using money for luxuries, I came head-to-head with this deep-seated belief: "People who spend money on luxuries are greedy. They should be giving all that money away to the poor." Shame back-washed over me as I convicted myself of selfishness. This belief is shared by many people in society, but that commonality doesn't give it absolute authority. I will never be able to use my creative energy, expressing as money, to fulfill myself as long as I care more about social beliefs than my own creative desires. To be able to enjoy the abundance that is available to all of us as expressions of the Divine, I believe I have to eradicate such thinking from my bodymind.

Some deep-seated beliefs are guaranteed to ward off riches because they convince the believer that money is inherently dangerous and evil. These beliefs are all based on fallacies and generalizations. Money does not make people happy because money is not the source of happiness or abundance. The God energy living within is the source of both. We can sell our lives in one form or another to try to get happiness and abundance from outside ourselves, but we will never feel satisfied. Only when we know that the source of prosperity is within, can we enjoy the outer expression with a satisfied mind.

Prosperity Secret #9: Create Space to Receive New Blessings

We clog the channels of abundance coming toward us by packing around too much "stuff" in the form of unresolved emotions and incomplete agreements. We live in a society that encourages limitless spending and activity without pause. When we clutter our lives with things and activities that are not giving us joy but which we're afraid to let go of, we prevent the possibility of something better entering our lives. We need to make room for the abundance we are consciously creating as well as the unexpected gifts that will materialize with perfect timing as we learn to trust. This involves clearing out anything we no longer need or use, either by selling it or by giving it away. Giving is an especially fine way to make space. Giving opens the door to life's riches because it is an expression of a life overflowing with abundance. We will feel more rich in time if we make space for creative stillness, giving away inessential or energy-draining activities, and share our time with someone who needs it. All these steps help us vibrate with the energy of plenty and attract more of the same.

We also need to clear out our emotional space. Many people walk through life carrying an emotional attic, stuffed with old unsettled feelings, especially anger. Over the years, the anger stored inside seems to grow, like a cancer, until there is no room for new blessings. Instead, we attract something with a like vibration, possibly the disease of cancer, possibly more experiences to resent. The antidote is forgiveness. As we forgive those we've been resenting and ask forgiveness for our part, conscious or unconscious, in the misunderstanding or injustice, we create emotional space. We lighten our life and create an emotional atmosphere hospitable to new gifts.

We all have times in our lives when we have not done what we promised or what we know we should do, as well as areas where our actions are incongruent with our values. These areas of incompletion hobble the camels bringing God's gifts our way. Perhaps we have long-forgotten debts. There are many reasons people overlook debts. Maybe we've  had a fight with the person who loaned us money. We may have decided the lender doesn't need the money as much as we do or has forgotten the debt. Maybe it seems too difficult to pay the money owed. Perhaps the lender is impersonal like a company, or a government, whose policies and leaders we oppose. None of these excuses changes the truth of owing money. We need to pay debts so we vibrate with an energy of completeness. Debt is like a series of holes in our energy field, through which our life energy leaks out, attracting even more debt into the vacuum.

Maybe the incompleteness in our lives is not about money but about time or willpower. Like the Board members in my spiritual community, maybe you have made promises to yourself or someone else and have not kept them because you just don't have time or can't muster up enough willpower. If we are failing to live according to our values, or are not doing what we agree to do, we radiate an energy of weakness. We need to live as the powerful creators we are by carrying out our agreements, or changing them. This is true whether the promises we make are to other people or to ourselves. Often we overlook the importance of promises made to ourselves. We promise to stop eating chocolate, or to start to exercise or meditate daily, and then we don't. We think we're only hurting ourselves by breaking these pledges but fail to understand the ramifications of self-injury. This was the lesson the Board of Trustees learned when we realized our personal lack of follow-through was being magnified in the spiritual community in the form of too few volunteers to implement our Board plans. By breaking promises we make to ourselves, we radiate an energy of limitation and weakness that has a ripple effect that keeps prosperity at bay.

Two other signs of incompleteness are dissatisfying situations that we don't redesign because we're afraid of provoking confrontation, and piles of clutter that drain energy, like standing monuments to our powerlessness. When fear drives us to settle for less than the good we desire and deserve, we align ourselves with limitation and lack instead of power and abundance. If we are creators, we must act like creators. We can acknowledge the fears of our limited consciousness, even while aligning ourselves with Divine whole-i-ness and creative power. This is a consciousness that attracts prosperity.

Prosperity Secret #10: Be Merciful with Yourself

As you take steps to open yourself to abundance, let it be okay for your progress to be halting. We don't expect our children to run marathons the day they begin learning to walk, yet so often we have super-human expectations for ourselves. You want to express your true abundant nature and are doing your best to remove blocks to receiving all the good available to you, yet your life's circumstances document continued struggle and lack. Breathe. Love yourself. We move slowly in this world of form, compared to the speed of our thoughts. Don't torture yourself with shame and impatience. There may be gifts in the slowness of manifesting abundance far more valuable to your soul than prosperity. Life is full of mystery. Trust the guiding presence of the Magic Child.

Intend to manifest your abundant essence in form and examine the outcome with curiosity, patience and trust. Be merciful with yourself.

Prosperity Secret #11: Use Words That Reflect Confident Thoughts

If we talk about how hard things are or what we think we can't afford or how we don't have enough, we vibrate with the energy of lack and struggle and attract more of the same. The truth is we can create everything we want. We build confidence in our God-power by thinking and speaking with the consciousness of God. Most of us are unaware of our negative thinking. We can observe our thoughts by monitoring our language. Start noticing how often you say the words "I can't" or "I hate." We can use language to change thinking by proclaiming instead, "I want," "I can," and "I appreciate." That is the language of a rich and powerful creator.

Prosperity Secret #12: Honor God within and Pay Yourself First

Financial planners and wealthy people agree that the first step to financial freedom is placing ten percent of all income into an investment program for the future. Why doesn't everybody automatically do this? I believe we are conditioned to pay ourselves last: after the bills are paid, after contributions to all the worthy causes have been made, after we have instant gratification, after we have spent nearly all that we have earned. Failure to establish a savings habit reinforces the scarcity habit of spending all that we earn. To be prosperous and enjoy financial freedom, value yourself enough to establish a pattern of setting aside a regular amount of money that is not available to pay out. The same holds true for the resource of one's time. When we allow everyone else's needs to take precedence over our own, we feel undervalued, and resentful, and often angry toward those we love and serve. The prosperous person knows the value of spending time nourishing the self.

Prosperity Secret #13: Exercise Financial Responsibility

Financial responsibility is an area many people avoid, because it just seems difficult and confusing, hopeless and depressing, or mundane and "unspiritual," yet it is a key secret to prosperity. If we want to attract more financial abundance into our lives, we have to know how much we need. This will remain a mystery if we ignore the facts about how much we currently spend and earn, as well as how much is required to meet financial goals. Knowing this information enables us to make spending choices that lead us toward our goals.

Ignoring financial realities is a widespread problem, yet I notice that one segment of society seems particularly inclined to shrug off the burden of finances. Mothers of young children, absorbed in the emotional tasks of mothering, often let husbands take care of the finances. This may seem like a sensible attempt to simplify a life that often feels overwhelming, yet it carries a high price. Because money is the symbol of energy and value in our society, these mothers often feel undervalued.

In turning over control of the family money, women unconsciously feed the social idea that money belongs to the man and it is his to dole out as he sees fit. Often the woman feels grateful for not having to worry about the difficult subject of money, when the children demand so much of her, and so leaves all money matters, including choices of how to spend it, to her partner. This is even more true if she has been socialized to believe that this is a husband's role or right.

In the early years of a marriage, especially when children first arrive, there may not be extra money, so this may not seem like a big problem. Yet regardless of the amount of a resource currently available, both partners need to focus their creative energy on creating and holding a vision of what they want. Spending choices need to be made as a team to support the creative visions of each spouse and the family as a whole. When this doesn't happen, women too often feel disempowered, unable to take control of their own lives, and depressed. They're usually angry but they seldom express it directly. The men, burdened with all the financial responsibility, feel resentful too, but they are more likely to express their anger by tightly controlling the ways they let their wives spend money.

Some women respond to this by retreating energetically from life in general and the marriage in particular. They go through the motions but don't invest their living with any passion. Their "wanting muscles" grow slack from lack of exercise, as recognizing their inner desires becomes a forgotten art. It shouldn't be surprising that women cut off from their own desires aren't very passionate sexually, yet their husbands are usually puzzled by the lack of sexual energy. I don't mean to imply that this is the only reason for passionless marriages, but it is a common one.

Most desires never even make it to the surface of awareness for women with such anesthetized spirits. Any that do emerge are usually rejected by the woman herself. She will dismiss her ideas as unrealistic or say her husband doesn't approve. I have had seriously depressed clients who had trouble getting money for counseling because they couldn't speak convincingly to their husbands about their needs, and they believed they had no voice in the family finances. Both partners comply in loading responsibility for two onto one set of shoulders. They both may think they're winning, but both suffer the consequence of diminished life force.

Not all women respond by completely relinquishing financial power. Some only yield the responsibility. They retain spending power and wield it indiscriminately, passively punishing the husbands they blame for controlling them.

I had that attitude with my first husband. David periodically complained about all the money I was spending, while I mentally ducked, waiting for him to stop lecturing me. My attitude was adolescent: rebellious, blaming, irresponsible and inequitable.

Unaware of my anger, I never realized my husband was controlling because I had handed him all the responsibility. Although he never expressed it until we were getting divorced, David was very angry that I had spent so much money that he had earned, for things important only to me. In his mind, the money he earned was his money and he generously shared it with me.

Another factor here is that mothers are often so focused on their children, sometimes subconsciously identifying with the children, that their own needs, or those of their husband, or the family as a whole, suffer. I could justify any expense as long as it would enrich our children's lives. But when I made decisions without my husband's participation, I deprived him of the opportunity to be a partner in guiding the children's development.

I discovered during the divorce process that my contribution of keeping a home and raising healthy children had marginal worth to my husband, because it had no direct financial value and because he had not participated in the child-rearing choices. I believe if we had created a vision, and worked together right along on how to achieve our goals, the divorce would have been less bitter and there might have been a closer tie between my children and their father.

Men can be just as out of touch with desire as women can, and just as irresponsible in the use of money. The dynamic of unloading financial responsibility is not restricted to young mothers or even to people who have a partner. I encourage you to examine your own attitudes regarding finances, whether you are in partnership or are single.

As one who diligently ducked financial responsibility for years, I want to testify that coming into integrity in this area has made a real difference in my feelings of aliveness. Accepting responsibility for one's life and actions always creates a greater sense of power and freedom and that is what has happened for me financially. I feel as though I have choices now.

There are, and probably always will be, more spending attractions than Ron and I have money to indulge in, so rather than use a standard budget, we prioritize our spending by setting financial goals together. When we focus on goals and contributions that matter to us, spending choices have a natural integrity. They clearly fit, or don't fit, in the whole picture of our chosen focus. Although the childish part of me continues to want to satisfy the whim of the moment and sometimes will sulk if deprived, I am now the authority setting the boundary. My wise self accepts the structure of restraint, and actually feels empowered by it, because I know it is helping us reach our goals. Ron and I know that together we can find a way to realize any goal we choose. Goals we set as recently as six months ago, which seemed outrageous at the time, are actually becoming a reality for us. When we choose not to buy something that beckons like the legendary Sirens, we make that choice because we have some other goal in mind. I feel good about knowing that we're consciously supporting our own financial objectives. I feel so alive financially that I believe any goal is within our eventual reach.

Prosperity Secret #14 : Invest Instead of Borrow

Few people manage to live without debt and few financial advisors even recommend such a practice. Our society is structured in such a way that debt can be prudent, but this is only the case when the debt represents an investment in ourselves. Impulse buying does not normally fall into this category. Because of the ready availability of credit cards, the ease of using them, and high interest rates, most of us pile up debt at rates that astound us when we get the monthly bills. Consider using ten percent, or even twenty percent of your income to pay off your debts each month. If you continue this practice while restraining yourself from habitual spending, you can experience greater financial freedom. When you incur debt to make an investment that will improve the quality of your life and your ability to function successfully, you will find that your ability to attract financial abundance increases as a result, and the repayment of your initial investment will be easier to accomplish.

Prosperity Secret #15: Radiate Richness to Others

Beings who vibrate with abundance naturally send out prosperous thoughts, regardless of whether those to whom they radiate riches will reciprocate or appreciate them. When we talk to, or even think about, other people, we can celebrate their prosperity, even if their consciousness tells them they are poor. Putting forth rich thoughts draws prosperity. When we lump people into categories of rich and poor based on five-sensory evidence, our hearts too easily constrict with envy or guilt. The truth is that the world has plenty for everyone because we are all aspects of the one abundant energy animating all life. Our hearts will remember this truth more easily if we actively envision a world where all people know the richness of their souls and mirror that in physical circumstances.

Prosperity Secret #16: Live on Purpose!

We magnetize riches when radiating harmony with our life's purpose. If we spend all our precious energy doing something that holds no joy, we are not living on purpose. Of course, babies don't arrive with their souls' purposes braceleted onto their ankles. Part of the mystery and adventure of life in form is the discovery of our purpose in being on earth. Often, initial careers are chosen in response to internal "shoulds" or other people's dreams for us. We might be lucky enough to be guided this way toward a soul purpose, but more often that approach leads to a life of dulled resignation. This semi-live state does not draw abundance because it doesn't radiate abundant life. Passion and joy are the guideposts to soul purpose. The very activities that most delight our hearts are the ones the world needs from us. When we are joyous, our spirits will naturally resonate with gratitude and attract greater abundance. We will be filling the world with positive energy.

Prosperity Secret #17: Acknowledge Prosperity's Source, the God Within, by Sharing Your Abundance with Whatever Feeds Your Spirit

The ancient practice of tithing ten percent to the feeder of one's soul is considered by many to be the most important prosperity secret. It sends out that energy of "I have plenty, enough to share" that attracts even more. Catherine Ponder, a New Thought leader and author of many books, declares, "You can't outgive God." When I consider who feeds my soul enough to merit my tithe, I have to focus on whether my soul is being fed. This questioning directs me to care for my soul's nourishment.

There are conflicting views about whether a tithe needs to go to a soul feeder or just to a good cause. However all prosperity teachers seem to agree that, regardless of the beneficiary, the practice of systematic giving radiates abundance and sets in motion the cycle of giving and receiving. The ancient teaching seems to recommend tithing to our soul's feeders, because in so doing we focus on the God-energy that showers upon us, breathes through us, and in essence is one with us. This is the most prosperous thought of all.

A friend of mine made a commitment to start tithing, a practice that had worked well for him in the past, but which he had abandoned over the years. Within two weeks of resuming tithing, he brought in $10,000 worth of new business, $6,000 of which he had already mentally written off as a failed prospect. I had a similar experience. For over a year, my husband and I had been systematically donating what seemed to us like large sums of money, but we weren't tithing ten percent. We committed to do so, and within weeks our accountant notified us that instead of having to pay the large income tax bill we anticipated, we were getting a huge refund!

One of my personal hurdles was tithing when the amount of my income got larger. Obviously, it seems hard to pledge ten percent when you are just scraping by, but committing hundreds or thousands of dollars can seem just as difficult. We all put personal limitations on how much wealth we envision for ourselves and the amount we can imagine giving away is directly connected to those limitations. The best way I have found to expand my personal sense of possibility is to act like one who has more by giving more. I believe Catherine Ponder's statement: I can't outgive God, and neither can you. I encourage you to make a commitment to tithing with the intention to expand into the fullness of possibility that is your Divine heritage. If you do, you will be living richly from the inside out.

Don't stop with tithing money. If time is scarce for you, tithe time to something that feeds your soul. If that something is an organization, volunteer. If it's nature, get involved in an activity like litter patrol or trail maintenance. If you experience a shortage of nurturing, tithe your loving energy. Know that the energy you expend in faith will be amplified and returned to you by the Divine source within.

We are all prosperous in our essence. Instead of looking for the source outside ourselves, we need to look within. As we discover that internal sun of wealth, we will naturally begin to radiate lavish abundance. As we radiate, so shall we attract. "The world will freely offer itself up to us, rolling in ecstasy at our feet." It will have no choice. This is prosperity from the inside out.

Wondersparks

1. How much of your energy do you spend in appreciation versus complaining and criticizing?
2. What promises have you made that you are not keeping? What excuse have you given yourself or others for breaking your agreement?
3. Are there any places where you are out of integrity with your finances, such as old debts that you never repaid or people or companies that you are cheating in some way? Do you help yourself to supplies at work, even though that's not a company perk? Do you freely use copyrighted material without permission? Does your allotted lunch hour often spill over?

4. Are you doing work that makes your soul sing? If not, why not?
5. Do you have dreams wrapped in tissue in the secret corners of your heart? Why aren't you unwrapping them and making them come true?
6. What are you holding onto that is no longer serving you? Stuff? Activities? Resentments? Why? How does that serve you?
7. How financially responsible are you? Do you have any financial goals beyond paying the bills?
8. If you are part of a couple, do both of you set the goals and plan how to achieve them?
9. What feeds your soul? Do you value it enough to support it with your tithe?

Elixirs for the Mind

The Abundance Book, by John Randolph Price. This tiny little book contains a forty-day prosperity program that was helpful for me. By following the author's program, I discovered some of my blocks to prosperity.

Dynamic Laws of Prosperity, by Catherine Ponder. This long-time Unity minister and author of many books on positive thinking combines biblical texts and personal stories to illustrate the laws of prosperity. This thick book is packed with inspiration.

You Were Born Rich, by Bob Proctor. This book is simple to read and inspiring. Proctor draws stories from his long career of helping people achieve abundance to illustrate his approach to wealth. He makes a convincing case that anybody can achieve what they want in life by thinking properly.

Think and Grow Rich and *The Master Key to Riches*, by Napoleon Hill. The mentor of Bob Proctor and many others who have mastered the art of abundance, Hill shares the legacy of Andrew Carnegie with all who care to inherit his proven philosophy of success.

Manifest Your Destiny, by Dr. Wayne Dyer. This well-known author/teacher considers this his most personal book. He believes he was guided, from the inside out, to learn how to manifest. The nine principles in his book were tested in the laboratory of his own life.

The Seven Spiritual Laws of Success and *Creating Affluence*, by Deepak Chopra, M.D. The author is renowned for creating a bridge between Eastern and Western mind. In these simple, readable books, he inspires readers to embrace the natural state of abundance and presents many nuances of wealth consciousness.

Simple Abundance, by Sarah Ban Breathnach. This book, presented as a daily reader, encourages readers (predominantly women) to find abundance in the everyday, through approaches like simplicity and appreciation.

The Nine Steps to Financial Freedom, by Suze Ortman. This well-rounded book explores emotional connections to economic health, gives detailed financial advice on how to protect and grow money, and explains the spiritual basis for wealth.

Creating Abundant Wealth, by Gay Hendricks, Ph.D., and Kathlyn Hendricks, Ph.D. This audio tape, based on a manifestation workshop taught by the authors, guides listeners to adopt principles of abundance.

Your Money or Your Life: Transforming Your Relationship with Money and Achieving Financial Independence, by Joe Dominguez and Vicki Robin. This is a practical, nine-step program for achieving financial independence by reordering priorities and living on less. Even if you want to create more rather than live on less, this is a good tool for getting your spending in balance while you develop an effective prosperity consciousness.

Never Take No for an Answer, by Karen Sheridan. This is the story of Sheridan's life, from her upbringing as a Mormon in Salt Lake City who believed it was her duty to stay home with the children, to her career as a successful professional financier on Wall Street. Currently Sheridan lives in Oregon and specializes in teaching women about finance. Her warmhearted book is filled with stories of conflicts that will seem familiar to many women. The book poses questions and offers exercises that will encourage you to examine your finances. Written for women, this book is also helpful for men who want to understand women's financial concerns.

The Wealthy Barber, by David Chilton. This book on financial planning is told as an easy-to-read story about a finance-savvy barber who teaches his ordinary clients basic commonsense strategies for becoming financially independent.

Unconditional Money, by David Cates. The author describes his personal path from just getting by, financially, to having plenty of money at his disposal and doing the work of his soul. The path includes an apprenticeship with the rich clientele for whom he served as a butler at a deluxe Hawaiian resort. He took advantage of his position to interview people who knew how to attract money. The second part of his path involved being on his own, learning to integrate what he had learned with daily circumstances, and finding the secrets of prosperity from the inside.

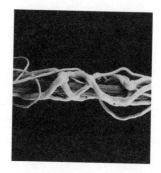

Chapter Ten

*Partners who fail to love us,
in the ways we need,
serve to reveal the parts of ourselves
that we have not yet loved enough.
These partners prod us
toward self-love without limits.*

Magic Wand
Embrace your life as the right experience.
Love yourself just as you are.

The Dance of Intimacy

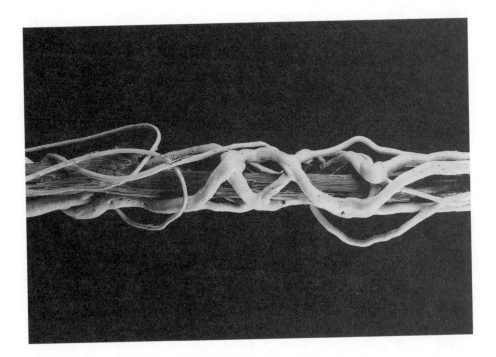

Our human hearts are tugged in two directions. The illusion that we are separate entities, with precious dreams others can destroy, draws us away from others, especially those we love the most. A strong desire for union, to experience oneness with all life, pulls us toward intimacy with others. One of our life stories, then, is the tale of this tug-of-heart.

I once had a dream in which two babies were sitting side by side. Growing out of the crown of each baby's head was a beautiful flower. The flowers leaned together, wrapping around each other, engaged in an energetic dance. The babies were in rapture. "No wonder babies always smile when around other babies," I said

aloud in the dream. "They haven't yet forgotten their connection." The Magic Child intuitively remembers the feeling of oneness with God and all of life and perceives the streams of glory that trail from our energetic bodies, dancing in ecstasy with the energy streams radiating out from all other living beings.

Most of us forget that connection, and our lives become an exploration of separation and a search for intimacy. The conviction that we are separate grows in us as we receive various wounds in childhood. Feeling disconnected from life, we begin to adopt false beliefs about ourselves. For example, we decide we are bad, unlovable, incapable of accomplishing our dreams, or not good enough in general. We then spend the rest of our lives unconsciously proving these beliefs true, while longing to discover they are false.

The beliefs that we hold about ourselves show up on the canvas of our lives, in the form of other people. Humans all hold the dream of true love and perfect intimacy, sometimes hidden deep inside the heart, sometimes preoccupying our thoughts. Yet the dream eludes us as long as we reject any part of ourselves. When we cast out an unwelcome quality or memory, it takes on flesh and bones and shows up in our lives to offer us a taste of our own attitudes. The purpose of this mirroring is not to punish, but to illuminate the places in our hearts where love's flow has been blocked by the belief in separation. Partners who fail to love us, in the ways we need, serve to reveal the parts of ourselves that we have not yet loved enough. These partners prod us toward self-love without limits.

Self-rejection always shows up, in some form, as disconnection and limitations on the love we receive. Examining life's frustrations through this lens can be very rewarding, but I caution you not to use this lens indiscriminately in an effort to explain away all the mysteries of suffering. Pain may be a reflection of the beliefs of the collective unconscious or some deeply subconscious business of our souls. I believe we abuse ourselves and others when, faced with the unexplainable, and feeling helpless, we accuse suffering people of causing their pain through lack of self-love or enlightenment.

We are all attempting to wake the slumbering Magic Child inside our hearts before finishing the earth game. When the Magic Child begins to stir and wake, our conscious minds remember that we are all connected and life is seamless energy. The rest of life becomes an examination of the ways we trap ourselves in the veil of illusion and an exploration of the possibilities available when we are consciously connected. The path of relationship is divinely designed to facilitate such learning.

When Phoenix and Gemma first arrived in my office, they were ready for a divorce. These high-school sweethearts felt alienated from each other after ten years of marriage and agreed that Phoenix was responsible for the difficulties between them. Apparently he just didn't love Gemma anymore, though he couldn't say why. His lack of love showed up whenever she got sick. She had undergone numerous medical treatments involving complications or misdiagnoses. The doctors' treatments sounded abusive as she described them. In the aftermath of these treatments, she was physically frail and needed her husband's help. Instead of offering nurturing care, he would get angry that she was interfering with his plans and leave her to tend to herself while he went to play golf. Furious at this repeated abandonment, Gemma was convinced that he was incapable of intimacy. She said she had lost all feelings for him and was unwilling to work on the marriage. He wanted to change and save the marriage, but felt hopeless about the prospects of success. Although they weren't able to commit to the relationship, both were interested in understanding their own behavior so they wouldn't create a similar disappointment in any future relationship.

As therapy progressed, both were surprised to learn that they shared a deep-seated fear of intimacy. Gemma had grown up in a violent home, where there was no safety. She distrusted men and was uncomfortable letting anyone close. Her initial attraction to Phoenix was based on all the space he was willing to give her because he had his own interests. He wasn't controlling like her father. Phoenix was abandoned by his dad in early childhood and raised by a mother who lived with one abusive man after another. He was raped by a stranger when very young, a fact he had never disclosed because he was so ashamed. Phoenix believed that the world was an unsafe place, devoid of tenderness, and that his only chance for survival was to wall himself off from other people. In the process, he had separated from himself as well. When he shared the story of his rape, I suggested he embrace his childhood self in his imagination, but he could not do that. Any kind of intimacy terrified him.

Gemma and Phoenix both needed to face their childhood fears, learn how to open their hearts to the child within, and become the source of safety for that child before either of them could learn to trust another person. By examining the conflict between them with curiosity instead of blame, this couple found insight into the unloved places within themselves.

Clients Kirk and Leah, a married couple in their late thirties, had a troubled relationship since the birth of their little girl three years earlier. Both had remote, unaffectionate mothers and highly critical fathers. With the added pressure of a child's demands, each felt so desperate for nurturing that neither had been able to support the other with tenderness and affection. Leah, convinced Kirk didn't approve of her, was afraid of making him angry and angered by his rejection of her. She felt particularly inadequate physically, described herself as a wimp and was sure Kirk despised her for that because he was a superb athlete. Kirk wanted to act in loving ways, but Leah's faults, and his own, were all he seemed to notice. She seemed whiny and unsympathetic. His fantasy woman would understand, even share, his desire for adventure and would support his efforts to be successful by nurturing and helping when business got hectic. The fantasy woman would offer unconditional love and support even though Kirk believes he is unlovable and too mediocre to ever succeed completely.

Both Kirk and Leah are struggling to overcome a belief, planted by their parents, that nobody would want to get close to them because they are inferior. They had an interesting breakthrough one day, realizing that each of them had reinforced this belief at a later point in childhood. As Leah focused on her fear of Kirk and feelings of inadequacy, she returned in memory to the third grade. Leah was a smart girl growing up in the deep South, where she learned to make up for the handicap of being a female with brains, by walking around in a fog. Tall and stringy at that age, she was called "Beanpole" by the other children. Leah sobbed, recalling their taunts. She remembered being put into a new class where she had no friends and how she was always picked last for every team.

Kirk surprised her by sharing that he had also been a reject in third grade. Although tall and large, he wasn't strong and was also the last pick for teams. Even worse, to him, the kids all knew he was stupid. Early in the year his mother took him out of class to be tested by the special education department. "They wanted to find out what was wrong with me," he said, "but they couldn't find it so they just sent me back to class. All the kids knew what had happened. They knew I was retarded." Although he hadn't been aware of trying to prove he was smart enough until later in his life, he realized now that this insecurity got a firm hold in third grade. Their wounds around intelligence interlocked perfectly. She was still bad for being smart, and he could never be smart enough.

Kirk and Leah were able to realize what a strong filter of disapproval they both had. For the other to be able to penetrate that filter and show up as loving and supportive would have been tantamount to cutting through Sleeping Beauty's enchanted forest. They were able to look lovingly into each other's eyes, past the illusion of rejecting third graders and rejecting parents, and begin sharing with each other the rich details of their appreciation. It was a very healing moment in their dance back toward intimacy.

Nadine, a fifty-two-year-old client, was uncomfortable around people she didn't know well. Her husband's work involved a certain amount of socializing, and he wanted her to accompany him. When we explored her discomfort through hypnosis, she revisited key incidents of sexual abuse, which had begun when she was only three. Reliving these moments, Nadine was distressed because she was so bad. Embedded inside these unhappy memories was unrelenting self-blame. As we reviewed the circumstances, Nadine conceded that maybe the three-year-old was not to blame because her trusted, beloved brother had claimed his touch was loving, but she refused forgiveness because she should have stopped the behavior when she got older.

We continued the journey through each major incident of sexual betrayal, right into adulthood. By the end, Nadine realized that her internalized self-blame kept her from loving herself. She continued to trust others, ignoring intuitive warnings, because outside approval was the only source of love.

Since Nadine was a deeply Christian woman, I asked her to imagine Jesus looking at her with eyes of love. At first she trembled with fear and self-loathing and could not look at Him. Because her belief in His all-accepting love was so strong, she was finally able to see herself with Divine compassion. Nadine reported later that she had never felt so free. Dropping a life's worth of self-censure created a huge new space within her. Nadine stopped worrying about what others thought of her. She loved herself and that was enough. Everything else was gravy!

The experiences of these clients are just examples of the roadblocks to love. We are all exploring separation and intimacy, unconsciously duplicating the patterns we experienced in childhood that convinced us we were separate and inferior. In reflecting on my own life, I realize that my idea of myself has shrunk or expanded depending on whether I felt separate or connected. I've had a lifetime to examine and revise my ideas about the chances for intimacy. Through desire for intimacy, I have created experiences of separation to learn how I was creating the walls myself. In learning to take responsibility for the separation, I am discovering intimacy from the inside out.

Plato told a story about the human "split-aparts." According to this tale, the gods, jealous of the happiness of the first mortals, split them each into two parts, male and female, and then scattered the two halves across the world. Ever since that time, human beings have searched for a soul mate, that ancient, split-apart, missing half. We go through life restlessly, imagining that somewhere outside our daily reality there exists a soul mate, with the power to make us happy. The search for a "split-apart" suggests our longing, not for another person, but for self-intimacy. The first secret to a great relationship is discovering the beloved within.

Mother Nature has thrown a red herring into the search for self-intimacy. That false clue is the hormonal reaction we know as "falling in love." Family therapist Dr. Pat Love, the president of the International Association for Marriage and Family Counselors, is the author of *Hot Monogamy*. She explains how the pituitary gland excretes a peptide called phenylethylamine (PEA), a form of adrenaline. When PEA starts racing through our systems, we have more energy and higher sex drive. We are numb to pain, and no obstacle seems insurmountable. If we are normally agitated, we feel calm. If we are usually depressed, we feel energetic. PEA provides about the greatest altered state available on the planet. The "catch" is that PEA is activated in the presence of the other. We have to be around the other to get the feeling. The other is literally turning us on. Under the effects of this natural drug, we are able to focus totally on the other person, to anticipate a partner's needs and meet them with great joy. Simultaneously, our partner is doing the same for us. We feel as though we have come home at last, and found our soul mate, and together we can do anything.

Another quality of the PEA hormone is that it's intensified by danger and adversity. Remember, it's a form of adrenaline. So people who are having affairs, and have to sneak around and worry about getting caught, experience even greater excitement. People who meet during wartime or other difficult circumstances, or teens whose parents oppose their love, all get an extra boost in their PEA pleasure.

Because life couldn't feel better than when we're riding the high of this hormone, many people rush into marriage. This is Mother Nature's agenda. To preserve the species, we are designed to meet, mate and procreate. Once that is accomplished, the hormone is no longer necessary, and it wears off. The honeymoon is over. This takes somewhere between six weeks to six months on the average, a few years at most. We look at our partners through eyes not glazed by PEA and wonder why they're not trying to make us feel good anymore. Instead of trying to please them, we begin shuffling through our power deck, looking for the card that will make them give us back those good feelings that we think originate in them. As if this change of view weren't daunting enough, our new way of looking shows us the faults in the other person, traits often maddeningly reminiscent of qualities we most hated in parents or former lovers.

The trick at this point is to realize that the other is not the source of either our delight or our misery. We alone are the source. Partners are designed to trigger introspection. They are mirrors of the unloved aspects of ourselves. This is one of the most important secrets to great relationships. The real dance partner is inside.

Our lives are a path to self-intimacy. I'm sure some people can read that sentence and fully digest its meaning. My mind doesn't work that way. I understand truths more readily through examples. For the benefit of those who learn the way I do, I've decided to share the story of my major relationships, to illustrate how life can be a path toward intimacy. I hope you will experience my story like a symphony, made up of motifs and patterns that repeat over and over and over. It is the power of the repetition that finally leads to the climax of awakening. As you read my story, perhaps, like music, it will enter your inner world and help you recognize how relationships and incidents in your life, seemingly isolated examples serving to confirm your separateness from others, have actually been motifs in your own symphonic story. In realizing that, perhaps you will begin to discover personal reasons for feeling separate. These illusory justifications give your life's music its particular texture. My great desire is that as you discover your own patterns, you will recognize yourself as the source of intimacy in your life, in order to enjoy intimacy with your essential self and with the other people dancing through your life.

My story is a journey from self-hatred to self-love, a process of realizing that love is not a product obtained from others, who are separate from and better than me, but a natural outcome of loving myself and my experiences unconditionally. Writing my story has not been an easy task. Reflecting on life through the lens of separation and intimacy, I understand, on a much deeper level, how the pain I have felt and caused in my life came from a belief that I was inferior and separate. I've cried my way through this tale, reliving the pain, knowing nobody else caused me to feel this way, realizing I could have avoided such pain if I had known separation was an illusion. Yet learning this truth is a life task, so I can forgive myself for not knowing sooner and also for not remembering all the time, even now. The great beings who have graced our planet over the centuries, like Buddha and Jesus, are the ones who were so deeply connected to their Divine essence that they experienced loving connection with everyone. They knew separation was illusion. For most of us, this knowing grows slowly.

As I share the story of the relationships that led me to recognize my innate capacity for intimacy, please realize my life has been overflowing with love and delight. I have enjoyed deep love and intimacy in every relationship, even though I have also created separation in each one. There was a time when I had little self-love, but I appreciate the inner strength which held me together and kept me moving on, even at my most lost and helpless. I have always experienced an intimate, though unarticulated, connection with the earth. Despite the haze that obscures childhood memories, I can recall all the flowering plants surrounding every home I ever lived in and all the trees outside my bedroom windows. I have lived in and traveled to very beautiful places on this planet and always felt an intimate, non-verbal connection with the living earth energy.

If, in this recounting, I seem to understate the fine qualities of my partners or to overlook the sensual, joyful intimacies of my life, please know it is not because positive aspects were missing or unappreciated. The story I tell is not the tale of intimacy enjoyed, but separation perceived. Over and over, I've unconsciously created experiences of separation, and assumed those experiences were mistakes. I needed years of self-examination and a depth of self-love and honesty gained through maturity to understand how I perpetuated the illusion of separation. At this juncture in life, I absolutely know, even if I don't always feel it, that we are all one, and so intimacy is the real truth of existence. I tell my story by way of illustration, not complaint.

I have talked in this book about accepting life in the shape it shows up in, because all experience is the "right experience." When I discovered this idea and made the shift from victim mentality to conscious responsibility, my whole life began to make sense in a way it never had before. I had always resisted life, in protest of the "wrong experience," holding myself apart from life because I believed I was a victim. In taking responsibility, I have discovered that lessons I needed to learn about intimacy and separation were embedded in the exact experiences that came along. Only by sorting through these experiences with a loving heart could I be honest enough to discern their teaching power for me.

A Cold Beginning

I was born in Syracuse, New York, on Christmas Day, 1948, in the middle of a blizzard. Sixteen months later, with the birth of a sibling, the illusion of separation took hold. I remember my mother saying, "You're Mommy's big girl, now. You can help Mommy with the baby." I didn't have words yet to convey my feelings. I didn't want to be a big girl. I was a baby! I wanted that newcomer out of the picture, and certainly didn't want to help take care of him. Jealous, hurt and angry, I felt set aside, separated from my loving mother. Temper tantrums didn't help, so eventually I resigned myself to being a good girl, outside the intimate circle, who, like Cinderella, had to glean whatever scraps of parental attention were left over. The fact that most first children experience this same wound didn't make it easier for me. There were no support groups for dethroned firstborns. Instead, I internalized a classic message of separation, namely, that I had been set aside because I was not good enough.

The next big lesson convinced me I was not just set aside, but completely alone. I formed this belief in response to my mother's death when I was seven. This was the major wound of my life, one I have examined and re-examined from every possible angle, and probably am not yet done with. If life is a school, then this incident and the beliefs I attached to it have been the subject of my thesis. In anger, grief and confusion, I divorced myself from God, my ultimate connection. I hated Him for taking my mother from me. Of course I couldn't admit that aloud, even to myself. When I wrote that letter to my father and scratched out "I hate God," I hid the truth of my angry estrangement. When Dad remarried, I was able to rationalize my mother's death as proof of God's wisdom. He had taken away my mother because she didn't have good enough discipline. In the two years since her death I had exhibited wild and angry behavior, which frustrated the adults in my life. I had projected all their frustration onto my mother. I told myself that she had failed to raise well-behaved children, so God replaced her with a better mother who knew how to make children behave.

My stepmother is a wonderful, loving woman who accepted four traumatized little children, and cherished and guided us like her own, but I eventually realized she wasn't sent in as a substitute for my defective mother. In early adulthood I made peace with God about my mother's death, but the God I reconciled with was still separate. Only in mid-life, did I make the discovery that God was an energy inside and all around me.

On the soul level, I had designed a life where I could learn to create an intimate relationship with myself. I would have to find out that I was good enough just as I am, that value comes from inside, and that I can never be alone. I started this course of learning by convincing myself the opposite was true. In the first seven years of life, the pain of losing my mother, first to a sibling and then to death, created a convincing illusion of my separate and inferior status. My course of learning had begun. How long would it be before I could see through the illusion?

Frenzied Friend Hunt

The next seven years reinforced that illusion. I spent my school years, like Kirk and Leah and so many unpopular children, trying to figure out the secret of making friends. In junior high, typically a low point of self-esteem, I remember poring over teen magazines looking for an answer. "Be yourself," they often suggested. What frustrating advice! I had lost all intimate contact with myself and didn't know who I was or how to be me. I was searching for clear steps to change myself from the wrong person, who never got a higher rating than "okay," to the right person, someone whom people wanted to be around. I was prepared to do almost anything to accomplish that if someone would just specify what to do. There was nothing about me so valuable that I wouldn't discard it to become acceptable and enjoy intimacy. I didn't know yet that a loving relationship with self was a prerequisite for intimacy with others.

I was raised in the Catholic Church by very devout parents and attended Catholic school, so I had plenty of Christian values drilled into me. Despite such well-embedded ethics, in ninth grade I asked my mom if it was okay to shoplift small items from the store. I was hoping two girls I'd gone bowling with might actually become friends but was convinced this would only happen if I were just like them. I was confusing intimacy and sameness. Because they bragged about shoplifting small items, I thought shoplifting would be the price of that friendship and was desperate enough for friends to considering paying that price. Luckily I was also naïve enough to ask my mother, and she was strong enough to give a very clear answer on that ethical point. By standing firm, Mom challenged me to rely on the inner strength she knew I had to get through this difficult time. That challenge was only evident with mature hindsight. At fourteen, I simply obeyed because I was even more afraid of risking parental anger through disobedience than of losing potential friends. Anger felt like deadly separation.

The same year, I decided that learning how to smoke cigarettes was critical, just in case anybody ever offered me one. I never pondered whether I wanted to smoke. Personal preferences were irrelevant. The only question I ever asked myself was whether an activity or behavior would raise or lower my standing in the eyes of others and increase the chance for friendship. Since my father, a chain smoker back then, had made a standing offer to teach us to smoke rather than have us sneak off to learn, I approached him for help.

Dad had one of those long parental heart-to-heart talks with me that night. He talked about the importance of being my own person and marching to my own drumbeat instead of following a crowd. Only now do I realize he was encouraging me to love myself enough to set a course from inside. I didn't love myself, and I wasn't ready to listen to inner guidance, but somehow my father partially got through to me. I think it was the power of his love, his belief that I had value even when I didn't know that, which steadied me and helped me continue until I could find some sense of worth. I never appreciated until writing this how much another's love can steady us through times of weakness. This realization highlights the importance of support systems: family, friends, God.

Smile and the World Smiles with You!

My life got better around the time I was fifteen. I moved to another new school, the seventh one, to begin tenth grade. Finally, I picked up a useful tip from the magazines. They suggested smiling, so I tried it. I walked through the halls smiling at everybody in sight. This technique was really helpful because it led me away from fixating on how alone and inferior I was, and toward connecting with other people and giving them a gift from the heart, a radiant smile. I'll never forget the day in the bathroom that a girl said to me, "Oh, you're the girl who's always smiling." I had a new, acceptable identity. I made more friends than I could count in that school and finally felt relatively happy. Only in later years would I come back to examine, on a much deeper level, the illusion of being acceptable.

The Divine Beckoning

During those years, while I was slavishly pursuing friendship at any price, a desire for intimacy with God wove its way into my life, like a contra refrain. My seventh grade teacher had challenged us to become saints. I remember being inspired to do exactly that, though I don't recall a plan for accomplishing that lofty goal. By the time I was fifteen, I began to sense a call from God to enter a convent, to choose a life where God was more important than any man or family. If you have not been raised in a Catholic environment, this may seem like a bizarre and unnatural choice. But for a Catholic, especially one coming of age in the mid-sixties, convent life was a respected option, a special calling reserved only for a few. For me, it was a way to express a core desire for intimacy through service.

Only in retrospect do I recognize a pattern of desire for intimacy with the Divine. At the time, I believed God was calling me, so I should obey. I was also attracted by the possibility for intimacy with the group of nuns, who had seemed warm, friendly and lighthearted during a weekend recruiting retreat. In their company I felt accepted and welcome, part of the group. I was a generous girl, willing to sacrifice if that's what God wanted, but was too young to appreciate what I was sacrificing. I hadn't had many boyfriends in high school and had no sexual experience. The life I would be giving up through this choice was still the stuff of storybooks and imagination. A long-cherished bridal fantasy was my biggest conscious sacrifice. As the oldest of eight children, I had enough practice baby-sitting to think I already knew everything there was to know about motherhood. I thought any maternal urges could be fulfilled through teaching. So, in the autumn after high school graduation, I entered the convent. It was 1966, and I was seventeen years old.

In the convent I found not only the friendship I so valued, but also an atmosphere of silence, rich with reverence. I was in the company of other women who placed a high value on spiritual growth. This was my first experience of the power of associating with people of like values. College teachers excited me about learning and encouraged me to stretch my mind. Practicing the vow of poverty taught me to simplify my needs. Life felt rich, never lacking. I felt peaceful inside and completely connected.

There was also a vow of obedience, which I accepted without qualms. Not a rebellious teen, I was accustomed to following adult guidelines. This part of the convent experience kept me at a distance from myself because it reinforced a belief that authority for life choices, big and small, comes from an outside source. It took years, and changes within the convent, before I finally began to chafe enough under the authority of the nuns in charge to start paying attention to my inner authority.

Seeds of Change

The convent was, at the very least, an atypical place to be during the tumultuous sixties. While contemporaries were exploring separation from the older generation and intimacy with each other through sex, drugs and rock and roll, I was exploring separation from everyday society and intimacy with God and community. I was out of the political mainstream. The only media exposure, aside from sneaking downstairs to watch the 1968 election returns, was Sunday evening College Bowl shows and an assortment of avant-garde films in English class.

Although the convent was a world apart, it was not a cloister, totally walled off from the world. A passion for social change and a new world order, the hallmark of that era, seeped into the convent world too, and indirectly changed my life dramatically. The year I joined the convent, the outfit the nuns wore was modified for the first time in centuries, to eliminate the heavy starched veil pieces. Within a few years, instead of long voluminous skirts and heavy black tops, we could wear knee-length skirts and vests. Two years after that even the veil was optional. Clothing became a free choice, though for the most part, those choices were fairly dowdy. This was an important issue because a person's clothing has always made a statement. For centuries, the nuns' clothing set these women apart, marking them as off-limits sexually, and reminding people that they were about God's work. The new style expressed a collective desire for a more intimate connection with God's people and the idea that attitude and lifestyle, instead of clothing, were the way to make statements. This was a radical idea, and not universally accepted. Most of the older women and some of the more conservative younger women held tenaciously to the old ways, sure that this new approach was dangerous.

Individual women began to look for a more intimate connection with the world outside the convent. By paying attention to modern society, they discovered needs that nobody was tending and looked for ways to meet those needs. For example, one friend of mine became active in the budding gay rights movement. Others wanted to be involved in helping the poor, whom, as private Catholic school teachers, we had no ordinary contact with. A group of socially aware women among us began to question whether our religious community was living in integrity with the vows we professed, and this self-examination spread through the entire group. If we took a vow of poverty, was it okay that we lived in such comfortable, middle-class homes? Maybe we were separating ourselves by being too materialistic. What about the whole governing structure of the convent? How could people follow the guidance of their hearts and live a vow of obedience? Older, more conservative women were wondering what was happening to the vows they had lived by because the younger nuns didn't accept or respect them in the same way.

Change was in the air. My friends and I spent many evenings talking, like revolutionaries and conspirators, instead of just relaxing, praying and going to bed, as we had in the early days. We were planning how we would save the community and some part of our world. We forgot to give God a role in this endeavor—at least I did. I hadn't yet learned about surrender. We had created a separation between ourselves and those who supported the status quo. We were the ones with the right answers and we could show the others "the way it is."

The convent authorities responded to our ideas by bringing in a consultant who gave us serious training in communication, negotiation, and consensus decision-making. They created a structure for examining and revising the community's basic philosophy and the rules we lived by. We met in small, like-minded groups and drafted documents describing our beliefs. Later we took those to the whole group and negotiated, and from the all individual group documents we made one that everyone could agree upon. I loved the process. I felt intellectually stimulated and excited about this chance to influence my own life and the shape of my community. The process created more intimacy for the whole group.

Ironically, this process that was designed to help us reach a consensus view of who we wanted to be as a group, was also the tool that led to an exodus of about one third of the nuns. I was one of them. I realized that by the time our small group document had been rewritten into a form everyone could accept, it had lost its soul. At the time, I had a much more radical view of who we ought to be. I finally realized I was being directed to follow my own inner voice instead of trying to herd an unwilling group to follow my ideas. I was beginning to learn that authority comes from the inside.

I separated myself from the convent community because it didn't measure up to my idealistic view, but there was another reason. Sexuality had become an issue for me, too. In all the time I was in the convent, sexual feelings were never addressed, except with one directive— "Don't flirt," and a single, personal comment from the nun in charge. She told me she preferred me overweight, because the less attractive I was, the less she would worry about me while I was off at college. Otherwise, we were simply taught how wonderful it was to be a bride of Christ and to devote one's life to God.

Divine intimacy is wonderful, but this approach promoted separation from our bodies by ignoring the existence of natural sexual urges and the desire for human intimacy. At first, this wasn't an issue for me, but in my fourth year of convent life I started going to a public college and interacting with men as well as women. The don't flirt advice didn't really apply, because I'd never learned to flirt consciously anyway. All I knew how to do at that point was to be open and genuinely interested in other people. A trusting person who assumed everyone had good motives and said exactly what they meant, I wasn't watching for hidden agendas. Because I wasn't looking for a boyfriend, it never occurred to me that a man would look at me in anything but a chaste way. I was so naïve. I didn't know how attractive the attitude of sincere caring was. I never actually got involved with anyone, though I remember walking with one man who was holding my hand. The connection felt sweet and romantic and confusing. He told me to decide whether I was a nun or a woman first. I didn't know what he was talking about. The two roles didn't seem mutually exclusive.

I was so busy studying and commuting home to the convent every night that I didn't have much time to get in trouble on campus. I finished those two years without any sexual incidents and started teaching fifth grade in private Catholic school. The only men I was around then were my students' dads, and we were all focused on the students' well-being. My sexual feelings remained dormant.

Moon

Aside from class preparations, I spent my time immersed in the radical discussions described earlier. A stimulating participant in these talks was a newcomer to our group who was about five years younger and different from the rest of us. One of the few people who had entered this convent in the last several years, she clearly reflected the mood and style of the new generation. Instead of a short, frumpy hairstyle, like the rest of us had, she had long, thick dark hair. She wore jeans, work shirts and combat boots. Her appearance and demeanor shouted *rebel*. She called herself Moon.

I was aware of Moon, and her ideas, from the group discussions but I didn't have much contact with her otherwise. Soon after her arrival, I was sent out of town for the summer. When I returned, my only intimate friend, Rita, was spending all her time with Moon. Rita, who suffered from rheumatoid arthritis, was frail of body. Her spirit seemed frailer now as well. She no longer seemed self-assured and outgoing, but fearful and distracted. She left the convent by the end of the year. I felt very sad because I never was able to connect with her during that time. She seemed lost within her problems and absorbed with Moon. She did reach out to me before she left. Our last conversation reminded me of a deathbed scene. She spoke to me and Moon together, and asked us to look out for each other. I wasn't particularly attracted to Moon as a friend, but I agreed to Rita's request. I didn't examine this promise before making it. I was in the habit of being agreeable, not discerning. Still unaware that inner authority requires paying attention to feelings, I automatically cooperated to stay in everyone's good graces.

I began spending time with Moon, but our friendship had a dishonest start. I never told her the truth of my feelings because I never admitted them to myself. Angry and jealous, I blamed her for stealing my best friend. Instead of admitting that, I hung out with Moon and, in the process, grew increasingly fascinated. Funny and irreverent, she was an artist with an unusual, colorful style that impressed me. At the time, I considered myself hopelessly lacking artistic talent. She also seemed very spiritual, with an intellectual edge, and had read everything by Thomas Merton, a popular monk/mystic. I hadn't completely understood even Merton's biography, so her enthusiasm for his more complex works convinced me that she was pretty deep. We had fun together, but I realize now I was attracted to qualities Moon had that I was unwilling to own in myself and only experienced through association with her. Self-intimacy by proxy, a contradiction in terms, is less than satisfying.

Through spending more and more time together and confiding in one another, we became close friends. In those days, a good friend was precious and rare. Though there was general kindness, acceptance, and community, the convent did not foster intimacy between individuals. In fact, "particular friendships" were discouraged.

As Moon and I grew closer, she became more and more important to me. Both my energy and sense of being special increased in her presence. I wanted to share everything with her. I was falling in love with her but didn't realize it because that possibility didn't exist in my conscious mind.

One summer night, my whole life changed. Moon came to visit me at a cabin where I was working as a camp counselor. A full moon poured light through the bedroom window. In this intimate setting, we sat together cuddling and feeling close. Then she kissed me. I was not prepared for this, yet it felt very good. Her kisses and caresses continued and soon we were making love.

My sexual energy had been awakened in a way I never would have imagined. I had never heard of lesbians. I didn't even know people made love to members of the same sex. That wasn't the kind of thing Catholic girls were taught about and, as I mentioned, the nuns had not addressed sexual energy at all in teaching the vow of chastity.

This awakening stirred up many emotions. I felt all the excitement of new love and the pleasures of a first sexual relationship but I also felt the discomfort and fear of being out of integrity. I was experiencing intimacy and separation at once. The delights of closeness with Moon also made me feel separate from God and my beliefs, a condition I thought of as sin. There was no way to justify such a relationship with the vow of chastity, but there also seemed to be no way to control my sexual hunger and stop what I was doing. Adding to this conflict was shame about having sex with a woman. No amount of pleasure could completely distract me from thinking this was the "wrong experience." I didn't want to hurt Moon's feelings by sharing my inner conflicts, and there was nobody else with whom I felt it was safe to confide and explore this experience. Unwilling to tell the truth to anyone, including myself, really, I let sexual passion rule my life and continued a clandestine affair with Moon.

In the fall, she was sent out of state for training. Our passion was fanned by the pain of being apart, the long letters, and joyful excitement on the rare occasions when we found a way to be together. At the end of the year, Moon left the convent. I was distraught over this separation, and felt desolate. Filled with discontent and questioning, I decided that convent life was not for me either. Moon had opened me up sexually and shown me the power of physical and emotional intimacy. I wanted more but wasn't willing to admit that truth publicly. Instead, I hid behind my idealism and righteously rejected the convent community because it didn't reflect my ideals of what a religious community should be. I left the convent in 1975. I was twenty-six years old.

I didn't plan to continue a relationship with Moon. I wanted boyfriends and eventually a husband and family. But when Moon came to visit, I was unable to resist the pleasure of her touch or to tell the truth about my feelings of shame and the desire to end our romance. I was an emotional cripple. The thought of hurting someone's feelings, or, more honestly, making somebody mad, paralyzed me with such fear that I was willing to betray my sexual preference and deceive a lover. I expressed love for her and withheld the truth that I didn't want to be with her. I was creating serious separation, from the inside out. When Moon proposed moving in together, I was too cowardly to say no. I had never said no to other people's needs, only to my own, and this wasn't a situation in which I felt strong enough to start.

Not long after we moved in together, I came close to a nervous breakdown. That was an unforgettable day. I was working in the sales office of a rubber stamp company. While sorting the mail, I started to cry. The tears grew like a tidal wave until they burst the dam of my self-control and forced me to leave work, having no idea what I was crying about. On the way home, the electric rail line broke down very close to a notoriously dangerous housing project. This happened in Boston, in the early, volatile days of desegregation. The crowded train was hot, and I was scared. In my distraught state, violent racial scenes were easy to imagine, especially for someone who had never been around people of other races or social classes. There was no real threat, but it was more appealing to let my imagination run fearfully away than to face what was actually troubling me.

Moon made an appointment for me with a counselor to whom I managed to confess the truth about my sexual involvement with Moon and my feelings of shame. Such a difficult admission! He responded with a variety of Gestalt techniques, like asking me to talk to myself in the opposite chair. Unfamiliar with therapy and unaccustomed to listening to my intuitive voice, I concluded he was a nut! I was clearly not sitting in two different chairs at once and was unable or unwilling to imagine what he was getting at. I thought the whole session was useless. Yet, at the very end, he said something totally perplexing, which I have never forgotten. He said, "You've got to stop saying 'no' to yourself." Had his advice made sense back then, my life might have gone very differently. Instead I continued to deny the truth: to myself, to Moon, to family and friends. I lived with Moon for four more years.

Now I see the harm that resulted from this inability to tell the truth. Moon was a lesbian and needed to be with a lesbian. We had many conflicts over the years because I would decide to date some man, and she would fall into a jealous rage. Because of my discomfort with her anger, I would stop dating, but I never completely understood or anticipated her reaction. She was expecting monogamous behavior, unaware that I didn't want to be with her since I still hadn't told her so. I lived as her partner, but when occasional opportunities to date a man came along, I acted like she was just a roommate, which is what we told everyone. Too cowardly and self-indulgent to admit to her that I didn't want to live as a lesbian, I resorted to a well-honed skill, denial, and continued living as if I were committed. We never discussed commitment or formalized it in any way. I was neither committed nor aware of the importance of commitment, and the safety it provides for two people to grow personally and together.

Lack of commitment was only one of the problems in that relationship. I behaved like a doormat and put Moon on a pedestal. I encouraged all her ideas and worked to help her accomplish all her dreams, but never indulged in dreaming myself. I felt more alive serving someone else. Moon tossed about in one direction and another. No sooner had she finished training to be a potter, than she was ready to try law school. She seldom made anything more than odd-job money while I knew her. We always pooled our money, like a married couple, without holding each other accountable for equal contributions. As a teacher, I had a huge salary compared to what she made, so technically I was supporting her, but I don't remember that as a conscious choice either. Looking back at this period in my life, I am amazed at how willing I was to be unconscious, just to avoid telling the truth and the risk of arousing her anger. Maybe if I had expressed my own needs, Moon would have acted more responsibly. As it was, she didn't need to be. I was only too eager to take responsibility for her life. I was far less willing to be responsible for my own. This backwards urge was the product of desiring intimacy with another while maintaining separation from myself.

It took many years for me to be honest enough to recognize my responsibility in this relationship and to give up the story that I was a helpless player in that scene. The eyes of honesty help me see not only my role, but the way other couples stay trapped in a similar drama, where one person doesn't want to be in the relationship anymore, but remains rather than risk the partner's anger or take a chance on being alone.

Eventually, Moon fell in love with another woman who actively wanted to be with her. I jumped at this chance to escape and freed her magnanimously, without blame or anger, avoiding truthfulness to the end. I can only speculate about what lessons Moon may have learned from our relationship. Since I believe we are here to learn and we are all connected, I trust that her lessons were important enough to compensate for those years of loving someone unwilling to tell the truth. I've lost track of her, but if I had the chance to talk to her again, I would apologize and share the whole truth from my heart.

As for me, the lessons from that experience were rich. Moon introduced me to the delights of sexuality. She helped me leave the convent, which was not my path, but which I might never have been brave enough to separate from on my own. It would be many years before I stepped through the doorway she opened, but Moon showed me the worlds of art, intuition and playfulness. I began learning the importance of telling my truth and dreaming my own dreams, though I had barely opened the book on those lessons. Only in these last years have I identified my lifelong pattern of encouraging others to be all they can be, while ignoring my own feelings and needs. I have often allowed, even urged, people to use me, because I didn't matter to myself. The only self-worth I could find was in pleasing somebody else. I have been so afraid of other people's anger that I could stuff any disappointment or desire rather than risk conflict. I've been like a placenta, placed on earth to nourish others, giving and giving and giving, everything but the truth, to everyone but me. I explored every niche of separation from myself I could find before considering the possibility of self-intimacy.

When Moon left me for the other woman, I felt like a bird out of a cage, so buoyant! It was 1979. At thirty, I had my whole life ahead of me. Temporarily lacking someone to take care of, I let myself follow a dream. Securing a job in another state, I took an exciting summer course in designing and building alternative shelters. I was delighted to be on my own.

Finally, a Man!

I was convinced that Moon's gender had been my only problem and that once the relationship ended, I would be automatically available for all good things life had to offer, particularly a relationship with a man. I was radiating enthusiasm for the possibilities in life, and David was the first "possibility" to show up.

David and I were rooming with the same family in the little town of Bath, Maine. He was working as a volunteer at an institute that made wooden boats, and I was studying at The Shelter Institute. David was excited to be using his hands and working with boats, having been stuck doing studies in a dead-end corner of the engineering world. He had just ended a complicated relationship and wasn't expecting to meet anybody in Maine. When I learned he was an engineer, I asked for help with heat therm calculations that were hopelessly complex to me and trivially simple for him. We digressed shyly from math to life.

I was surprised and pleased that he wanted to spend time with me. Most men I had met since leaving the convent were married teachers. In the four years I spent with Moon, only two or three men ever asked me for a date, and those relationships were always short-lived because of Moon's angry reaction to my infidelity and my unwillingness to be honest about what I wanted. So I had very little experience with men.

Though I had long wanted a heterosexual relationship and had set out with optimism about finding one, deep inside, I had no idea if there was anything about me a man would like. I certainly didn't seem to think I was worth getting to know, ignoring my feelings and desires the way I did. David's interest in me seemed to grace me with a value I didn't possess before he noticed me.

Within days, we were enjoying a passionate summer romance. David told his truth right away: he did not want a relationship. Still unaware of the value of commitment, I only cared about getting attention in the short term. We enjoyed an intimate affair and by summer's end were reluctant to end our relationship. So when David returned to California, I stayed in Maine, and we began a long-distance romance. I soon decided this was definitely love and I wanted more intimacy, or at least the chance to live in the same city. In what I then interpreted as an amazing coincidence, I started losing interest in teaching. Commitment to my job, or even to the teaching profession, complicated my desire to be reunited with David immediately. So, calling on the familiar skill of denial, I convinced myself that I was not just missing my lover and scared that geography would separate us permanently, but was really disenchanted with teaching. I left Maine with a clear conscience and joined David in his new home in Texas.

We planned to live apart, but since I was making a career transition, he invited me to stay with him while I got established. Content with our companionship, we stayed together by default. I never took responsibility for moving out as planned, and he never asked me to leave. We didn't change our agreement either, but instead, continued living an unexamined but pleasant life, never discussing commitments or mutual visions.

I didn't yet know that vision and commitment flow from relationship to oneself. I continued to ignore my feelings and deep desires, such as the unexpressed desire for a husband and family. I probably assumed, without admitting it aloud to myself, that eventually we would get married. Even though David had clearly stated that he wanted companionship without commitment, I didn't really believe him. I was self-centered enough to assume that he would ultimately want the right thing, in other words, what I wanted. Until that happened, I was ready to meet his needs for uncommitted companionship. I was still unconscious, unwilling to examine or take responsibility for my life.

"I'd Cross an Ocean for You!"

We continued in that pattern until David's company sent him to Thailand for three months. At the end of that period, the job was extended for another nine months, and he came home for long enough to announce the news and to invite me to join him. I jumped at the opportunity, leaving a big city with all its diversions, and my job as an engineering recruiter making big bucks for the first time in my life, all for the chance to be with David again, as well as to have a foreign adventure.

Instead of moving to the bustling city of Bangkok, which David didn't like, we settled in a little house in the rural village of Ban Chang, close to his work site, where we lived for two months. We were wakened at six o'clock in the morning every day by the crackling town loudspeaker announcing the daily news and playing haunting, dissonant Thai music. There were four dirt roads in the town, and two destination points: the American diner or the exotic, colorful market. I must have been the only fair-skinned redhead who had ever walked down those dirt roads, because each day when I passed by, everyone, from old ladies to toddlers, stopped moving and stared until I was out of sight.

There wasn't much else to do, until the weaving loom I'd brought was eventually liberated from the customs warehouse. Occasionally I was invited to attend local Buddhist ceremonies and festivals and I was fascinated by the colorful pageantry and ritual. Everyone was friendly, but without a common language, deep conversation was impossible.

Before long, loneliness and boredom set in, so I asked to accompany David on his weekly trips to Bangkok, where there was so much to do. To my surprise, David completely ruled out that possibility, saying simply, "It won't work." This didn't make much sense, but I swallowed my frustration, and accepted his decision. Frustration and boredom were safer than demanding my way and risking annoying David. He was not a violent man and, in fact, had never expressed anger at me, but my fear of disapproval and consequent rejection squelched all risky behavior. He was far more important to me than I was to myself.

After two months we moved to a house in Pattaya, a nearby resort town with boutiques and other interesting places to see, but a sense of purpose and challenge were still missing. Unaccustomed as I was to turning inward, the idea of spending this time in meditation and self-discovery never occurred to me. Stuffing my days with handweaving, cleaning and shopping, I hushed my restless spirit.

Wild Black Hairs

In the beginning of November, as David lay reading in bed one evening, I was in the bathroom getting ready for bed, and straightening the bathroom shelf, when I picked up his hairbrush and noticed three long black hairs tangled in the bristles. I stared at them, frozen. Moving in what felt like slow motion, I walked into the bedroom carrying the brush and made a feeble joke about what these might mean. Laughing tensely, he responded with another joke. We looked at each other, the truth hanging heavily in the air between us. Then he began to tell his story.

During the first three months in Thailand, he had tried to avoid intimate contact with the beautiful Thai women who worked in the bars. Fellow workers were all enjoying the perks of being wealthy white men in Thai society, but

David constrained himself because of our relationship. In time, his resolve weakened, and he began seeing a nice woman nicknamed Nan. He stopped dating her before coming home to get me.

This was an issue we could have addressed much earlier had we been in an honest relationship. Before going to Thailand, we had each sought medical treatment because David had contracted a venereal disease. At the time, he had apologized, but otherwise we never talked about it. I had also had a couple of sexual encounters during our time apart, which I acknowledged to him, indirectly. We shrugged all this off and skipped the opportunity to talk about what we thought we were doing together. My own actions indicated that I shared his desire for companionship without commitment, although in truth it had more to do with acting impulsively and unconsciously.

Except for declaring, before I moved to Texas, that living together was only a trial, we had never discussed the subject of commitment. It's hard to be out of integrity with an agreement that hasn't been made. I was unaware that my own behavior was inconsistent with a desire for commitment, because I hadn't let myself admit that I wanted commitment. I preferred to stay in the unconscious limbo of trusting that we would be together forever, and acting as though our behavior had no bearing on that. If I had admitted to myself, or to David, that I wanted commitment, I would have had to examine my own record of sexual integrity and also risk discovering that he still did not want to make a commitment. The possibility of losing him was more painful than ignoring my desires. I just assumed everything would somehow work out and saw no reason to spoil the excitement of our pending travels with an unpleasant discussion.

The stage was set for further problems. Were we committed to a monogamous relationship? In leaving a good job to be his companion, should I expect anything more than pleasant company and a travel adventure? These were important questions, but instead of discussing them, we each made our own assumptions.

Over the years, I had made plenty of choices based on emotion and sexual passion, without thinking about consequences, so I understood David's actions to some extent. That night in Pattaya, he confessed that he had not intended to resume a relationship with Nan; he thought they were done. Now that I am more mature, I realize that didn't necessarily mean he intended to be faithful to me. Anyway, he described how, one evening, at a Bangkok bar, he saw her with a young American escort who was treating her badly. David felt compelled to rescue Nan from the abusive life of prostitution. He set her up in an apartment and paid the tuition for sewing school, which was her dream. In return, of course, he had a place to stay every week in Bangkok, a place where he obviously couldn't bring me.

As David told this tale, he reassured me that he never intended to hurt me, he felt very remorseful, and he had been dreading this outcome for two months. He shared that he had been trapped and tormented—torn between two women he cared about, unable to talk to anyone—having to keep up the deception. He painted himself as quite a victim, and I went along with it. I was living my life as a victim and believed that much of life just happens to us. My heart melted with compassion, feeling how terrible it must have been for him.

Never once did I express, or even feel, any anger about his betrayal of the commitment I assumed we had. My feelings of anger were buried in a sealed metal vault in the darkest corner of my inner world, guarded by military police and vicious attack dogs. I wasn't going anywhere near the anger that I was sure would lead to abandonment. Even now, when I had already lost him, I couldn't take that risk.

Nor did I ever stop to examine my responsibility for this story. If I had asked for a commitment, or been faithful in Texas, or challenged his refusal to take me to Bangkok, would we be experiencing this pain now? Probably not, but I didn't think about any of that then. Instead, we made love very tenderly.

The tenderness of that night yielded to practical problems by day. I was not willing to stay with David while he had an active relationship with someone else, and he wasn't willing to let Nan go. We did finally talk about what we wanted, after deciding to end the relationship. David had spent most of his life in one place, and he wanted to continue traveling the globe, doing engineering field jobs. He still did not want to commit to a relationship. Finally I admitted aloud that commitment was important to me.

As a therapist, I now know that commitment is a problem for many people. If you're in a relationship where the *C* word is not openly discussed, I encourage you to ask yourself what truth you're afraid to tell. You may convince yourself, as I did, that avoidance of thorny issues creates harmony, but it ultimately leads to greater pain than whatever you think you're avoiding. Lack of commitment is an attempt to enjoy intimacy while defending the right to be separate. This position assumes that commitment will destroy freedom and that intimacy is possible without commitment. Once we experience self-intimacy though, we can enjoy both intimacy and space with another. Commitment fosters, rather than destroys, that possibility by creating an atmosphere of safety for exploration of both togetherness and privacy.

Starting Over

I returned to Texas and, within a few months, was involved with three different men on a regular basis and an assortment of others casually. For the first time, I had plenty of male attention and I felt genuinely attractive and special. The quantity of physical intimacy masked the absence of inner intimacy.

David and I had parted intending to maintain a friendship, but the letters he wrote seemed cold and lifeless. Since the only excitement in my life derived from involvement with other men, I thought I didn't have anything to share in letters to him, either. Finally I decided to treat him like a girlfriend and just tell him the truth. By now you can appreciate what a startling concept that was for me!

Telling the truth always seems to bring surprises into my life. Even though I clearly told David in a letter that I didn't love any of the men I was dating, he was sure I would marry the one buying expensive presents and jet-setting me around the country. Five months after David and I had separated, he called me early one morning from Australia, where he had a job. He said he didn't want to spoil anything I had going but he wanted me to know he still cared. The international phone connection was faint and crackly. I had trouble hearing him and I could hardly believe what I thought I was hearing.

I didn't wait this time hoping he would offer a commitment. The small shoot of self-esteem growing inside enabled me to state clearly that he would have to propose before I would agree to see him again. David assured me that he was willing to get married and have kids because he knew that's what I wanted. I was moved to tears. I now realize that a large and stormy moor lies between the land of being willing and the land of actively wanting, but at the time, I thought it was the same place. I didn't notice that he failed to say he wanted to get married and have kids. I didn't mind that his proposal didn't make it on the top ten most romantic list. I still loved him and was happy about the prospect of being together again.

David offered to return to Texas, saying I had done enough of traveling to be with him. This was a major offer, for he highly valued those overseas jobs. But, as an engineering recruiter, I knew that he could not quit a project mid-job and land a new position. Engineering jobs were scarce in 1982. That's how I decided to take off for the "Land Down Under." A trip to Australia seemed like an intriguing adventure and local universities would surely provide plenty of refuge from boredom. I made plans to move in five months.

In the intervening time, David and I spent long hours writing and talking to each other on the phone, negotiating a new relationship. It was an incredible period of communication and honesty. I was finally having a relationship with myself and, for the first time in my life, actually paying attention to my own needs and truthfully expressing my concerns. As a result, I felt as though we were able to share our souls. We wrote poems to each other during this time. I'll never forget one that I received from him:

For Jane

Lying asleep in my arms
We breathe together as one.
With you, I find the strength to be
soft, to be gentle, to be free.
Jani, the one I have found to trust,
to freely show my fears, my laughter,
my tears and my love.
My walls of ice melt before your faith,
and I am released from the armor
I knew as strength.

Now free, now fluid, I am afraid
without the shell I have worn for so long
and built so carefully.
Trust in you, trust in me. We discover
new strengths there within us.
May you ever know how I have changed,
as I hold you in the night.

I really believed David had changed. I still think he did, for awhile. However, the open, vulnerable side he showed in the letters that I loved so much was too frightening for him to expose in person, and gradually he shut down. I had learned to say what I meant regarding important matters like commitment, but once I was living with him again I didn't have the courage to express my feelings about ordinary situations. Nothing in my daily experience seemed significant enough to fuss about and risk conflict or disapproval over. I still didn't understand the importance of telling the ordinary truths.

David and I got married. It was 1983, and I was thirty-four years old. Over the next three years I gave birth to two daughters, one born in Australia, and the other in Texas, where we spent another eight years. It was there that the door to my inner world was forever opened, and my life changes set in motion.

During that time I discovered primal therapy, metaphysics and spirituality. As I learned to recognize and express feelings, there was more space in my life. Into that space roared unlimited creative expression and a passion for learning about non-physical reality. I felt more truly alive than ever before and comfortable in my inner world. I was getting to know myself and liking the person I was meeting. I desperately wanted to communicate with David about our inner worlds and to begin making choices together based on spiritual teachings. Innately skeptical, mistrustful of anything remotely psychic, and very reticent to poke around in the cellar of his stuffed emotions, he was not a likely tenant of the inner realms. He did, for my sake, experiment with some new modalities, experiencing some profound breakthroughs, but he never made the kind of commitment I was hoping for. I wanted him to share my commitment to healing and growth, but he wasn't interested. Instead, the more

I learned to express myself emotionally, the more he retreated into believing that feelings, like geology or auto mechanics, were an optional interest, one he didn't happen to share.

Looking back, I realize that I always saw him as that poem-being, free and fluid, available for intimacy, filled with a light greater than his fear. Because of that, I overlooked his fear. Or maybe the poem-being was the man I loved, and I just pretended he lived with me. I clung to his potential, ignoring the reality he chose to express. Still afraid of telling any truth that involved possible conflict, I never challenged the man who was back in armor. I didn't tell him I felt angry and abandoned because he had retreated. How far away he'd gone and why he'd left were mysteries I didn't understand. I also didn't yet appreciate the corrosive role my own dishonesty and cowardice were playing in our lives.

How does a long marriage begin to end? It seems there should be a certain point where we pushed a button and started a time bomb ticking. No specific event signaled the onset of our retreat from one another. The end was seeded at the beginning. We embarked on life together, silently agreeing to withhold truth and avoid conflict, maintaining a desperate veneer of peace. Each time we shrugged and turned from those inconvenient feelings, the shadow of our life force, squatting in the space between us, shifted its weight and stretched. As that shadow took more space, we compressed the parts we were willing to share into tighter and tighter corners. Our fears led us away from intimacy and increased the sense of separation.

Reflecting back, I realize that David and I lived like victims. Believing we had no control over our lives, we never created a vision for ourselves. Avoiding the risks of disappointment and conflict, we also avoided claiming responsibility for our lives. We floated aimlessly through life, supported by the feathery parachutes of vague wishes. In the absence of the impetus of striving toward a goal or the passion of feelings fully expressed, anger howled through the hollow corridors of our relationship. In the end, our marriage blew apart like a dandelion in the wind. Nothing, not even our children, could hold us together.

By then, David only knew that he wanted to explore and live in new places, and do hands-on engineering, moving from project to project. That desire conflicted with my need to live in one place, establish a counseling practice, and offer our children a stable environment. He wanted adventure; I wanted a home. We didn't know how to combine those needs.

But beneath the geographical conflict, the difference in our desires for intimacy and commitment formed a gulf between us that we could no longer span. It seemed to me that David ended where he began. I think deep intimacy was too threatening for him, and the truth was he didn't want a commitment—not to me, not to a family, not even, perhaps, to his inner spirit. His tumbleweed commitment to adventure blew him back to Thailand.

In a sense, I came full circle, too. I started out wanting someone to commit to me, but ignoring that truth, and I learned that only passionate commitment was enough for me and that I was the one who had to commit to myself. It was 1994, and at forty-five, I was finally determined to become all I could be, to start listening to my feelings and my inner voice and to tell myself and others only the truth, even if it meant risking conflict, disapproval or rejection.

Life's lessons come along in spirals. The same issue reappears over and over again. If we choose to ignore it, back it comes in slightly different shape or louder voice, saying "Do you get it now?" Even when we think we've understood, the issue returns, at a deeper level, so we can practice our new skills. We get practice situations and "pop quizzes" to test our understanding until we've satisfied our need for knowledge about that issue. I was ready to test my ability to practice self-commitment through honesty.

A New Beginning

Ron walked on stage even before my marriage ended, but until I decided to get divorced, he waited quietly in the wings. I met him in January of 1994, but for several months our contact, usually in a group setting, was uneventful. David returned from a two-month stay in Thailand at the end of March, asking to end our marriage. I spent the next month bargaining for a way to keep both the marriage and my soul, grieving the loss I knew was inevitable. One month can't be enough time in which to dissolve a long marriage, and yet, because of all the emotional work that led to this point, it was enough for us.

Ron and I often crossed paths while walking on Pilot Butte, a volcanic cone stretching 3,800 feet into the sky. A mile of road spirals around this butte and has become a Mecca for local walkers. One day in spring Ron invited me to walk the butte with him. That was our real beginning. My chance to practice truth-telling started right away. For three days in a row we walked up and down Pilot Butte, twice in a row, talking non-stop for the whole hour it took. Not yet done with divorce details, I certainly was not looking for a relationship. I had imagined myself pulling inward with my children, living in a cocoon for a couple of years. Yet, when I talked with Ron, the possibility of truthful intimacy stirred inside me. He seemed like the kind of man I wanted to share my life with.

I was surprised by strong feelings of grief and loss. I was still grieving the loss of my marriage, but now was also grieving because, since Ron would surely find somebody else long before I was ready for a relationship, I thought I'd lose him too. I wasn't very gentle with myself. Maybe I wanted to stuff that grief. I told myself, very judgmentally, that my feelings were neurotic and that I was a neurotic person who desperately grabbed the first relationship at hand.

My first instinct was to share all these feelings with Ron. A second reaction swept through my mind like a housewife on a cleaning binge. "NO!" shouted a voice inside. "You don't tell a man something like that! He'll get scared and run off. Keep it to yourself." There it was: my first opportunity in a new relationship to choose between telling the truth and hiding unacceptable feelings. The next time we met, I told Ron the truth. Hurrah for me! I was astonished when he admitted feeling the same fear of loss. He also said if I had chosen to withhold my feelings, he would have sensed that I was withholding something, magnified it, and begun withdrawing, fearful of whatever he would have imagined I was hiding. What positive reinforcement! The truth hadn't scared him off, but instead had brought us closer.

Over the weeks and months that followed, our connection expanded from walking partners to good friends, to lovers, to partners. At each step of the way, we got to practice truth-telling.

I've already related our "death-defying" acts of truth-telling in the bedroom. Parenting together was like walking through a mine field. As conflicts arose with the children, Ron and I talked about how to handle them. David and

I did not have a conscious parenting style, so I appreciated such unfamiliar parenting support, and the disagreements we had about approaches brought many new feelings to the surface for both of us. I had to deal with shame for mistakes that I felt I'd made raising the children. Ron, who had never had children of his own, got to face fears, lingering from childhood, regarding chaos and control. Amongst eruptions of anger, hurt and fear, we discovered layers of defiance and explored their effects on our ability to be effective and loving authority figures for the children. We told the truth while struggling to balance differing needs for intimacy and independence with each other and with the children.

We supported each other in realizing career dreams. When we met, my counseling practice, which had never grown past the struggling level, had evaporated totally while I focused on the divorce process. I'll never forget the day Ron called and asked about my work. He wanted to know how my career was going, my goals, and if he could help me. Although David had financially supported my career, he wasn't a businessman and he didn't know how to help me grow it. More importantly to me, he had never supported it emotionally. I had to plead with him just to get him to read brochures I had spent months laboring over. During the divorce process he revealed his resentment over all the money flushed down the toilet to support my little "hobby." I didn't understand how that attitude drained my energy and ability to be successful until Ron showed me what support could feel like. Ron helped me craft an effective marketing program and, by participating in the Hendricks Conscious Relationship Training with me, made me a counselor with a conscious partner. In less than a year my practice was very successful.

Ron had just finished a long contract as a Chief Financial Officer that culminated in the sale of the organization he worked for. With my support and encouragement, he took a year's sabbatical to begin to pursue his lifelong dream of creating a CD. Approximately three years later, Ron's *Magic Child* CD was a dream come true.

We have challenged each other to move past self-limits, laughed uncontrollably and often, and loved ourselves and each other, just as we are. Ron has been a true companion, a reflection of the love I am finally giving myself.

The level of honesty we have brought to this relationship has enabled us both to peel away the masks of personas that seemed to be our essences. The most dramatic shift in consciousness, for me, happened six months into the relationship, during the first Conscious Relationship Training. Gay and Kathlyn Hendricks had been stressing the importance of integrity and truth-telling. They told us any breach of integrity, even from long in the past, which we have simply swept under the rug of awareness, is draining energy and affecting our present relationship. To avoid that energy loss, I decided to confess to Ron all the places where I had been out of integrity in the sexual arena.

Other than my initial liaison with Moon, I'd never had a prolonged affair while in a committed situation. All my sexual infidelities were impulse-based and short-lived. There had been a couple of friends with whom I found both emotional intimacy and the lusty sizzle of sexual attraction. Though I chose not to act out that attraction, I did keep the fire going and never told David the truth about my feelings for these "friends." Feeling ashamed of my actions, when I told Ron I unconsciously cloaked my behavior in innocence, to avoid the judgment I felt sure I deserved.

Luckily, of the pair of us, I was the only hanging judge. Ron didn't condemn me, nor did he whitewash what I'd done. He helped me to recognize a pattern in my behavior. In every situation, I described how surprised I had been by whatever happened sexually, as though I had been walking around anesthetized, oblivious to any sexual cues.

During primal therapy, memories suggested that I may have been sexually abused by a family friend when I was a child. At this point I am inclined to believe they are past-life memories. However, at the point of my confession, I was convinced that I had been abused and so decided my adult behavior was a replay of the energy of that abuse, which certainly would have taken me by surprise. My sexual encounters all happened "without any warning," and then I would be stuck. I was ready to release myself with a "not guilty" verdict. No wonder all these things had "happened to me." I couldn't help it!

Ron wasn't interested in verdicts or judgments. He wanted to help me understand the pattern and take responsibility for it, so the pattern wouldn't control me anymore. Still stuck in judgment, I did my best to convince him I was a victim. I pleaded helplessly, saying that my past actions were beyond my control at the time they happened. I felt scared defending my helplessness because, as a helpless victim, I couldn't guarantee that the fog would never come over me again. There was no way to protect myself. I felt sure of losing Ron, knowing he would not tolerate any behavior that deviated from my commitment to him. I worked myself into quite a dramatic victim frenzy.

Ron still wasn't buying excuses. Not unkindly, but firmly, he continued to insist I was responsible for my behavior. That was one of the most difficult pieces of inner work I have ever done. Because Ron was able to stay so firm and yet so loving, I finally stopped whining and got to a deeper level: the need in me from which all the other behavior had issued. That wound was the need to feel special. This is when I discovered my Daisy persona, the part that believed specialness had to be conferred from an outside source. I experienced intimacy when somebody reassured me that I was special because then I would feel worthy enough to let the other person come close. I prized this feeling of validation more than safety or integrity. I would let myself be mesmerized by the swaying cobra head of admiration, ignore any consequences, and go for the validating pleasure of the moment. Discovering this pattern, which had controlled me for so long, felt like ripping the skin off my face. To my surprise, that skin was not my real face. Underneath it, I found an innately special, shining essence: the Magic Child. On the other side of all the pain I had just gone through to face myself, I discovered freedom! Now I could confidently promise to be faithful, knowing that my sexual choices were really choices and that my value didn't depend on what I chose. I felt grateful to Ron for his strong refusal to let me live as a victim.

How do I end the tale of a life that isn't finished? I still have many opportunities to listen to my inner voice, speak the truth, and honor the commitment to self-intimacy. Some days I automatically say what's true. Other times I get sidetracked with excuses and imagine that situations are happening because somebody else is acting a certain way. I can still get quite righteous at times. But the commitment I have made comes to my rescue when I go back into victim mode. Either I remember, or Ron reminds me, and I drop the pretense. I am absolutely committed to being true to myself, to acknowledging aloud, whenever it's appropriate, the truth of my feelings, and to experiencing life as a journey of intimacy rather than separation. As soon as I notice myself feeling separate or "less than," I explore, with mercy and curiosity, how I am causing that feeling of isolation through my own fears and judgments or integrity violations.

I don't waste much time anymore blaming myself or life. I know life is showing up as "the right experience" and that, with enough loving attention and honesty, I can discover a gift in whatever is happening. Now that I love myself, my life is full of loving people. I feel connected to God and everyone else. I know I'm not through with feeling separate. One argument with my kids can catapult me right back into that space! The difference is, now that I absolutely know separation is illusion, I have a rope to haul myself back to center. Most of my energy these days is expended on love and creativity, and I feel great! I feel more truly alive than I have ever felt in my life!

I invite you to reflect on your life. The Magic Child in you can awaken and come forth. Your sleep cannot be any more sound than mine was. Begin by examining your evidence for believing you are separate, both from the people you love and the people you don't love. In considering this evidence, look for patterns and explore their origin. This will reveal the veil of illusion covering your beliefs. Listen to the voice of the Magic Child, prompting you with intuitive whispers. Intimacy with others is absolutely contingent on your ability to honor your own feelings and dreams. Only when you master the art of self-intimacy, through this honoring, can you lay aside the veil of separation.

This book is filled with magic wands, tools of love and passion to help you transform your life. As you begin to use these tools, great relationships will be a natural by-product of the richly rewarding relationship you develop with yourself. As your loving intimacy with the inner partner grows strong, you will naturally choose partners who reflect the appreciation you have for yourself and want to join you in expressing essence.

You can have the relationship of your dreams. Your beloved is waiting within. I share this love song that Ron wrote for me. Let it be a song that you sing to the Magic Child in you. Discover your own preciousness, and never again stray from loving yourself.

Kiss the Sky!

You wanted to know what would I do if I loved you
Would I jump and kiss the sky the way that you do?
You ought to know,
I'll be your friend, without break or decay
Till the moon no longer shines, and strays away
And the flowers have faded from memory, and turned to
stone
You ought to know.

You ought to know,
I'll be your friend, 'til moisture cannot be found
I'll follow your soul till the scent fades away
and bury my heart for you in sacred ground.
You ought to know—you ought to know
that I'll jump and kiss the sky the way that you do.

Wondersparks

1. What are the major traumas from your childhood? What beliefs about yourself did you form as a result?
2. Have you had other relationships or experiences that seem to support these beliefs?
3. If these beliefs were not true, how might you interpret those experiences instead?
4. How would you rate yourself as an intimate partner to yourself?

5. Do you keep the promises you make to yourself?
6. Do you admit your true feelings to yourself? Do you admit them to others?
7. Are your needs as important to you as other people's needs?
8. Do you believe you are a worthwhile, good person, or have you condemned yourself for certain behaviors, attitudes or qualities?
9. Is there anything that could happen to you that you imagine would seriously damage your sense of self-worth? If so, why?
10. Do you see any connection between the level of honesty, nurturing and commitment you have toward yourself and the level you show toward others?
11. Challenge! Write the story of all your relationships. Don't worry about your writing style, just tell the story. Notice the patterns that emerge.
12. Can you appreciate your life, exactly as it has been, as the crucible that formed the precious gem that is you? If not, where are you still holding resentment?
13. If you still resent your life, what do you require before you'll accept it?

Elixirs for the Mind

The Conscious Heart, by Gay Hendricks, Ph.D., and Kathlyn Hendricks, Ph.D. Learn about conscious commitment and the ways we create separation, both from ourselves and from those we love. This book, the fruit of over twenty years of experience working with thousands of couples, is densely packed with principles that can change your relationships as dramatically as they have changed mine. It definitely belongs on the Desert Island pile.

Centering and the Art of Intimacy Handbook, by Gay Hendricks, Ph.D., and Kathlyn Hendricks, Ph.D. This little book published in

1993 is packed with activities designed to help partners come into greater intimacy with each other.

The Path to Love, by Deepak Chopra, M.D. This is one of the richest books I have ever read, because it contains so much food for thought. Chopra weaves Hindu philosophy into explanations of the bliss and fear of relationships and presents loving another person as a spiritual path with specific stages. He teaches how to love yourself even when that seems impossible. Unlike some of Chopra's other books that focus simply on powerful principles, this one is filled with stories that made the book far more helpful to me. It too holds a spot on my desert island bookshelf!

To Love and Be Loved, by Stephen and Ondrea Levine. This audio series on the difficult yoga of relationship, showcases the Levines' gift of compassion. They inspire the listener to face the fears that close the heart, and to replace it with mercy for yourself and your partner. Their messages seeped into my heart, profoundly influenced me and became an important part of my Desert Island Collection.

The Passionate Marriage, by David Schnarch, Ph.D. The author combines his two fields of expertise, marital counseling and sex therapy, into a new approach that uses sexual issues as a metaphor for intimacy issues. It is designed to help committed couples increase their intimacy and their sexual satisfaction.

Getting the Love You Want, by Harville Hendrix, Ph.D., and Jo Robinson. The premise is that we enter into a partnership in order to heal unresolved issues of childhood. Hendrix describes the mystery of choosing partners with both the positive and negative qualities of our parents and suggests concrete, effective techniques for healing the old wounds and creating a heart-centered relationship with our partner.

Hot Monogamy, by Pat Love, Ph.D., and Jo Robinson. This book focuses on sexual differences between partners and ways to communicate with one another about sexual needs. This informative book should alleviate any fears you may harbor that your needs or sexual conflicts are abnormal, and abounds with practical ideas for turning up the heat on your love life.

Gay Relationships, by Tina Tessina, Ph.D. Although gays have all the same issues around intimacy and separation that straight people have, they have additional concerns that are not commonly addressed in most relationship books. Tessina addresses issues such as meeting partners, dating etiquette, homophobia, coming out, dealing with society's restrictions, commitment issues and much more. Her book is designed to help gays find, develop and maintain healthy relationships.

Chapter Eleven

Vision invests life
with the vital fluid we all need
to feel fully alive.

Magic Wand
Use starvision to create miracles.

Follow the Star

One of the most painful limitations of five-sensory reality is the illusion that our choices are defined by our past and present experiences. Many of us waste precious life energy struggling in the mud of life as we know it, not daring to explore open fields of possibility. We convince ourselves our limitations are the hub around which our experience collects. Believing the lack in us is innate, we think we have no power to alter reality. As we begin to reject the authority of the five-sensory world, we realize we can create anything. The first step in that creation process is to decide what to create. To do this, we look for inspiration, for that flicker of starlight calling to us from across the universe inside our hearts. If we find our star and follow it, we can connect heaven and earth and bring a beckoning possibility into form.

Possibilities call to us through desire our entire lives, but often, we fail to respond or even acknowledge that call. Metaphorically, we have settled ourselves and our belongings inside an ordinary house, in a neighborhood full of similarly ordinary houses. We tell ourselves we don't need a custom home with lots of space. This one will do. Who are we to expect more from life? We never hear the dreams calling because we're busy arguing the legitimacy, lineage and omnipotence of our limitations.

Of course, I'm not talking about dreams of custom houses, but about a willingness to dream. Many of my clients, especially the depressed ones, can't imagine what they want in life, except to feel happy again. Others of us harbor wild dreams in secret rooms but never consider the possibility that these dreams could come true.

Songs of Limitation

Why don't we reach for the stars in our lives? Most of us can't reach that high because we're busy singing songs of negativity. These limiting refrains, usually learned in childhood, are chanted by various personas. Without awareness of our personas and the tunes they're humming, we accept limitations without question. The limiting chorus most of my personas join in on is "not enough." Cynthia and Mildred, for example, have to do all the work because there isn't  enough help. Lily, the little girl on guard for disapproval, is never good enough and never has enough of what she needs. Everything is too hard. As Lily, I can imagine anybody else on the planet manifesting a dream but I am convinced such possibilities are unavailable to me because I personally am "not enough." Limiting beliefs usually defy logic with undaunted boldness.

"Not enough" is only one popular refrain in the song book of limitations. "I don't/can't know" is another. We convince ourselves we can't be trusted with the dreaming power in our lives, telling ourselves we're not qualified to know our own desires, fearing that if we ever happen to get what we think we want, either we won't like it after all, or it won't be good for us.

Others of us have found our stars and know exactly what we want, but sing a refrain called "It's impractical." We intone discouraging messages that prove our heads are in the clouds. We're sure there's no market for what we want to do or else there's too much competition in the field of our desire. We imagine these dreams cannot be realized because our standards are impossibly high. We know we could never have enough resources to accomplish such an unrealistic pipe dream.

Another limiting song is "My dreams are dangerous." We fear that if we get our desire, somebody else will be disappointed or angry or have to do without. Even if nobody suffers we imagine people we care about will shun us for the crime of becoming successful. Many people in our society label successful individuals as conceited, selfish and unethical. There seems to be some unspoken code of victim camaraderie which penalizes success.

"My dreams are too costly" is a popular refrain. Fearing dreams will require the sacrifice of something precious, we don't let ourselves dream. To manifest the vision of a healthy, happy relationship, for example, we may have to let go of a beloved but incompatible partner. Creating a dream job usually means giving up the job we hate, but do so well at and make good money doing. And, of course, there are no guarantees, while dreaming, that someone or something better is really out there for us. To get something better we often have to let go of the lesser good our hands are filled with and be willing to wait with empty hands for those dreams to come true. Many people are too terrified of this emptiness to take the chance on dreams. They convince themselves that the most precious dreams are coated with barnacles of misery. Since dreams carry such a heavy price, people with this song of limitation prefer to live in bland acceptance.

Ron spent over two years creating the *Magic Child* album. During that time, he often pondered his musical fate. Each time the issue of promotional tours arose, two of his strongest personas would step in, to discourage him. Edna would sigh with exhaustion, and Clyde would scornfully announce that success in the rock and roll business was not possible for a man in his forties and chasing that dream would definitely lead to a loss of both family and financial stability. It took Ron two years just to admit aloud that he had always dreamed of touring, singing the inspirational music of his soul.

"I have too many responsibilities" is another dream-stopper song. We believe we have no right to pursue dreams when people are depending on us. The unspoken assumption is that nowhere, in the field of possibilities, is there a way to realize dreams and simultaneously act responsibly toward people who rely on us. We also usually fail to question whether other people's dependence on us is reasonable and healthy.

If none of these refrains sound like your special tune, you can do an exercise at the end of this chapter designed to help your body reveal your limitations. I learned the technique from Steve Siskgold, a vision coach in San Francisco. Steve specializes in helping clients discover and realize their life purposes. He tells the story of a doctor whose practice limped along despite his best promotional efforts. As Steve helped the doctor notice messages conveyed by his body responses, the man remembered asking, as a five-year-old, why other people had nice things and his family didn't. He remembered his father's reply, "Money makes you sick, son." The doctor's dreams were clearly "too costly." Once he cleared out that belief, his practice doubled in a month. Our bodies are wonderful conductors of the unconscious beliefs that limit us. Since the beliefs are hidden from conscious awareness, we have to detect their presence from concrete clues. The sensory messages of our bodies and the circumstances of our lives are two powerful forms of evidence that, if we explore them through loving conversation, can lead us to discover and dispel hidden, sabotaging beliefs.

Creative Tension

Once we know what is holding us back, how can we learn to sing a song of empowerment? I learned an effective process from Kris King, president of

Wings Innovative Learning Seminars in Eugene, Oregon. Her teaching was based on *The Path of Least Resistance*, by Robert Fritz. I have blended her process with techniques learned from the Hendrickses, Steve Siskgold and my own instincts.

Kris says to imagine standing in the middle of a large room, facing your fondest vision displayed on the wall before you, with your back turned to a wall covered with limiting beliefs. Imagine industrial strength rubber bands encircling your waist. One is attached to the front wall and the other to the back wall. Since every point of tension requires resolution, as you move toward vision, you'll be pulling against the rubber band attached to the back wall. Eventually the pressure will be too much and you'll start to move backwards, following the path of least resistance, away from your dream. As soon as you get far enough away, the pressure will begin in the other direction, pulling you toward your vision once again. The end result is that you remain stuck in the middle, wondering why you're not moving forward. If that sounds like your life, but you're ready to move past being stuck in the middle to manifest your dreams, follow this dream-stepping guide.

Dream-Stepping

1. Identify the limiting beliefs written on that back wall.
2. Love yourself, just as you are, complete with those unhelpful beliefs. Think about how each belief formed. If your parents were hypercritical, you may feel incapable of doing anything right, including manifesting a dream. Guilt and blame will not serve you. Your parents could only give what they got themselves. Accept how it was for you back then. Accept that, until this moment, you have been unable to change the belief. As you lovingly accept yourself, you will find the energy for the next step.
3. Create a new tension. Throw out the tension between what you want and the belief that you can't have what you want, and create tension between what you want and where you are right now. You can choose your starting point. The Hendrickses recommend facing your present situation first. If you can't imagine new possibilities, it may work best for you to

do this first. I have listed this as step six, because of Kris King's opinion that the excitement of the vision softens the pain of self-examination. Play with the order and see what works best for you.

I recommend that you start by envisioning what you want. The vision has to be very detailed, dripping with juice, because desire is the force that propels us forward. The vision has to stoke desire to a big flame level. It isn't enough to imagine a wonderful relationship. You have to picture details of what wonderful means to you. For example, imagine yourself cuddling in bed every Saturday morning or going for long hikes in the woods.

Visioning is especially important in relationships, both current and future ones. When Thea, a former client and expert horse trainer, got the idea of detailed visioning, she exclaimed excitedly, "My partner will know how to ride, and he'll love horses. I won't have to teach him to ride or persuade him to do it." In contrast, clients Ariane and Mickey, who were months into their relationship, ran into trouble when they discovered that she wanted plenty of space to pursue her many independent activities and he wanted plenty of time for togetherness. They had a lot of issues to work out to save their relationship, whereas Thea got clear on her needs prior to her next relationship.

4. Imagine how you'll feel when living your vision. You may use symbols to express that. When I envisioned a new relationship with money, it was the symbols that conveyed the feeling of lavishness I desired. I imagined sun-bright, standing-under-a-waterfall ease and fullness of money; possibilities shot through with rainbow colors and rocket fuel. I pictured myself as a sun radiating out in every direction. Whenever I think about those feeling images to describe my relationship with money, I feel expansive, spacious, lavish. This is more real to me, more exciting, than when I simply recite affirmations or give myself a pep talk.

5. Once you get clear on the vision, bring it into concrete form in some fashion. Some ways to do that are: tell someone you trust; make a collage of images and hang it somewhere you look frequently; be dramatic, putting a full voice and your whole body into proclaiming your vision.

The goal is to energize this vision, magnifying its power to draw you forward. I like to incorporate Steve Siskgold's full-bodied manifestation process, outlined at the end of the chapter, to shake out the feelings and beliefs in conflict with the dream. One technique that manifestation experts like Norman Vincent Peale and Bob Proctor recommend is writing down the goal on a piece of paper. Put the paper in your wallet and look at it daily. Write something like "I have a brand new four-bedroom house in a country setting by (date)." This serves notice to your subconscious mind, which then gets busy bringing your vision into physical form.

6. The second part of creating a tension to pull you toward your dream is to get searingly honest about where you are now. This is a deepening of step one where you acknowledged limiting beliefs. Now you have to look your life in the face, with its makeup off, and acknowledge the real-life effects of your limiting beliefs. This process requires admitting the absolute truth, in detail, without any sugar coating, rationalization or excuses. If you pretend your situation is better than it really is, you lose the tension between reality and your dream. When I examined my relationship with money, I realized my feelings about it were all tight, like I was measuring life out with an eyedropper, and receiving bounty through a narrow gauge funnel.

   Once you've looked your life straight in the eye, you're ready to move on to the next step. Don't linger here by sharing the details with others or making collages. You're ready to let go of this version of your life. You may notice at this point that your energy is sagging. Self-appraisal without shame is hard to accomplish. When I was acknowledging the truth about my money attitudes, I felt like a block of cement was weighing me down. Shame is an albatross that hangs around most of our necks at one time or another, but we don't have to leave it there. It comes off with the next step.

7. Accept and love yourself for creating only what you knew how to create. This is a repeat of step two, but now there's more to accept. We can't overdo self-acceptance. I found this step was easier to do with the dream

of what I wanted to create oozing its juice all over me, distracting me from self-pity and despair. Self-love mixed with dream juice prepares us for the next critical step.

8.   Take one step. Choose something you can and will do that will move you closer to your goal. Cultural anthropologist Jennifer James, author of *Living in the Future Tense*, says change is so difficult for humans that we need very small baby steps. When James decided to start swimming for exercise, her first step was to buy a bathing suit. The next step was to hang the suit on the doorknob where she would see it as she went to work each day, allowing herself to get used to the idea that she was going to start swimming. She gave herself lots of steps before she made herself get into the pool and actually start swimming.

Many of my clients learned to practice these steps that allowed them to believe in their dreams. Lena worked as a graphic artist, but she dreamed of being a fine artist. She had a fine collection of her own beautiful paintings, but at the time she came for counseling her life was consumed by caring for a small child and working for a living. Her dream had been drifting further and further away, until it seemed beyond reach and she became depressed. In session, we talked about small steps. Lena realized she could spend one evening a week painting. In that amount of time, she might not be able to develop her skill, or amass a large enough body of work to support herself through fine art, or experience national acclaim as an artist (her dream at its maturity), but one night a week was an achievable first step. For the present, she just needed to water the dream and give it a little sunlight to help it grow to maturity. I saw one of her paintings in a gallery recently, so the small-step approach seemed to work for her.

Even if the task is a difficult one, like leaving a relationship, we can break it into small pieces, so it seems friendlier. For example, write down a plan instead of just thinking about it; take time to find a new home; get counseling; begin to do more activities on your own. Every life change can be broken into manageable steps. The small steps give us time to make prayers of surrender and grow more confident about our direction and a successful result.

Now that I'm writing a book, I hear many people say, "I've always wanted to write a book." If you're somebody like that, don't keep putting off the dream. Write. Do it even if you don't know what your book is about. Spend a certain amount of time each day or each week writing whatever comes to you. Don't demand that it be a book, fully conceived, before you'll agree to write the first word. As you grow accustomed to writing, you'll discover whether you enjoy it. You'll begin imagining yourself as a writer. Eventually you'll discover what it is you want to say. One day you'll finish your book. No matter what your dream, the process is the same. Take the next step. I put off my dream of writing for years because I didn't know what I wanted to write about. I still didn't know when I finally started on my book, but I discovered, through the writing, what I had to say. The accomplishment of that dream is in your hands.

9. Surrender is the next dream step. I am not suggesting that we race out the door of our current lives, leaving behind spouse, children, home and livelihood to follow a dream that excites us, trusting God to provide. We have to use our powers of discernment and planning. Surrender implies that we trust our hearts and follow our vision. In doing so, we discover the magic of synchronicity, where we are in the flow, and everything we need just seems to show up as we need it, step by step. This is not the same as having a genie magically change our lives for us, delivering all the circumstances we need at once, with a single puff of smoke. It is a much more organic process. As long as we continue to focus on a dream and take the next steps, even if they're risky, we will keep moving in the direction of our dream. The exact outcome, if we surrender the details, will be our dream, or something infinitely better. We take the step we know how to take now and trust God with our dream.

10. The final step is always to say thanks, even before we experience our dream manifested in form. At this point in the process, the dream has already been realized in the non-material world, so it is important for us to show gratitude and faith and expect the miracle of our dream moving into our material lives.

Putting the Steps into Action

The day I took the manifestation workshop with Kris King, I returned home, full of excitement about my new vision of money. When I walked through the door, I was greeted by my husband and twelve-year-old daughter.

"We found the car!" they chorused. "Let's go look at it." Ron had been making noise for a few weeks about replacing my old, completely paid for car, and I had been ignoring him, worried about the burden of car payments. Now, fresh from the workshop, I was face-to-face with the opportunity to practice what I had learned, and challenge my former attitudes and beliefs. The first thing I did was burst into tears. After I stopped crying, I went to the car lot with my family.

First I drove a big brand new Ford Expedition. I've always been nervous about big vehicles because I lack a good sense of spatial relationships, but this time I just noted how spacious the car felt. Then I tried out an Explorer. My elbow kept bumping the CD compartment on the front seat and I kept noticing how much smaller it was than the Expedition. The vehicle felt tight to me. "Hmmm," I thought, "tight is how I said my life feels now and spacious is the feeling I said I wanted." I decided to get the Expedition and stop worrying about "not enough." It was a daring decision for me, but one I have never regretted.

Finding Your Star

Desire is the spark that fires the creation process. We are all creators. The only choice is whether we prefer to create consciously or unconsciously. There is a difference between choosing what you want and being attached to the limits of your conscious vision. As you entrust your dreams to the higher power, you can practice detachment by adding the phrases, "if this is for highest good" and "this or something better." Through surrendering we let go of ego attachment, but we still allow ourselves the creative power of dreaming.

What if you don't currently have a dream? You most likely also have limiting beliefs that have anesthetized you so heavily that you are going through life without bothering to wonder what you want to create. You already know it's no use; you never get what you want. Some people in this state are just depressed and tired and never bother to ask themselves what they want anymore. Others speak of their lack of desire in spiritual terms, describing wanting as a state of ego. They think it's better to just go through life taking what comes, knowing everything is always in Divine Order. That sounds enlightened, but is a deadening attitude for someone who wants to be truly alive.

We all need to be doing something we love that's part of a vision stretching past the horizon of what we know how to do. If we don't allow ourselves to dream, our lives may still be full of nice things, miracles even, but we'll be missing passionate aliveness, the life that flows when we're bringing the starlight of dreams into vision and form.

Vision is important in every aspect of our lives because we create what we focus on. We need to envision the kind of relationships we want, the way we want to spend free time or money or old age, and alternatives for everything we complain about. However, I think vision is most critical in regard to the work we do or the careers we choose.

Many people work at jobs that are dissatisfying, lacking the starlight of vision, because of limiting beliefs. Since work occupies so much of our days, life often seems flat and unfulfilling to people whose lives are devoid of vision. Throughout the long work day, they simply go through the motions of living, without the animation the vision star infuses. Then they come home exhausted from spending all that time out of harmony with their souls. Many people just numb themselves with food, television, alcohol, drugs or sex so they don't have to feel the pain of visionless living.

How do we find that life vision, that star to follow? Some people just always know what they have to do. They may not know how and they may avoid their dream for many years, but they always know what it is. My friend Jody Miller Stevenson, author of *Soul Purpose*, knew when she was only five years old that she wanted to be a writer. She spent the next forty years having many interesting experiences, telling herself that she'd write about them someday. By the time she was forty-five years old she was so burned out with the pace of her work that she couldn't get out of bed without assistance. She went to an iridologist who said her thyroid and adrenal glands were very weak. Jody realized her spirit was leaving and she still had not fulfilled her dream. She felt so much grief realizing that she might die without ever writing, that she promised herself that if she lived she would start writing.

Ron remembers going to church as a boy of ten to sing with the congregation. Every week he would hold the hymnal and try to sing but only tears would come out. Singing was a part of his soul and he was scared to let it out. In high school he had a rock and roll band but then he put away his music when it was time to become an adult and be part of the "real world," which had no room for dreams. It took Ron over twenty years to bring his dream out into the sunlight, to start singing the songs of his soul. The first song he wrote expressed the importance of reviving his dream.

Coming Home

I am coming home
I am coming home to me
I've been gone so long
I've left my dreams alone
Given my soul for my heart
I am coming home.

I am coming home to me
Part of the journey along the way
To know that my love for me is okay
To walk into a brighter—brighter day
I am coming home
I am coming home to me
Look at what I tried to give to you
I wanted you, not me, to make me well.

I am coming home to me
It's the only way that I can give
To show the love that truly is
To let you be who you are
I am coming home to me.

Those who haven't found their star need to engage in dream-tracking to get close enough to see their dreams clearly. This process is easier in the inner realm because that's the home of the Magic Child, the keeper of dreams. You can use any of the intuitive tools mentioned in chapter 2 to get into the inner realm, though I do believe hypnosis is particularly helpful in this application.

The Magic Child is waiting within, holding dreams bigger than what we know how to do, and more soulful than we can ever consciously imagine. The inner journey to find the dream-keeper-self is a vision quest. The Magic Child leads us to an intuitive dream-spring. As we gaze into its waters, we find our soul's star reflected there, the true vision of who we are and what we have come here to do. The visions people see in this inner spring always surprise them and also resonate deeply in the person's heart, offering a new dimension of purpose and satisfaction.

However, we have to come home to ourselves and bring our dream-stars to earth by connecting body, mind and emotions. This frightens many. Others are more lost than frightened, blind to the light of their own dream-star, with no guiding vision to inspire them. It's as if their inner landscape is under a spell of overcast skies. My friend Reenie speaks wistfully of having a job she could love the way I love mine, but she has no idea what it might be. If you are like Reenie, what can you do? How can you find your dream? First, you have to imagine there might be a dream for you. Reenie used to show up for work every day, hating it and telling herself she had to have that job. The money seemed so critical to her survival that she never stopped to wonder if there could be a job she would enjoy. Reenie has already taken a first step. She's wondering, and she is willing to discover her dream.

It may be that it's not time yet for you to have a clear vision of your dream. You may be going through a birthing process, bringing your starlight out of the void of unknowing. When this happens, we must do what parents have always done: wait and trust. Expectant parents are filled with curiosity, dreams, love and eagerness. They long to hold the baby in their arms and discover who has come into their lives. While they wait in the dark of unknowing, they are trusting. They are confident about one thing: a wonderful baby will be born. So we too, if we are at a point of gestating a dream, must nourish it with our confidence that it will be a wondrous dream, perfect for us, and will be revealed to us in the perfect timing.

Some people remain in the darkness unnecessarily because they are wearing blinders. Paulette was a client in her early forties who had always worked in the nursing field. Her current job involved a long, tiring commute. Although she was good at the job, she wasn't satisfied, and couldn't imagine staying in it long term. She longed to spend more time with her children while they were still young, but blinders prevented her from accomplishing that dream. When a

friend was suddenly killed in a car accident, Paulette felt an inner urge to make a change—she was no longer willing to squander precious time. The first step was to pull off her blinders.

The heaviest blinder involved financial "reality." A recent divorce had left her with a huge debt load that seemed to necessitate keeping the high paying, stressful job. As we explored her feelings, I realized financial fear was only part of her difficulty in creating something new. More limiting were the blinders she wore about career options. Without the passion of vision, moving through fear of limitation is almost impossible. Every time Paulette considered career options, she drew a blank. We finally realized this was because, like many women who have been socialized to give selflessly and unendingly, she was only considering options that were service oriented. I posed an "outside the box" idea. "Suppose you were not allowed to choose a service occupation?" Initially, Paulette's chest tightened in panic. But she also felt a rush of lightness. There were many steps ahead of her, and other blinders to remove, but Pauline was beginning to relax and to consider exploring new possibilities.

Later, when Paulette traveled within herself, she came to a crossroads. In one direction lay the road of service; in the other a path of self-expression. Despite lingering twinges of guilt, she turned away from the service path and began to explore the new direction. I suggested that, while traveling this road, she should try to envision activities she loved so much that she would feel as though she were getting paid to play, if her job consisted of them. The feeling that you're getting paid to play is one indication that you are following your life's star.

As Paulette continued to notice things that delighted her spirit, the Magic Child, disguised as a future self, revealed a dream. She wanted to travel and explore, to spend time biking in nature, and then write about the adventures. Paulette felt excited about this idea. She didn't know yet how to make a living doing that or how to resolve her financial problems, but now that she knew where she wanted to go, she felt more optimistic about getting there.

Dan was a client who enjoyed his work in pipe manufacturing, a business he'd been in for twenty years. When he initially visited his inner realm, he realized his extremely busy schedule made it very difficult to take time to travel there independently. He wondered if there were another kind of work that would offer more balance and happiness. Dan thought he'd like teaching because he liked kids, or maybe he would enjoy photography. He really had no firm ideas. On the vision quest to the intuitive spring, the Magic Child returned an old dream in much clearer form. He saw himself living in a very beautiful, isolated part of the country, with his family, raising springer spaniels. There were other animals too, like llamas and cows. The ranch was called Murphy's, which puzzled me at first because that wasn't his last name. Murphy turned out to be the name of Dan's childhood dog, a springer spaniel.

Dan told me that long ago he and his wife had talked about having a ranch and raising animals someday, but they hadn't thought about it since. Now he was excited, though. The vision was so clear that he could readily picture himself in that life. He didn't run out and quit his job. This wasn't a vision to accomplish right away. It was a starlight dream to gaze at for awhile. He'll probably spend several years laying the groundwork to bring this vision to earth. In the meantime, he has a star to guide him.

This takes us back to the steps I laid out earlier. Once you have a juicy vision, acknowledge your life as it is now, love yourself for creating that situation, and take a step toward achieving your vision. Ron bought himself a keyboard and converted a spare room into a studio where he could play music. When Jody Miller Stevenson recovered her health, she kept her promise to write. She started by writing an article for a magazine. Later she got busy on her first book. Dan might do some research on springer spaniels, or put a new savings plan into place. If we believe we can realize our dreams, there is always at least one step to take in that direction.

Some dreams may take many years to bring into form. We may not be ready yet to live inside that vision. Still, we have to keep the vision alive: keep reading that note in the wallet and imagine the dream as manifest; continue to plan ways to accomplish it; and keep giving thanks. Many dreams die prematurely, abandoned because the dreamer couldn't immediately and easily accomplish it.

My friend Shannon dreamed for years of having a tea house. She knew what she would call it and imagined the activities that would go on there. She lived in several different states, searching for the right location for a tea house. All the time she kept saving money and stoking dream embers, keeping the dream burning in her heart. Finally, she opened the door of her tea house, A Cup of Magic, in a beautifully renovated house, with moons and stars and suns stenciled all over the walls. Eventually she wants to serve many kinds of teas, but right now customers are more interested in coffee. She imagines having evening poetry readings and discussions there, somewhat like a nineteenth century salon, but for now she's just focused on making the breakfast and lunch business successful. The other parts of her dream will come later. That's the way it is with dreams.

Sometimes a dream grows into a very different form than what was originally imagined by the dreamer, yet it still contains the same essence.

Kris King told the story of her husband's metamorphosis. He was very successful in the corporate world, but grew disenchanted with that life. Wanting to work with his hands, he quit the job and went to massage school. After getting licensed, he started working in a room with a window that looked out at a large tree. All day long while working on people's bodies, his attention was drawn to the tree. Even though he was working with his hands, he still felt discontent. One afternoon, he stopped by a friend's house. The friend had a tree that needed to be pruned. "I can do that!" her husband said, and soon he was enthusiastically trimming the tree. Something clicked inside. He wanted to be working on trees, not bodies. Now he is happily and successfully employed using his hands to shape tree people instead of human people. The essence of the dream is the same. Only the clientele has changed.

Magic Circle/Mastermind

In addition to the ideas for dream-stepping, one more powerful support is available for calling dream-stars into form: a Magic Circle. In essence form we are all Magic Children. In daily living, we are prone to forget that truth. If we could simply flip a channel and think as the Magic Children we are, manifesting any dream would be easy, but most of us don't know how to do that. However, when we come together to focus on realizing dreams, we increase the capacity of each group member to access the magic responsible for creating the world. Jesus said "Whenever two or more of you are gathered together in my name, I am there in the midst of you." A popular saying is "The sum of the parts is greater than the whole." Both of these statements illustrate an important principle of manifestation. When we come together with positive, focused intent we collectively access a power that often eludes us as individuals.

Masterminding is a process that has long been used with great effectiveness by people of superior accomplishment. It is like creating a magic circle where wonders can be worked. The idea is that the harmonious focused intent of many "small" minds, i.e., limited rational minds, flips the switch for the whole group and gains them access to the master mind, the unified field of energy responsible for all creation. From that consciousness, the group can create anything.

Mastermind groups may consist of members of an organization who share the common purpose of growing the business, married partners who share joint goals, or a diverse group of individuals committed to supporting one another in the achievement of personal dreams.

There are many formats for conducting mastermind groups. The process I share here is one I have devised by adapting principles and group processes from various sources. I have utilized futurist Dr. Barbara Marx Hubbard's *Guide to Evolutionary Circles*, Dr. Wayne Dyer's *Manifest Your Destiny*, and the mastermind principles developed by Jack Boland, who adapted the Twelve Steps of Alcoholics Anonymous to resonate with New Thought beliefs.

Use this approach if you like, or create your own. The critical aspect is not the wording or techniques but the process goals. It is important to align as a group with each other and with the mastermind energy. The group needs to be a place where members are held accountable, given encouragement, and fed with the insights, knowledge and experience of one another.

As I explained in chapter one, I needed to choose one word for the Divine and be consistent, so I'm still using God, which I believe is what the mastermind energy is. If you bristle at that three-letter word, substitute whatever term you prefer.

Overview of the Process

In the attunement section, the group aligns with Divine energy, the Magic Mind that flows through each partner. Members consciously open their hearts to this love energy, affirm a willingness to be a channel of this loving guidance for each other, and accept God's direction through the insight of the partners as well as through personal intuition.

To channel the mastermind energy more fully, we need to examine any ways we are blocking that love. Everyone has a shadow side, the part that pulls in the opposite direction of our conscious desire to love. We tend to hide this shadow from other people, and even from ourselves, because we judge it to be unlovable and feel ashamed. The shadow-self is not bad, only scared. By inviting this hidden self into the safety of the mastermind circle, we allow God's healing love, flowing through our partners, to help us love the parts of ourselves we had rejected.

Our shadow-self resists life by holding onto blame, toward ourselves or another person, by giving in to fear instead of acting on intuitive guidance, and by breaking the promises we make to ourselves. In the sacred safety of the mastermind circle, we acknowledge to one another the ways in which we are off the mark.

The partners receive our admissions without judgment and invite us to let Divine love move through the hardened places in our hearts. This is a process of atonement. That word has acquired a connotation of obligation and making amends, but the word broken into syllables reveals its true intent. At-one-ment means using whatever means are appropriate to regain our sense of oneness with the Divine, and with one another. The partners' acceptance of us, with our weakness, gives us strength to accept ourselves and move forward.

The next stage in the process is a time for listening to God's voice. Simply by stopping to notice, we can become aware of new forms of Divine energy pushing like tiny green shoots through the hard ground of our conscious minds. Each partner now considers all the ways that God may be wanting to express something new in our lives, or may be calling us into service. Perhaps a dream image keeps returning or an unreasonable thought won't leave us alone. Maybe underneath a fear that pulled us off the mark, we discover a gift trying to emerge. Sometimes, the habit of focusing on what is wrong with us makes us forget that we are on a spiritual path. Articulating the focus of our spiritual path may illuminate the next step of the path. Although we may enter the group already knowing what direction God is nudging us in, a time of quiet reflection at this juncture allows all the partners to listen for the unknown.

After quiet reflection, partners share insights about their own paths and what God is wanting to bring forth. We reveal the dreams we want to manifest. It doesn't matter if we don't know how to bring them into form. The power of the mastermind circle is that through linking energy we allow God's wisdom to emerge through any individual in the group, and we serve to remind each other that anything is possible when aligned with God. We surrender the manifestation process to God, then listen for further instructions.

One by one partners share their dreams, asking God to manifest that or something better; each person is then asked by their partner what the next step might be. The partners reinforce the person's trust by affirming belief in the individual's ability to manifest that dream through Divine partnership. They share images and insights to encourage or further the person in the manifestation process. Group members not only bear witness to their partners' potential, but also remind them of the character strengths and accomplishments they already have but may tend to downplay.

Some teachers believe that problem solving doesn't belong in a master-mind group. In my opinion, that belief erects unnecessary blocks to the flow of God's wisdom. As long as group members have first attuned to the mastermind energy and are pausing to listen intuitively before speaking, there is no reason to assume God prefers to work miracles without the "interference" of human partners.

On the other hand, group members need to be committed to listening to their guidance before speaking. Most of us love the sound of our own voices and enjoy talking about personal experiences. This can be helpful, but it can also be overdone. I have found that when the urge to share comes from a desire to fix somebody so I won't feel helpless, or from a desire to impress others with my knowledge and accomplishments, I am more prone to assault people with my ideas instead of listening for insights that may be flowing through me. Such clarity is difficult for us humans to maintain. That's why the attunement process is so important. Even then, individuals may miss the mark and talk too much, but this doesn't have to be detrimental. The person being advised has the power and responsibility to sift ideas that are shared, and determine which ones resonate. Each member of the group also has the right and responsibility to speak up if it seems as though another group member is monopolizing the sharing.

After sharing dreams and receiving guidance and encouragement, the group may join together in chanting the sacred sound "Aaaah." As Dr. Wayne Dyer explains in *Manifest Your Destiny*, this is the sound of creation, embedded in names for the Divine found in every language. By chanting this sound, we participate in the act of creation in a very primal way.

Because we believe that God, expressing as the Magic Child in each of us, is longing to make miracles in our lives, we know that our dreams are already coming true, and so give thanks even before seeing the results. This gratitude step could take the form of recounting our blessings or chanting the sacred sound "Om," the universal sound of gratitude. This sound can simply be chanted three times or allowed to build and flow in a prolonged chorus of thanksgiving. This chanting serves well as a closing ritual or the group can invent some other ritual to close the circle.

In the process outlined here, I have separated the mastermind principles into sections corresponding to the different stages of the process. Your group may like to read these in unison, take turns having different people read aloud, read them silently, or phrase the ideas in your own words. All these options can work. Experiment to find a format that your group prefers.

The Process

Attunement
- Play beautiful music to open the heart to Divine energy and create a field of resonance, or harmony, amongst group members.
- I BELIEVE God is love without limits, expressing in physical form as endless miracles. I believe that, in my essence, I am one of those miracles and that God responds to me in a personal, loving way.
  Touch palms or hold hands, to increase energetic connection.
- I REACH OUT to my partners, knowing this harmonious connection lets us escape the prison of what we think is possible.
- Together with my partners, I SURRENDER control of my life to God's miraculous power.
- I OPEN MY HEART to the flow of Divine love expressing as me.

Facing the Shadow
- In what ways are you off the mark? (Holding onto blame, giving into fear, breaking promises...) Share this in the loving safety of the circle.

Atonement
- I PURIFY MY HEART OF RESENTMENT. I stop blaming myself and others for mistakes and seeming injuries. I take responsibility for my life and recognize that all the experiences and people in my life have provided oppor-

tunities for greater self-knowledge and deeper self-love. My acceptance of life aligns me more completely with God's creative power.

- I SHOW MERCY toward myself for the fear and weakness that, until now, have kept me off the mark of complete love and creative magic. I now call upon God's power to enlighten my mind, open my heart, and strengthen my will.

Listening for God's Voice

- I DEDICATE MY LIFE to expressing God's love and power in the physical form known as me.
- I LISTEN to hear if I am being called to serve as an expression of God in some way. By responding to God's intuitive prompting, I believe I will come into service of others in a way that feels joyful to me and is in harmony with the greatest good.

  Spend time in quiet reflection listening for additional Divine whispers.

Sharing Dreams and Directions/ Asking for God's Help/ Supporting One Another

- I know that everything I need for happiness and success is available to me right now, as my Divine inheritance, and so I refuse to worry. Instead, I ACCEPT all life's rich delights as a personal gift from God.
- I ASK God to transform the specific dreams and goals of my heart into physical form, either in the way I imagine them or in a more miraculous and delightful form.
- I COMMIT TO TRUST God and follow the intuitive guidance I receive.
- I INVITE God to speak through my partners and I listen to their insights with an open heart.
- Each partner reveals the dreams we want to manifest and any insights from the listening step.
- Partners ask: What would you do to manifest this dream if you knew you couldn't fail? Remind each other that anything is possible when aligned with God.
- Share insights and brainstorm ideas to help the partner manifest the dream.

- Remind the person sharing of positive strengths and qualities and steps already taken. Build confidence.
- I APPRECIATE the way God is already manifesting in me and in my partners. I know this is an ever-expanding process.
- Chant the sacred sound "Aaaah."

Gratitude

- Recount and express thanks for the blessings that have already been manifested .
- I THANK GOD, even before my senses perceive the results, because I know the physical world always conforms to the miracles created on the spiritual plane.

Closing

- Although we close the physical form of this Magic Circle now, the love energy that connects us remains present, supporting and guiding us in our resolve. WE GO FORWARD, on our own soul paths, with a spirit of enthusiasm, expectancy and peace.
- Chant the sacred sound "Om."

The Mother-Star

The dreams I have been describing so far are very clearly defined dream-stars. Jody wanted to write; Ron wanted to sing; Dan wanted an animal ranch; Shannon wanted a tea house. These essential dreams change our lives, and often the lives of others whom we inspire to dream. Yet there is an even more basic, more powerful aspect of vision. Steven Covey, author of *Seven Habits of Highly Effective People,* calls it a mission statement. Jody Miller Stevenson describes it as soul purpose. I believe we have all come into this world for a reason more encompassing than having a particular job to do. A job flows from our mission. This soul purpose gives a dream-star its bright light. It is like a mother-star, a great energy that births all the individual dream-stars that beckon us forward.

I wrote my first mission statement on July 6, 1995. It was inspiring and long-winded.

> *"My mission is to shine the light of loving acceptance of what is and empowering vision of what lies hidden on myself and all those in my life—and to have fun doing it. My love has the power to transform the dark, scary, unloved places so the inner treasures of joy, love, and creativity are revealed. In this way, I am a spark-lighter. People burst to fullness all around me. My life is full of joy and excitement because I love this mission so much. I am free to feel and express all of my feelings; to speak all of my truth. I accept and celebrate myself, and others, in entirety. I dance through my life, delighting in the depths of my stillness, and in the heights of my expansiveness. I surrender my belief in limitation."*

I loved the words and they described my life, as I was living it, fairly well. They did not, however, make any difference in my life. A year later, I realized the importance of brevity. A soul purpose statement has to be something you can say without reading, and can recite to yourself over and over. My new statement read:

> *"My mission is to light a global bonfire, to impassion people all over the planet with the joy of being alive in a body, on this beautiful blue green planet."*

That statement was easy to remember and recite, but I noticed it didn't make a difference in my life either. Also, people whose opinions I valued highly told me that statement didn't sound like me. I was insulted, but their opinions gnawed at me until I finally realized my discontent was unrelated to a need for approval. The statement really was not quite me.

While contemplating goals for 1997, I began once again puzzling over why I was here. Without realizing it at the time, I went back to the essence of my first mission statement, but this time, composing it mentally on a long walk, I came up with something shorter.

"My personal vision is to make the world a more loving place, by helping myself and others love the parts of ourselves and other people that we thought were unlovable and so freeing personal and planetary energy for creative expression instead of judgment and destruction."

Not only did this statement totally resonate with the work I was doing as a counselor, it also infused my creative projects. Days after articulating this soul purpose, I gave a talk to my spiritual community on the theme of Divine connection. As I spoke, I physically felt a sacred presence swell inside me, dimming all the judgmental thoughts I had about other people's beliefs. All I cared about was communicating the truth that we are all love and nothing more. The response from my audience was dramatic. I had addressed this community many times and always had a warm reception. This time, there was a hushed sense of reverence as if people had swallowed something very holy. I had no illusions of being some great guru; it was my own magic soul, inseparable from the Divine, the mother-star, that was speaking.

After that experience, the mother-star led me to examine the working draft of this book. I began combing through every page, asking myself whether the words written would lead people to be more loving. I know my book is more focused and loving because it is infused with the power of my soul purpose. If you think you have articulated your soul purpose and it's not making this kind of difference in your life, examine your purpose again. Either it's not quite yours, or limiting beliefs are preventing you from expressing it.

Ben, a photographer who attended a workshop I was co-leading, had a goal to develop a contract with Coca-Cola. That accomplishment represented the greatest success he could imagine. He also had a wish to work in film but "knew" that he was too old to get into that field now. We pressed Ben to move beyond his limits and create a bigger vision. He was quiet for awhile and then very simply said to the group, "My mission is to make the world a more positive place by creating visual magic." I felt like an electric current had swept through the room. Ben's eyes were brimming with tears. The group cheered. Ben still didn't know how to pull this bigger dream into form, but now he had a new and more powerful compass to guide his life. He had found his mother-star.

The mother-star is an organizing energy as well as a compass. With soul purpose, I have found energy and discipline I was sure I did not have. For example, I have wanted for years to change my eating habits, but my will was always weaker than momentary urges. When I made the connection between my eating habits and the energy I needed to accomplish my soul purpose, I finally found the strength of will to change. Infused with purpose, I mattered more to me than I had without purpose.

This is a common thread I notice in clients who are depressed, overweight or drinking. In addition to the problems that led them to that state, they share a lack of vision. If they have found a dream-star, they're too busy singing a song of limitation to follow it. I have yet to have a client, who has found the mother-star, suffering from lack of motivation.

If you haven't found your mother-star, take some time to reflect on your life, tune in to the inner realm, and identify your soul purpose. Let that purpose birth individual dream-stars to guide you through life with energy, passion and love. Although I cannot offer you evidence more concrete than the stories I have shared, I absolutely know, from the inside out, that vision invests life with the vital fluid we all need to feel fully alive. You are a Magic Child and so dreams sparkle in your blood. Journey within, and set them free. Starvision is your birthright. The whole world is waiting for the magic that only you can express in your special way, and which Rainer Maria Rilke set to words in the *Book of Hours:*

> *I believe in all that has never yet been spoken*
> *I want to free what waits within me*
> *so that what no one has dared to wish for*
> *may for once spring clear*
> *without my contriving.*
>
> *If this is arrogant, God, forgive me,*
> *but this is what I need to say.*
> *May what I do flow from me like a river,*
> *no forcing and no holding back,*
> *the way it is with children.*

Then in these swelling and ebbing currents,
these deepening tides moving out, returning,
I will sing you as no one ever has,

streaming through widening channels
into the open sea.

Wondersparks

1. What dreams do you have?
2. Do your dreams vibrate with the light of your mother-star? What is your soul purpose?
3. What excuses, limiting beliefs, keep you from living your dreams?
4. Do you give yourself time, or even permission, to dream? If not, when will you start?
5. What do you hope people will say about you after you are dead?
6. Are you living your life in a way that people are likely to say such things about you?
7. To help you find your soul purpose, write a eulogy for your imaginary memorial service. Describe a life lived by your best possible self. Read the eulogy aloud, and notice if it quivers with starlight.
8. To identify limiting beliefs, write this sentence in big, bold letters: I can have exactly what I want. Then listen to your mental protests. Steve Siskgold suggests to notice if your body tightens, gets sweaty, or reacts in some way. If it does, breathe and focus on the physical sensation, asking your body for more information. Maybe a memory will surface of the last fateful time you made the "mistake" of dreaming. If it does, love yourself, love the memory, until the pain shifts and you feel freer.

9. Use the same process to embody your visions. Say aloud, to somebody else, exactly what you intend to do. Then pay attention to mental and physical reactions. Love yourself for experiencing resistance until you feel a shift toward peace and freedom.

Elixirs for the Mind

Building Your Field of Dreams, by Reverend Mary Manin Morrissey. This is a detailed practical description of how to take a dream from inspiration to manifestation. Morrissey's masterful storytelling style illustrates her message in an entertaining and memorable way. The stories made such an impression on me, I have to include this on my desert island bookshelf.

Soul Purpose, by Reverend Jody Miller Stevenson. The inspirational stories, reflections and exercises in this book are designed to lead you to awareness of your soul-purpose. Stevenson further shows readers how to make life adjustments so that expenditure of time and energy reflect soul purpose. If you are not living your soul purpose, put this book on your desert island bookshelf!

First Things First, by Steven Covey, Roger Merrill and Rebecca Merrill. The authors approach time management by encouraging the setting of priorities and explain how to put the most important things in your life first. There is also a mission statement workshop in the appendix.

Chapter Twelve

This is not the end...
Your next step is just the beginning.

Magic Wand
Walk forward in trust.

The Next Step

I hope this book has already made a difference in your life. I have shared my story and the stories of friends and clients in an effort to inspire you. None of us are unusual. We are all the kind of people you meet every day. If we can become conscious of our inner magic and learn to love ourselves more completely, you can too.

I know that the key idea of this book, that we are each God expressing as a physical form, can be very threatening. It sounds arrogant, prideful and crazy. Yet the logical consequence of believing anything less is that we must remain disempowered victims, subject to the plans and whims of whatever powerful force we imagine is pulling the strings of our lives. We have to realize that our marvelous rational minds represent our limits—not our possibilities—and surrender control of our lives to the mind of God expressing as the Magic Child in each of us.

If you can make the shift and begin acting on the belief that you are God in form, you will unleash an unlimited supply of love and magic to enjoy and to share.

If you look inside and can find God, then you will have found both the source and object of love. You will feel whole, holy, and naturally radiate and notice love everywhere. Because love is innately creative, your life can become a miraculous process of bringing dreams into form.

If you want to experience the world as a Magic Child, the starting point is to believe that no matter what the circumstances of your life or how you feel about yourself you still are magical at your core. Then accept every situation and person in your life as a teacher, designed by your own soul, to help lead the Magic Child out of hiding.

This approach eliminates the negative, resistant energies of blame and complaints because all life now becomes a perfect opportunity for learning. Instead of being a justification for rejecting experience, discomfort can be interpreted as feedback that indicates the blocks piled atop the Magic Child. Even the painful experience of being physically separated from loved ones by death illuminates the rich possibilities of life in form.

If you can accept yourself as a physical expression of God, you can end the age-old war between mind, body and emotion. All three levels are aspects of God in human form. All are important parts of yourself that can help if you regard them as friends and allies. Instead of being paralyzed by self-judgment and rejection, you can learn to accept and love your whole self and approach your mystery with curiosity and respect instead of fear.

We are all wondrous beings, who are prone to forgetting our miraculous nature, and to acting out the beliefs that keep us feeling separate from God. When viewed with compassion, our distinctly ungodlike behavior reveals the masks we have mistaken for essence, the parts that are ready for love's transforming power. Without the ball and chain of self-hatred, we can freely explore habits, reactions, feelings, memories—even ancient ones—yearnings, inspirations and whims, and allow all of it to lead us home to the Magic Child within our hearts.

This is possible for you. I encourage you to use the Magic Wands presented throughout the book. Although the Wands don't create instant magic, they do cause lasting, powerful changes and they can help you interpret your life experiences as feedback. I know these Wands can make magical life changes, because at one time I lived my life without practicing any of these principles, and now that I'm using them, my life is filled with vibrancy and joy that wasn't there before.

You don't know how much time you have left to live in your current physical form. Can you bear to let go of life here without knowing how wonderful it could be, without unleashing your magic and bringing your dreams into form, without ever really loving yourself? You don't have to let that happen. Begin today. Commit to love yourself completely, and express every bit of magic inside you. Don't worry about knowing how, believing you can, or doing it perfectly. Surrender those details. Stay focused on the goal: to love yourself and express your magic. Trust God to help. Then watch the miracles appear! The Magic Child is you. Love and miracles are your birthright and your destiny. Step forward and claim them today!

Appendix

**The treasure is yours,
if you want it.**

 Magic Wand
Use all your magic; spend all your treasure.

The Magic Child's Treasure Chest

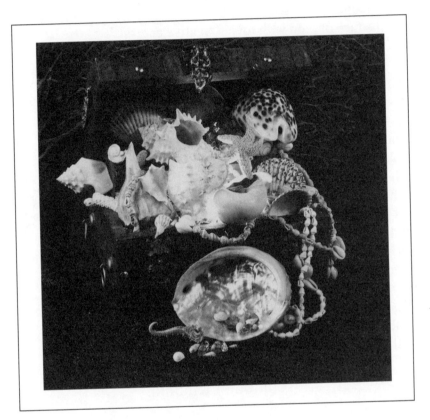

Every child has a secret stash of precious things: rocks, feathers, marbles, and assorted magical findings. The Magic Child is no different. But in this treasure chest you will find ideas. This section contains summaries and lists that have been presented throughout the text, for easy reference. The treasure is yours, if you want it. Use it with abandon and watch your life acquire a new sparkle!

Magic Wands

- Find the magic inside your own heart!
- Soothe the face of pain with love's creative caress!
- Follow the path of your heart!
- Know that you are never alone!
- Remember who you are!
- Treat your body like a beloved friend!
- Claim full responsibility for your life!
- Surrender to your higher power!
- Approach the banquet of life as a lover, savoring the whole feast!
- Kiss the past good-bye!
- Admit your true feelings!
- Study the roles you're playing!
- If you would be rich, shine your light lavishly!
- Embrace your life as the right experience!
- Love yourself just as you are!
- Use starvision to create miracles!
- Walk forward in trust!
- Use all your magic; spend all your treasure!

Intuition Kindling

1. Treat physical sensations and pain as body messages. Approach them with love, patience and curiosity.
2. Invite intuitive insights about the meaning of the physical message.
3. Honor the ideas that come to you.
4. Notice if the idea raises or lowers your energy. Genuine intuition raises energy.
5. Notice if the idea feels right. It may seem strange, yet exciting, and somehow right.

6. If the insight makes you uncomfortable, check for limiting beliefs.
7. Act upon your intuition.
8. Express appreciation to the Magic Child who has been whispering so helpfully.

Responsibility Rules

- Loss of power is the price of defining yourself as a victim, controlled by the whims of people and circumstances.
- The only result of blame is hurt.
- Assume life is showing up as the right experience. Start asking "Why me?" with genuine curiosity.
- Make requests, not complaints.
- As an indistinguishable spark of Divine creative energy, you have creative responsibility for your life. Design whatever you want!

Surrender Mini-Manual

1. Intend to surrender to the Magic Child.
2. Ask for guidance in setting goals.
3. Surrender the means to achieving the goals.
4. Surrender the outcome.
5. Be quiet and listen for insight.
6. If thoughts of worry intrude, love yourself, and then stop worrying!
7. Expect a miracle.
8. Say thanks even before the miracle shows up in physical form.

Desert Island Bookshelf

Coming Home, by Martia Nelson
Seat of the Soul, by Gary Zukav
Energy Anatomy, by Carolyn Myss, Ph.D.
The Conscious Heart, by Gay Hendricks, Ph.D.,
  and Kathlyn Hendricks, Ph.D.
The Aware Ego, by Hal Stone, Ph.D., and
  Sidra Stone, Ph.D.
To Love and Be Loved, by Stephen and
  Ondrea Levine
The Path to Love, by Deepak Chopra, M.D.
Manifest Your Dreams, by Wayne Dyer, Ph.D.
Building Your Field of Dreams, by Reverend Mary
  Manin Morrissey

Guidelines for Great Relationships

Things to talk about (first with yourself, then with your partner):

- your vision for your life
- your goals for your life
- your vision for a relationship
- how you feel about intimacy
- everything about your past
- the relationship hot spots: sex, money, power, politics, children, spirituality

  (Don't wait for these to become an issue before you talk!)

Seventeen Secrets of Prosperity

1. Remember that you are one with God.
2. Know that, as all-powerful God in form, there is nothing you cannot create.
3. Decide to create.
4. Watch "coming attractions instead of "reruns."
5. If not in the flow, check who's running the show.
6. Focus on the outflow and the inflow will be automatic.
7. Experience life through a grateful heart.
8. Realize that money is energy.
9. Create space to receive new blessings.
10. Be merciful with yourself.
11. Use words that reflect confident thoughts.
12. Honor God within and pay yourself first.
13. Exercise financial responsibility.
14. Invest instead of borrow.
15. Radiate richness to others.
16. Live on purpose!
17. Acknowledge prosperity's source, God within, by sharing your abundance with whatever feeds your spirit.

Points to Remember

- Conceding is different than wanting.
- Be willing to let the relationship go if you really want different things in life.
- Something better will come along if you focus on self-intimacy.
- Your partner's seeming inability to give you the love you want mirrors the ways you don't yet love yourself.
- One hundred percent responsibility, loving commitment, merciful acceptance and appreciation create a container where we can grow whole.

Ways to Talk to Each Other

- Share everything you're feeling (even if it seems petty, especially if you're scared).
- Describe what you're feeling, including physical sensations.
- Breathe deeply in your belly as you talk and listen.
- Never blame!
- Be merciful toward your partner.
- Remember that your partner, and you, are Magic Children, confused by illusion and fear.
- Wonder what the current situation or feelings might have to do with your past.
- Take responsibility and assume there is a connection.
- Share your wonderings.
- Turn complaints into requests!
- Tell each other what you appreciate about each other—often!
- Appreciate yourself as well!

A Guide to Dream-Stepping

10.   Say thanks and expect results!

9.   Turn the dream over to God

8.   Take a step in the direction of your dream.

7.   Love yourself for creating only what you knew how to create.

6.   Tell the truth about how your situation is now.

5.   Bring the vision into concrete form, involving your physical senses.

4.   Envision what you want—in detail, with feeling.

3.   Create a new tension between what you want and where you are now.

2.   Love yourself, just as you are, complete with limiting beliefs.

1.   Identify your limiting beliefs.

The Mastermind Principles

1. I BELIEVE God is love without limits, expressing in physical form as endless miracles. I believe that, in my essence, I am one of those miracles and that God responds to me in a personal, loving way.

2. I REACH OUT to my partners, knowing this harmonious connection lets us escape the prison of what we think is possible.

3. Together with my partners, I SURRENDER control of my life to God's miraculous power.

4. I OPEN MY HEART to the flow of Divine love expressing as me.

5. I PURIFY MY HEART OF RESENTMENT. I stop blaming myself and others for mistakes and seeming injuries. I take responsibility for my life and recognize that all the experiences and people in my life have provided opportunities for greater self-knowledge and deeper self-love. My acceptance of life aligns me more completely with God's creative power.

6. I SHOW MERCY toward myself for the fear and weakness that, until now, have kept me off the mark of complete love and creative magic. I now call upon God's power to enlighten my mind, open my heart, and strengthen my will.

7. I DEDICATE MY LIFE to expressing God's love and power in the physical form known as me.

8. I LISTEN to hear if I am being called to serve as an expression of God in some way. By responding to God's intuitive prompting, I believe I will come into service of others in a way that feels joyful to me and is in harmony with the greatest good.

9. I know that everything I need for happiness and success is available to me right now, as my Divine inheritance, and so I refuse to worry. Instead, I ACCEPT all life's rich delights as a personal gift from God.

10.   I ASK God to transform the specific dreams and goals of my heart into physical form, either in the way I imagine them or in a more miraculous and delightful form.

11.   I COMMIT TO TRUST God and follow the intuitive guidance I receive.

12.   I INVITE God to speak through my partners, and I listen to their insights with an open heart.

13.   I APPRECIATE the way God is already manifesting in me and in my partners. I know this is an ever-expanding process.

14.   I THANK GOD, even before my senses perceive the results, because I know the physical world always conforms to the miracles created on the spiritual plane.

15.   WE GO FORWARD, on our own soul paths, with a spirit of enthusiasm, expectancy and peace.

Audio Products by the Author

Journey to Inner Peace: Side one is a basic relaxation guide, designed to teach listeners to take themselves into deep relaxation. Side two is a guide for meditating, affirming that inside you are love.

Journey from the Shadows: This album contains four audiotapes, including an introductory tape describing the nature of the inner journey. Other tapes in the series are designed to lead the listener, using powerful hypnotic imagery, to heal the pain of the past in order to move forward. Individual tape titles: "Remember Who You Are"; "You Can Trust Again"; "Bring the Lost Parts Home"; and "Send Your Love Across Time."

Nighttime Messages for Children: Side one is a guided journey that leads young listeners while they sleep to an inner sanctuary where they can reliably find love, safety, healing and guidance. Side two offers a series of affirming reminders that they are precious, protected and full of possibilities. Jane's reassuring voice is interwoven with Ron's calming lullabies to suggest the enveloping safety of mother-father love.

Chicita and Other Tales: This is a storytelling tape of original stories told by the author in a delightfully dramatic style. The stories, aimed at elementary-age children, have characters of both genders that are both strong and sensitive, and myths that are tailored to our times, without sacrificing good storytelling style. Jane worked as a weekly volunteer in school classrooms for several years honing her narrative skills with young people.

Magic Child: This CD of original music by Ron Meyers features powerful lyrics that flow from Ron's personal journey of transformation. His voice pulses with emotion and the music is innovative, melodic and professionally produced. You can sample the style on "The Magic Child" web page.

Permissions

The following selections are reprinted in this volume by the kind permission of the copyright holders hereinafter acknowledged. Any omissions are inadvertent and will be remedied in future editions.

Dossey, Larry, Candace Pert, and John Kabat-Zinn. Excerpted material. Reprinted by permission of Jeremy P. Tarcher, Inc., a division of The Putnam Publishing Group from HEALERS ON HEALING edited by Richard Carlson and Benjamin Shield. Copyright © 1989 by Richard Carlson and Benjamin Shield.

Rilke, Rainer Maria. Poems. Reprinted by permission of Riverhead Books, a division of the Putnam Publishing Group from RILKE'S BOOK OF HOURS edited by Anita Barrows and Joanna Macy. Copyright © 1996 by Anita Barrows and Joanna Macy.

The Upanishads. Excerpts. Reprinted by permission from *The Upanishads,* by Eknath Easwaran, founder and director of the Blue Mountain Center of Meditation, copyright © 1987.

Attributions

Detailed acknowledgement of all sources of information used in preparation of this text is not practical and perhaps not possible. However, in an attempt to be thorough, a list derived from data given by the author is offered to represent works cited in this book, or used as reference material.

Aborigine song. *The Essential Mystics: The Soul's Journey into Truth.* Edited by Andrew Harvey.
Aurobindo. Quote found in *The Essential Mystics.*
Dalai Lama. Poem found in *The Essential Mystics.*
Griffiths, Bede. *Return to Center.*
Mirabai. Poem found in *Women in Praise of the Sacred.*

Roth, Gabrielle. *Sweat Your Prayers*.

Rumi. "Admit It and Change Everything": in *The Way of Passion*.

Sarton, May. "The Great Transparencies" in *A Grain of Mustard Seed*. Permission requested.

——. "The Voice" in *Halfway to Silence*. Permission requested.

Welsh Black Book of Cumarthan. Poem.

Williamson, Marianne. Poem quoted by Nelson Mandela in his inaugural address.

Wordsworth, William. "Intimations of Immortality."

Making Contact

Jane Meyers is a professional speaker available to speak to your group. Call, or check the web page to find a current list of programs or to design something tailored for your audience.

Website: magicchild.com
E-mail: meyers@teleport.com
Phone/fax: (541) 388-2929
Mail: 1880 NE Maker Way, Bend, OR 97701

To order additional copies of

Magic Child

Book: $19.95   Shipping/Handling: $3.50

Contact: ***BookPartners, Inc.***
P.O. Box 922, Wilsonville, OR 97070
Fax: 503-682-8684
Phone: 503-682-9821
Phone: 1-800-895-7323